Civilizing Authority

Civilizing Authority

Society, State, and Church

Edited by
Patrick McKinley Brennan

LEXINGTON BOOKS

A division of
ROWMAN & LITTLEFIELD PUBLISHERS, INC.
Lanham • Boulder • New York • Toronto • Plymouth, UK

LEXINGTON BOOKS

A division of Rowman & Littlefield Publishers, Inc.
A wholly owned subsidiary of The Rowman & Littlefield Publishing Group, Inc.
4501 Forbes Boulevard, Suite 200
Lanham, MD 20706

Estover Road
Plymouth PL6 7PY
United Kingdom

British Library Cataloguing in Publication Information Available

Library of Congress Cataloging-in-Publication Data

Civilizing authority : society, state, and church / edited by Patrick McKinley Brennan.
p. cm.
Includes index.
ISBN-13: 978-0-7391-1806-1 (cloth : alk. paper)
ISBN-10: 0-7391-1806-4 (cloth : alk. paper)
1. Authority—Religious aspects—Christianity. 2. Authority. I. Brennan, Patrick M., 1966–
BT88.C58 2007
303.3′4—dc22

2007021858

Printed in the United States of America

∞™ The paper used in this publication meets the minimum requirements of American National Standard for Information Sciences—Permanence of Paper for Printed Library Materials, ANSI/NISO Z39.48–1992.

Contents

Acknowledgments

A providential 1998 encounter with Joseph Vining's *From Newton's Sleep* (1996) awakened me to the simultaneous indispensability and elusiveness of authority in human living, including but not exclusively in law. Turning next to Vining's earlier *The Authoritative and the Authoritarian* (1986), my initial interest was confirmed as my hope for an easy solution was dissolved. The necessary connection, even in the quotidian practice of law, between authority and the eschatological was fixed in my mind by these and similar paragraphs in Vining's two offerings:

> A command to levitate either means something other than what at first glance it seems to mean, or it is not the law. If it is a "command to levitate" it is unenforced and unenforceable. It cannot be obeyed. It is ignored, laughed away. It is not serious, unmeant really, only a bit of play, a joke—perhaps a cruel joke and serious in its consequences, but a joke nonetheless.
>
> A claim unenforced and unobeyed may not be the claim it seems to be, and read differently may turn out in fact to be enforced and obeyed. It is not, merely because unenforced and unobeyed, therefore not law. That would be "what is, is right" in negative form. There could be no thrust of hope, no eschatological thrust in law if that were so, if no eschatological thrust no authority, and no law. Law speaks to the spirit, which can fly. But there may be something like gravity in the world where the spirit moves, and a spiritual determinisim, such that statements purporting to be law that demand the spiritually impossible are, in that perception, perceived to be not law, just as a demand is seen to be not law to the degree it demands the physically impossible. Levitation does occur. Gravity is transcended. But the spirit, when it takes flight, does not find itself with nothing around it, in the nothingness of infinity. (*From Newton's Sleep*, 126)

The question of the relationship of all authority to the transcendent remained in my mind and ripe for further investigation seven years later when there arose the opportunity to hold the chair for the Study of the Culture of Law in the Intercultural Forum for Studies in Faith and Culture at the Pope John Paul II Cultural Center, Washington, D.C. What better place to pursue the rabbit of authority whithersoever it might lead? The venue did not disappoint, nor did the invitees—the Christian lawyers, theologians, and philosophers who accepted my invitation to come together to study the place and experience of authority in our post-Christian culture and society. During a two-day symposium in December 2004, nine leading scholars and I presented early drafts of the papers that are now collected here as chapters of a book. The product reflects many of the interconnections that emerged as those trained variously in law, theology, and philosophy crossed boundaries and created new bridges in search of authority.

To all nine authors who answered my call to come together and frame an ecumenical Christian discussion of authority, but above all to Joseph Vining, who framed the question for me in the first instance, I am exceedingly grateful. To accept my invitation was not without risk, for, as Yves Simon once observed, "the issue of authority has such a bad reputation that a philosopher cannot discuss it without exposing himself to suspicion and malice."

For support and encouragement throughout my stay at the center, I owe considerable thanks to Karen Calabrese King of the Intercultural Forum and to Msgr. William Kerr, executive director of the center. For making the chair for the Culture of Law possible, we are all in the debt of His Excellency Donald Wuerl, Archbishop of Washington, D.C., and a member of the executive committee of the center. It is a distinct personal pleasure to record my gratitude to the Very Reverend Richard Schenk, O.P., then-director of the Intercultural Forum, for his kind invitation to hold the chair. The Church needs more Schenks, for reasons beyond numbering. For his continued support of this project, I thank Father Schenk's successor as director, Reverend Dennis McManus. I am grateful to Lexington Books for permmission to reprint a variation on chapter nine in volume 83 of the *Notre Dame Law Review*. At Villanova I thank Terri LaVerghetta and Susan Coady for their secretarial contributions, and Roman Galas, Erin Galbally, Christine Green, Edward Heffernan, Carolina Robinson, and John Wagner for their research and editing assistance. I also extend my thanks to Villanova Dean Mark Sargent for his support of this particular project, but moreover for his commitment to creating the institutional conditions that nourish work in the Catholic intellectual tradition. Above all, I am grateful to my wife, Jaime, whose support I enjoyed from the moment Father Schenk's invitation arrived until the last page was proofed.

Patrick McKinley Brennan
Rome
July 2007

Foreword

H. Jefferson Powell

The most salient political characteristic of the modern West, many think, is its "attempt to call political power to book against a yardstick of fundamental human requirements, universally applied," or, in other words, the affirmation in "modern liberal political culture . . . of universal human rights—to life, freedom, citizenship, self-realization—which are seen as radically unconditioned." Charles Taylor, whose formulations I have borrowed, sees this fundamental commitment to individual rights as both invaluable and dangerous, for the very real accomplishment of putting respect for the individual at the heart of the political agenda has been trailed by a dark shadow, a tendency to reduce human experience and understanding to the preservation of biological existence and the enhancement of physical comfort. Modernity, Taylor worries, threatens to "close the transcendent window, as though there were nothing beyond, more, as though it weren't a crying need of the human heart to open that window, gaze, and then go beyond." In doing so, modern Western culture betrays the truth about us as human beings—"human beings have an ineradicable bent to respond to something beyond life"—and by identifying freedom with freedom from the transcendent, modern liberalism undercuts its own social and political goals; in that regard, Taylor borrows Dostoyevsky's warning: "'Starting from unlimited freedom,' we may arrive 'at unlimited despotism.'"[1]

Taken as a whole, the chapters of *Civilizing Authority* offer an analysis of Western modernity that is deeply compatible with that offered by Taylor. In a culture dedicated to individual freedom, this volume asks: "What has become of the concept, and the practice, of authority?" Most or all of the authors agree that authority is typically understood and experienced as heteronomous, an imposition from without, by its very nature a limitation on individual freedom. This could hardly be otherwise, they suggest, because modernity has systematically cut authority loose from any roots in human nature or a divine ordering of creation.[2] The consequences are dire, and by no means merely academic: anomie, the ascendancy of consumerist "mass diversion," attempts to substitute process ("democracy," constitutional adjudication, "the market") for substantive decision in the public sphere, the withering of social and civil relationships in the face of overweening and centralized state power, and a growing loss of the ability to act on or even talk about truth.[3]

The creators of Western modernity had, of course, a solution to the problem of how to reconcile freedom and authority: legitimate authority rests on "the Consent of the Governed," as the American Declaration of Independence informed the world, and the reign of laws, not of men. In reality, however, this relocation of authority has become empty or even dishonest,[4] for without a substantive account of human flourishing, popular sovereignty can only be a legitimating fairy tale.[5] Western modernity, it seems, cannot explain its own political practices, except perhaps along the lines of the despairing restriction of politics to shared self-preservation about which Taylor worried.[6]

For anyone unpersuaded by the chimera of anarchism, this is a grim and even alarming account of the fate of authority—and some of the contributors to *Civilizing Authority* are pessimistic indeed about our social and political prospects. Taken as a whole, however, these chapters suggest the possibility of a solution to the problem of authority that preserves the very real accomplishment of holding the exercise of power accountable while avoiding the threat of nihilism. Western modernity reflexively understands authority and freedom as opposites, but that is at its heart a failure of imagination and also a failure to understand the legacy of the premodern West. The (truly) authoritative and the (heteronomous) authoritarian are, or at least can be, distinguished; legitimate authority admits of and depends upon the free choice of those subjected to it, not by the fiat of a political myth, but through authority's substantive commitment to the common good.[7] Rather than being opposites, authority and freedom can be correlatives: authority creates the possibility of genuine freedom while freedom is itself intrinsic to the existence of authority. When we think in this manner, all sorts of additional, odd ideas occur: freedom as the internalization of authority, authority as dependent on truth (not just on process), and friendship as the matrix of authority. Merely to entertain these ideas suggests radical changes in how we think about law, democracy, and social relations.

The chapters of *Civilizing Authority* provide, I believe, an exciting and even inspiring account of how we might think about authority. Modernity will not simply disappear—the authors avoid the nostalgia for a mythicized past that infects much social critique. Nor should it; Taylor is right to applaud modernity's critique of public cruelty. But societies shaped by Western modernity cannot indefinitely put off a reckoning with the destructive aspects of a concept of authority that is a libertarian version of Thomas Hobbes. The contributors to *Civilizing Authority* do not walk in lockstep, and some readers may question the overall thrust of the book's quite distinctive viewpoints—as Charles Taylor suggested years ago, liberal political arrangements may well be compatible with a nonliberal understanding of human flourishing.[8] That said, *Civilizing Authority* is a remarkable, and provocative, challenge to any belief that we can simply keep on going as we have been—or that we are bound to do so. Our freedom includes the possibility of genuine authority.

NOTES

1. Charles Taylor, *Sources of the Self* (Cambridge, Mass.: Harvard University Press, 1989), 26–27, 32 (quoting Fyodor Dostoyevsky, *The Devils*, 404 (David Magarshack, ed., 1971)).
2. See, especially, the chapter by Michael J. White.
3. "Mass diversion" is Glenn Tinder's nice phrase. Russell Hittinger and Thomas C. Kohler explore the relationship between destructive modern views of authority and the genuine communities formed by personal friendship and broader social allegiances. Steven D. Smith's chapter in particular addresses the role our loss of any coherent notion of authority plays in our increasing unwillingness to speak directly of what is true, or what you (or I) believe.
4. See especially, in addition to White, the chapters by Joseph Vining, Tinder, Hittinger, and Smith. J. Budziszewski vigorously critiques the contemporary American Supreme Court's constitutional jurisprudence as a sustained exercise in (my term, not his) public deception.
5. Patrick McKinley Brennan's chapter persuasively argues that the Enlightenment's strategy of moving the locus of authority away from the actions of persons with authority is incoherent.
6. An additional problem is that the dominance of popular sovereignty rhetoric makes the practice of authority in a body such as the Roman Catholic Church almost literally incomprehensible. See the chapter by Avery Cardinal Dulles.
7. Joseph Vining's *The Authoritative and the Authoritarian* (1986) is seminal, and within this book the chapter by John Coons is especially radical in its reworking

of what authority entails. Most of the chapters in *Civilizing Authority* draw similar distinctions along these lines, but it is particularly striking that Cardinal Dulles, whose contribution, it seems fair to say, is the most difficult to reconcile with modern Western liberalism, finds it appropriate to distinguish pronouncements that are "juridically authentic" from those that are "we may say, personally and pastorally authentic."

8. Taylor, *Sources of the Self*, 532, n. 60.

Introduction

Patrick McKinley Brennan

> It is my contention . . . that authority has vanished from the modern world.
>
> Hannah Arendt

The year was 1956 when Hannah Arendt declared authority vanished.[1] In 1974 Frederick Edelmann, S.J., could say in serious circles: "It seems evident to anyone giving thought to the matter, that at the root of contemporary social ruptures lies an attack on the theory and practice of authority."[2] And by 1976 it was fashionable to assert, as R. Baine Harris did in introducing the anthology *Authority: A Philosophical Analysis*, "Authorities are now being challenged in all areas of human life. . . . We are now witnessing a challenge to the very *idea* of authority. The crisis of authority is more than a reconsideration of how authority should be expressed in society. It extends also to a reconsideration of the *meaning* of authority."[3]

Civilizing Authority stands in the tradition of those who wonder about the possibility of authority in the modern world. Half a century after Arendt wrote, three decades after Harris wrote, Glenn Tinder reports: "That the Western nations today are in the midst of a crisis of authority is sensed very widely."[4] It is the judgment of Michael J. White that "it is not unfair to characterize modern thought, beginning in about the seventeenth century, as exhibiting a profound skepticism concerning the classical idea of natural authority."[5] And Thomas C. Kohler speaks not for himself alone when he reflects, "threat seems to lurk in the shadows that the word [authority] casts. From this perspective, authority stands as a challenge, if not an affront, to my insistent self-sovereignty."[6]

The reports could be multiplied almost endlessly, and no student of modernity could fail to see their point. Quite simply, according to Joseph Vining, "[i]t does seem to be a hallmark of modernity to dismiss 'authority,' the very notion of it."[7] Whatever authority once was, something has changed.

Notwithstanding all this, and perhaps despite it all, in 1985 Richard De George could observe in beginning his minor classic, *The Nature and Limits of Authority*: "Authority pervades society. . . . [W]hat can be called the *authority experience*" is common throughout our societies.[8] Will anyone deny this outright? The evidence remains that children heed the authority of their parents, citizens obey the authoritative orders of the courts, the faithful adhere to the authority of the pope and Church councils, and so forth. The tantalizing possibility of disobedience, sometimes seized, only testifies to antecedent authority. As Joseph Vining sees it, "the truth is that authority and the response to it we call 'deference' or, in its full presence, a 'willing obedience,' are to be found everywhere in the modern world." John E. Coons elaborates another perception of authority:

> Employing the voices of nature, revelation, and positive law . . . [authority] then assists imperfect reason in the search for the behavioral content of the right in specific cases. The effect is transformative, delivering the human will from what is otherwise a repertoire of unmeaning possibilities for choice. When authority confers consciousness of good and evil, it allows the capacity for choice to become a real actor in a real story in which decisions cease to be arbitrary preferences. Its first gift is the news that there is a point to this freedom.[9]

Coons's verbs are in the indicative mood, not the optative.

And again, the reports could be multiplied, as they are throughout this book. Ranging from Church to civic life, the "authority experience" remains common. Still, what *is* authority? The dictionaries and encyclopedias abound with recorded usages, but what of the phenomenon?

This volume responds to the perception of a paradox. Reports of authority's disappearance persist even as most people's experience of authority (and authorities) perdures. Tinder follows his observation of the "crisis of authority" with this: "[N]either the nature nor the cause of crisis is clear. Nor is it clear even whether it is altogether a bad thing, since it presumably consists in a weakening of authority and that, given the evils of 'authoritarianism,' may be desirable." The danger of the authoritarian is *concessum*, but can authority survive a "weakening"? Relatedly, can authority make its appearance in a world driven by Darwin, bureaucracy, atomization, and indifference? In a word, whither authority in McWorld?

All ten authors of this book affirm the possibility of genuine authority—that is, of authority that is not mere human artifice "all the way down." While affirming that there are principles of human unity that transcend mere contingent human agreement or imposition, they differ in their assessment of authority's nature and operation.

Tracing the ideological legacies of Thomas Hobbes and Jean-Jacques Rousseau, Michael J. White observes the elusiveness of authority that is not merely the contingent consequence of the consent of the governed. As White notes, "[f]or someone like Bertrand Russell or Professor Richard Dawkins, who holds that 'Science [note the capitalization] presents for belief' a world that is 'purposeless' and 'void of meaning,' I suspect that the notion of natural [that is, non-contractual] authority can have little, if any, purchase." White does not count himself among those for whom genuine authority has vanished from the world. But whence authority in our frequently denatured world? Steven D. Smith, whose "'Hollow Men'? Law and the Declension of Belief" brings the volume to a conclusion with the help of the insights and observations of Joseph Vining and the poem "God's Grandeur," by Gerard Manley Hopkins, S.J., suggests this answer:

> [Oliver Wendell] Holmes's famous essay was called "The Path of the Law," and Holmes's Path is one that for generations now we "have trod, have trod, have trod." The path leads to a dead end, I think, and so at the moment the picture can be a dispiriting one. The whole enterprise "wears man's smudge and shares man's smell." Yet even here, if with Vining we pay close attention to the underlying commitments and presuppositions that pervade law and that we seem constitutionally unable to relinquish, we may glimpse "the dearest freshness deep down things." "[T]hough the last lights off the black West went," even so, transcendence "will flame out, like shining from shook foil." And so we can say that the world—and even the law—is "charged with the grandeur of God." That vision is at least part of what a Christian jurisprudence should help us see.[10]

The symposium out of which this book grew was intended as a contribution to Christian jurisprudence. It is instructive that David Stagaman, S.J., in *Authority in the Church* (a book mentioned by Avery Cardinal Dulles in his chapter of the same title herein[11]), relies on the work of Joseph Vining, *The Authoritative and the Authoritarian*,[12] to articulate a theology of authority in the Catholic Church.[13] The traffic on the roads to Rome flows in two directions, in other words. A working premise, variously supported and qualified throughout the text, has been that authority as it appears in the body politic and the state is not *toto caelo* apart from other manifestations of authority.

Still, what *is* the "authority experience"?

The English word "authority" is derived from the Latin word *auctor*, which Lewis and Short's *New Latin Dictionary* defines as one who "brings about the existence of any object, or promotes the increase and prosperity of it, whether he originates it, or by his efforts gives greater permanence or continuance to it." But, as Cardinal Dulles observes in this connection, "[f]or better or for worse, the term has taken on a modern meaning, which might be summarized as rightful influence or rightful power over the minds and behavior of persons." Dulles continues: "When we speak of authority in a society, we generally have in mind something more than influence. Authority in the strict and formal sense means rightful power to perform certain official acts, such as the issuance of laws and commands that require obedience or the formulation of doctrines that require assent. Authority implies dominion over free human agents." Rather than of command or dominion, Coons identifies an authority of invitation—and he goes on to indicate some practical consequences of an authority that invites rather than commands. But which thing authority does—command or invite—is a question of fact. More generally, it remains a question of fact for us descendants of Holmes whether the universe and we are constructed in such a way that we have access to authority, or is the design such that, as Arendt believed, authority is absent now? The possible is not necessarily necessary. One thinks of that other line from Hopkins's poem: "The soil is bare now, nor can foot feel, being shod."

Cardinal Dulles's concern in defining authority was the life of the Catholic Church, a society that differs from other societies because of the particular unity therein of both human and divine elements. However, this definition or a variation on it vies for acceptance in all the perfectly mundane societies to which each of us belongs. Indeed, it is the Catholic view, as Russell Hittinger explains, that authority attends authentic society as such; authority is not an imposition *ab extra*, a dolloping out of direction from someplace else. As Hittinger goes on to observe, it is the existence of the multiple societies, such as families and churches and clubs, each with its own proper authority to govern within its respective sphere, that constitutes the bedrock within which that particular society that is the modern state must take its place, not usurping rightful dominion that is not its own. The Catholic contribution to a Christian jurisprudence includes the insight that authority is to be found in human persons' various social unities; it is not the mere concession of the bureaucratic instrument that is the state.[14]

Furthermore, in a world such as our own, in which suffocation by bureaucracy and the blows of authoritarian sovereignty have been felt, the superabundantly cautious are tempted to dispense with authority altogether in order to avoid the menace of the authoritarian. If that temptation is refused, how is genuine authority to be recognized, the pretenders rusticated? This characteristically modern quandary receives attention throughout the volume. Consider, by way of introduction, this catechetical colloquy:

> Then again I asked him: "Supposing the Pope looked up and saw a cloud and said 'It's going to rain', would that be bound to happen?"
>
> "Oh, yes, Father,"
>
> "But supposing it didn't."
>
> He thought a moment and said, "I suppose it would be sort of raining spiritually, only we were too sinful to see it."[15]

Thus Evelyn Waugh introduces the modern readers of *Brideshead Revisited* to the notoriously Catholic concern with authority, in this case the authority of the Bishop of Rome. How is it to be recognized? In an overeager display of obedience, the catechumen Rex Mottram, under instruction in order to make possible a "Catholic wedding," posits the existence of an authority at Rome that can predict or even command the weather; those unable to verify the satisfaction of the pope's authoritative pronouncement, Mottram is willing to suppose, are "too sinful to see" what is plain to the virtuous. This extravagance combines with others to lead Father Mowbray, S.J., the long-suffering instructor of the catechumen, to conclude that Rex Mottram "doesn't correspond to any degree of paganism known to the missionaries." But, in the end, Father Mowbray agrees to receive Rex into the Church, it being necessary "to take a chance sometimes—with semi-imbeciles, for instance."

As so often happens in *Brideshead*, the unsophisticated see and somehow communicate deep truths. Though Mottram was wrong concerning the particulars of the pope's authority, he was right in sensing that authority is, as Abraham Lincoln said of equality, a tough nut to crack. Nobody comes stamped with authority, not even the pope.

As to some matters, including the weather, the pope speaks as all nonmeteorologists speak; as to other matters, the pope can speak with authority, much as Christ himself, as scripture records without qualification, "spoke as one with authority." As Cardinal Dulles observes, "[t]he question of authority in the Church has been much discussed since the Second Vatican Council"; in a representative democracy, "authority comes from below," whereas "in the Church, authority comes from God through Jesus Christ, who instituted the Church as a hierarchical society." Still, what authority to attribute to statements of the pope on matters of faith and morals not delivered *ex cathedra* is the subject of ongoing debate in good faith of theologians trained in the heart of the Catholic tradition. How the members of that hierarchical society identify and embody that authority received from Christ is one of the questions Dulles pursues. Others will give it a different answer; David Stagaman already has, with the help of Joseph Vining, in the aforementioned book. Does this work or witness a destabilizing of authority? Cardinal Dulles quotes Karl Rahner, S.J., as follows: "The Catholic does not demand a juridical norm by which the Pope could be impeached, he relies on the power of the grace of God and of the Holy Spirit in the Church."

Outside of the Church, the phenomenology of authority, as we might call it, is—though lacking in supernatural elements—surprisingly complex. Consider a quotidian example from the world of law. The opinion of the Supreme Court of the United States in *Plessy v. Ferguson* (1896), which gave compulsive, legal effect to the "separate but equal" doctrine, is still, as they say, "on the books." However, without a jot or a tittle of the text having been altered, someone trained in American law would say that the decision has been divested of what authority it once carried; the untrained eye would miss this altogether. To take another example that exemplifies the same point from a more oblique angle, if the question is what authority can be found in the judgment of the Supreme Court in the case *Bush v. Gore* (2000), which rendered George W. Bush the president and Al Gore a citizen, the answer will have to come from a mind trained in the dynamic logic of our legal tradition; though the case has not been overruled or even questioned by a majority Supreme Court opinion, the question of its authority is by no means transparent, and the best-trained minds have in fact reached differing conclusions. The official written pronouncements of even our most august civic bodies carry no imprimatur of authority; indeed, as J. Budziszewski shows, the writtenness of law sometimes tends to, and in the judicial culture of the United States today sometimes does, undermine law's authority, while allowing the state to grow through the unlawful usurpation of power by those in positions of legal authority.[16] Those agreeing with Budziszewski's diagnosis of the current American situation will look again to the path sketched by Hittinger, according to which authority is located in societies, not conceded from time to time by a unitary sovereign.

A cognate issue is developed in the chapters by Thomas Kohler and the present author, both building on the classic essay by Bernard Lonergan, S.J., "Dialectic of Authority," which first appeared in the 1974 anthology quoted at the beginning of this Introduction. On Lonergan's understanding, legitimate governments create authorities or offices, but a person's de facto occupation or possession of such an authoritative position or office does not guarantee that the he or she will embody authority. As one influential account observes, one can be *in* authority without being *an* authority,[17] and the conditions of the latter frequently are hard to satisfy. Kohler links embodied authority—that is, *being* an authority—to friendship and solidarity; Brennan traces such authority to contextual satisfaction of the unrestricted human desire to know the real and the good.[18]

Both authors insist that an ongoing dialectic is necessary to avoid authority's declension into the authoritarian. Harold Laski saw the need of such a dialectic, and commented on it as follows in his *Authority in the Modern State*: "If we remember St. Francis we must not forget the inquisition; if we insist upon the wrong of Hus' condemnation, we must not neglect the splendid ideals of the Cardinal of Cusa. We have to remember, in brief, that the realization of the Kingdom of God involves the holding of property, the making of contracts, the appointment of officers, the determination of dogma. The fact that the Pope is the Vicar of Christ does not exclude scrutiny into the details of his election. And our judgment upon the state must be in similar terms."[19] By a comparison of texts' respective places in the law of the state and in the life of the Catholic Church, Brennan clarifies the existential conditions of authority. Kohler's conclusion in this vein is both sobering and emboldening: "[A]uthentic authority requires authentic friendship, embodied in shared judgments about what is objectively and verifiably valuable."

Hannah Arendt denied that the conditions of authority can be satisfied in today's world. The authors of the present volume have been unwilling to limit the conditions of the possibility of legitimate power over the free individuals of a community, as Arendt did, to the Roman trinity of religion, tradition, and authority. If Kohler is right and friendship is a necessary condition of authentic authority, then perhaps the obtaining matrix of atomized individuals and sovereign state renders authority elusive or impossible. But perhaps deeper within that matrix there lie enough genuine societies in operation, each with its authentic authority and animated by the bonds of friendship in pursuit of the truly valuable, that we are not as bad off as sometimes appears in the emergent McWorld.

Withal, it remains a question of fact. The contribution of the present volume to Christian jurisprudence is a fresh collection of theological and philosophical insights into the human capacity to separate the authoritative from the authoritarian, across the spectrum of human living. Across the spectrum of human living, the fact proves the possibility, though the fact may prove difficult of achievement. Will transcendence "flame out, like shining from shook foil"? Will there be what Joseph Vining called that "eschatological thrust in law"? Holmes denied the possibility. The authors gathered together here affirm it. But it is a conditioned possibility, as Joseph Vining explained in one of the texts that raised the possibility of the current study, *Civilizing Authority*:

> Legal analysis consists of working with texts, as others work with texts. There is much else in addition in the practice of law and much else in the

deciding of a wrenching case. But this is what the legally trained do when asked to find the law and say what the law is, whether they are judges, or among those who are, in fact, the source of statements of law in that greater part of human affairs that does not and never can reach a court.

Are they foolish to engage in this kind of activity? Is it a front, a cover? Is it beside the point, superfluous or superstructural? The question is always with us and may be asked now. . . . The shape of the answer that will emerge should be evident. It is an answer of the not-if kind. Not foolish, not superfluous, if law is to have authority. Not if law is to hold us, evoke our willing acceptance rather than our resistance. Not if law is to be a source to be looked to in discovering what we ought to do. Perhaps we do not or ought not to want that; but if we do not, then we cannot complain about disintegration, disappearance of authority, of respect, and of self-respect, or loss of meaning in the modern state.[20]

NOTES

1. Hannah Arendt, "What Was Authority?" in Carl J. Friedrich (ed.), *Authority: Nomos I* (Cambridge, Mass.: Harvard University Press, 1958), 81. The paper was delivered in 1956; the volume came out in 1958.

2. Frederick J. Adelmann, S.J. (ed.), *Authority* (The Hague: Martinus Nijhoff, 1974), 1.

3. R. Baine Harris (ed.), *Authority: A Philosophical Analysis* (Tuscaloosa: University of Alabama Press, 1976) 1.

4. Glenn Tinder, "Authority and Liberty," in this volume, 59.

5. Michael J. White, "The Disappearance of Authority and the Elusiveness of Nonnatural Authority," in this volume, 23.

6. Thomas C. Kohler, "A Rock on Which One Can Build: Friendship, Solidarity, and the Notion of Authority," in this volume, 99.

7. Joseph Vining, "Authority and Reality," in this volume, 4.

8. Richard T. De George, *The Nature and Limits of Authority* (Lawrence: University Press of Kansas, 1985), 12 (emphasis added).

9. John E. Coons, "Does Authority Invite or Command?" in this volume, 82.

10. Steven D. Smith, "'Hollow Men'? Law and the Declension of Belief," in this volume, 213.

11. Avery Cardinal Dulles, S.J., "Authority in the Church," in this volume, 36.

12. Joseph Vining, *The Authoritative and the Authoritarian* (Chicago: The University of Chicago Press, 1986).

13. David A. Stagaman, S.J., *Authority in the Church* (Collegeville: The Liturgical Press, 1999), 35–38, 46–47, 51–55.

14. Russell Hittinger, "Society, Subsidiarity, and Authority in Catholic Social Thought," in this volume, 130–38.

15. Evelyn Waugh, *Brideshead Revisited: The Sacred and Profane Memories of Captain Charles Ryder* (New York: Alfred A. Knopf, 1944), 174–75.

16. See J. Budziszewski, "How a Constitution May Undermine Constitutionalism," in this volume, 149–53.

17. See Richard A. Flathman, *The Practice of Political Authority: Authority and the Authoritative* (Chicago: The University of Chicago Press, 1980), 16–19.

18. Patrick McKinley Brennan, "Locating Authority in Law," in this volume, 185, 190–91.

19. Harold J. Laski, *Authority in the Modern State* (New Haven, Conn.: Yale University Press, 1927), 68.

20. Vining, *The Authoritative and the Authoritarian*, 40.

I

THE SPECTRUM OF THE AUTHORITY EXPERIENCE TODAY

1

Authority and Reality

Joseph Vining

"Imagination" has been introduced as a term of art in discussion of the social and political world. Some years ago James Boyd White turned to it in *The Legal Imagination*,[1] his monumental work on the foundations of secular law and legal practice. A prominent example of its use today is Charles Taylor's *Modern Social Imaginaries*,[2] tracing changes in the common mind leading to what we now call modernity.

The term can have a large scope and at the same time a rather definite meaning. "Imagination" is at the center of Mark Massa's comments on the contrarian position of the Catholic Church in American life, contrasting David Tracy's well-known and distinctively Catholic "analogical imagination" with imagination that is "dialectical." American culture, it is said, is skeptical and even dismissive of tradition and authority. The "dialectical imagination" is allied with "individualism" and an "instrumental" approach to the world.[3] A similar picture of what lies at the roots of American social and political thought appears in the report of the American Catholics in the Public Square Project, referring repeatedly to the "individualist core" of American culture, which is a "culture of choice," the very terms of debate being "set by radical individualism."[4]

It is a useful term, "imagination" or "an imagination," even if it has a tendency to squeeze out the normative aspirations clinging to the older term "ideal." Certainly all that it brings to mind takes the sources of social and political arrangements beyond the total theories of mindless system and process being pressed so strongly today. It puts human capacity and experience into visions of the nature of "stars and stones and everything else"[5] and helps keep human society distinctively human.

But "imagination" does carry with it an implicit contrast with "reality," and it is this I want to pick up and emphasize in this initial chapter, the reality that imagination feeds and is fed by. Imagination may mold reality. But the reality of things can mold the imagination, and I will suggest that the reality of things speaks clearly to any view of the social and political world that is skeptical and even dismissive of authority. Attending to this somewhat more than has been done can put Catholic experience in particular to the service of a realistic idealism or an idealistic reality (if I may use the older term "ideal"). Catholic thought can help ground secular imagination of a better world in what is possible.

THE PERVASIVENESS OF AUTHORITY

It does seem to be a hallmark of modernity to dismiss "authority," the very notion of it. But the truth is that authority and the response to it we call "deference" or, in its full presence, a "willing obedience," are to be found everywhere in the modern world.[6] Nothing could be less atavistic or more modern. Authority is the heart of joint effort and organized human life, making the ideal of a universal regime of truly free contract between individuals more a bulwark against authoritarian tyranny than a real possibility. Founders even of the Chicago School of Economics[7] saw this and introduced it into the very definition of "free enterprise," where exchange relationships of an arms-length kind are between "business entities" rather than between human individuals, and "authority" continues within the business entity.

If the "invisible hand" of a competitive economic system is marvelous in the way it makes joint life possible, so too is authority marvelous in what it makes possible. The language of the law of the authority of an agent, "agency law" on which the law of business entities such as the corporation is built, is startling on first encounter, with its three duties of "care," "loyalty," and "obedience." Property law, joined with the law of contract and the law of business entities as the foundation of the modern world economic order, is not just or even primarily a law of relations between human beings and things, but is rather the context of "orders" constantly being given and heard everywhere. "Property" locates the human voice that will speak an order to another human being, and provides the sanction, exclusion from a flow of material goods or necessities if (a most important "if") the law as a whole gives the order the authority of law. An illuminating analog of this aspect of "property" and its setting within the law as a whole is to be seen today in what we now and newly call "animal law" as a course of study and field of legal practice, in which a growing web of criminal, administrative, and constitutional provisions focuses an "owner" of a "non-human sentient being" on the interests of the animal itself and requires they be taken into account in making decisions that can have the authority of law and be protected or enforced "in the name of the law."[8]

Then of course there is government with its government agencies great and small, wrapped around with "administrative law," which is entirely about a search for authority, for a reason to obey or for a reason to give up a challenge to an order.

Sometimes, it should be said, this decisionmaking on the part of one making a decision and speaking it, and then the decisionmaking on the part of one hearing it and making a decision to defer or obey, is discussed in terms of "power"—which fits more easily into an imagined universe in which things merely are and events merely happen. "Power relationships" is the phrase. But there is and always has been a distinction between power and authority in the law of human organization (as, for that matter, there is in the Gospels). Power is a negative thing, authority a positive. Employers may think to themselves that it is power to fire—to stop a flow of money and respect to an employee—and to countermand what the employee proposes, says, or orders, that enables them to cause employees to take initiatives into the unknown future for the sake of joint enterprise. But it is not their power, certainly not their power alone, but their authority, if they have it. With recognition of authority, the one who is ordered recognizes the other who is ordering as a source, and he puts his own imagination to the task. It is authority, not power, that releases imagination and initiative in the service of the goals of joint enterprise. Organized life, except on a most rudimentary level, would not be possible without it.

It may be noted too that within science, so central to any conception of modernity, authority and authorities are to be seen despite strenuous denial that there is anything of the kind. There are central texts. There is deference, there is good faith and taking-on-faith, there is office and exclusion from office, teaching and discipline of teaching—most of the detailed features associated with the creation and presence of joint effort and decisionmaking based on recognition and acceptance of authority. The phenomenon of authority within science is, I think, nicely revealed by the near universal hostility among scientists to its elimination through a folding or absorption of science itself into the very processes it undertakes to examine on the assumption that they are all there is.

THE WORKINGS OF AUTHORITY

From this brief pointing to the pervasiveness and, indeed, modernity of authority, let me turn to the workings or structure of the phenomenon, if "phenomenon" is not too neutral and static a term for something that is so much inside us and part of the promptings of life. Even in a sketch of it, I believe the contributions Catholic experience can make to the social and political imagination may be seen to emerge on their own.

I want to try some equations or equivalences for authority in practice, the way it emerges and fades, appears, disappears, and reappears. A book by a physicist on the basic phenomena of space and time will be found full of equations, each a summary, and a summary when knit together. We would not want to cast aside discussion and offer formulaic theses to take its place, but we can play with equations of a sort for the equally basic phenomenon of authority, and gain some of the brevity the device offers, perhaps even some of its mnemonic advantages.

Begin at the most particular level—that is, the sound or shape that identifies itself as the voice of a person—and consider that:

- Who a person says he or she is, and whether to start paying attention to what he says, may be the same.
- Whether a person is who he says he is, and whether to continue paying attention to what he says, may be the same.
- Whether to obey and whether to continue paying attention, may be the same.
- Therefore, who a speaking person is and whether to obey may be the same.

Introduce other terms of discussion and there can be other "equations" of such rough pointers to the presence or not of authority. For example:

- Whether to continue paying attention, and whether there is a mind perceived, may be the same.
- Whether there is a perceptible mind, and whether what appears to be a person is believed to be a person, may be the same.[9]

Now behind and beneath the ingredients and working of authority are presuppositions—of the existence at all of the mindful and the caring, of the responsibility of speakers for what they say, of the authenticity or not of statements made, of persons or "entities" beyond individuals, even of the transcendence of space and time as they are commonly conceived in ordinary life. The contribution of Catholic thought and experience to the understanding and further development of modern social and political organization may consist in some large part in making these presuppositions plausible, understandable, comfortable to entertain, and an ordinary part of what might still be called secular thought. Contrarian the Church may be and remain, a witness and a challenge. But far from being set against the workings of the modern world, the Church's explicit acknowledgments, even its language, may be a reservoir of perception of what makes the modern world actually work.

AUTHORITY AND THE PERSON

Principal among these is the person. Acknowledgment of and speaking of and, ultimately, believing in the person is also, to borrow the title of Steven D. Smith's new book, "law's quandary."[10] It is always an individual from whose thought and mouth speech comes, that most particular level at which playing with equations of authority would begin. The individual never fades from the picture. Recognition of the individual as of unique value, the individual as not fungible but irreplaceable, individuals as access to and sources of identity each for the other, is indeed the source of what we try to express as *equality*, whether in Catholic or secular thought.[11] But when an individual speaks with authority, he or she does not speak for himself or herself. "I order you to stop!" she may say. "So what?" is the natural reply. "Do you have longer legs or stronger arms?" When she goes on to say, "I order you in the name of . . ." and then comes a name of a person beyond herself, speaker and spoken-to both step into the world of authority. Living in those whom all of us refer to as "persons" are the connections between us as "individuals," and these living connections make possible the political, economic, or environmental arrangements by which we live as individuals. These living connections stretch far beyond our individual life spans. They make possible the very thought of sacrifice of any kind. They make possible science itself, the very thought of science.[12]

The world of true authority is one in which a person beyond the individual does exist, and the difference between a world in which authority can be present, and one without authority or the possibility of it, is the difference between a world that can work, a world of hope, and a world in which there can be nothing more than empty sound and forces playing upon forces. The latter, of course, is the cosmology of total theory in the physical and biological sciences to which I have referred, and most interestingly, those who urge it strenuously upon the rest of us demonstrate in so many ways that they do not believe it. They—call them "they"—are test cases for the relation between the modern imagination and reality. They do believe both in the unique value of the individual and in persons behind and beyond the individual, however hard it is for them to bring themselves to say so.[13]

In fact, and in the most general way, what draws one of us to another of us is a sense of the authentic or the real in that other. In situation after situation, field after field of study and discussion, what makes us turn to a voice we hear, and stay with it among all the competing claims on our attention, is perception of the authentic, the real. So too, it should be said, what draws individuals to the Church is not primarily "neediness," which would and does give rise to the charge of imaginative wish fulfillment. We all certainly do have needs and are needy, but that is to the side of the primary thing, which is movement toward and opening up to what is most real. Deliverance from need, from bondage, from exile, there certainly is in this movement, and it touches on all that is meant by salvation. But the deliverance from bondage is from bondage to the inauthentic, the unreal, the not really meant; the exile is the strangeness of being away from home, which is what is most real. "Truth," it is sometimes called. This was the novelist Walker Percy's answer to those who pressed him on his adult conversion. It was not comfort that drew him. It was, he said, "that what the Catholic Church proposes is true."[14]

These connections between authority, reality, and the personal are obvious to some, but I know they are not obvious to others. Most of us surely believe in an objective truth about the material world, that there is such even if we do not grasp it all. We believe in a historical and physical reality. We believe in historical time and a past. We believe in a future ahead. We believe in science and medicine and engineering and each day show that we do. But it may take a very long time to realize with any clarity that most of what we know and believe about the reality of the physical, social, and historical world, the "real world" we say, is what I, or you, don't actually have direct, hands-on experience of. Nor does any scientist or mathematician have it, however fine or broadly competent. Life's too short. I am too limited as an individual and I venture to say you are and they are. Most of what we know and believe comes from what others testify, say to us, tell us. We trust them. We may choose whom to trust and believe, but we can't get away from that reliance and that trust in the person.

To believe anything full and rounded about the objective real world, to do that, we must first believe in each other and believe each other. The person is primary, first, the bedrock. The person whom we listen to and join with isn't a product, something manufactured by all this mighty world around us. It's the other way around. All this mighty world depends on the reality of the person, as does the Church. I hardly dare essay here anything about the Eucharist and what the Eucharist does, but I will try because it is pertinent to our subject, almost *is* our subject. The Eucharist is a celebration of ultimate reality. It is a celebration of the personal and the person in which we are joined and in whom we live without losing ourselves. But not just a celebration of the person or the personal as if what is celebrated were somewhere else. It is touching the thing itself, which of course is not a thing—a being-with that, a taking that reality into ourselves and identification with that reality, coming as close as we can come to the authentic, the bedrock, and leaving it each time refreshed, more real, more at one with oneself, and more anchored in the world.

An unremarkable thing to say, I hope, that this is what the Church offers, but it may not be realized how much to the point it is. Look home to the real or reality as a source, perhaps the source, of the various contributions Catholicism can make to the secular world. Within Christianity, Catholicism is marked by the fullness of its commitment to the actuality of spirit in the world, not called to mind as if from memory by symbol of it, but present. Spirit present, apprehended as a person. To the question who or what is Catholic, one could not do better than starting there; and if the connections between us that allow any of us to survive in the here and now, not to say flourish, are to be aided by a distinctive contribution from Catholics, Catholics could not do better than start with this. No backwardness, shyness, or embarrassment about it, no giving over the "real world" to imaginary visions that have no place for spirit or person in the general social and political world, any more than appeal to the empirical can be given over to those who categorically deny large parts of human experience.

REALITY AND THE PERSON

Let me continue with this connection between the personal and the real, to which we come through the connection there is between the authoritative and the personal.

Admittedly, any person takes us as individuals beyond place and ordinary passing time. Human language is but vibrations and marks without a voice heard through it. Hearing a voice takes attention, work, and time. The very undertaking to understand the meaning of the always changing physical evidence of sounds and sights by associating some of the evidence with a voice and some not, continuing throughout to pay attention despite all the competing claims on attention, fairly leaps beyond ordinary space and time.

It is also true that as persons, for we are persons and individuals both, we are mutually created as we seek the authentic in the different bits of evidence we each present to ourselves and others over the passage of ordinary time, and that others present back to us. Creation is continuously "at work," as we who work might say, in our seeing persons around us: those whom we name with "proper names," those with more general names like "Church" or "People of Israel" or "Court" or "Congress," and those with the largest names.

But though transcendence of time is involved, and creation is at work, when a person is seen and heard the person is here and now, as real as anything else in the here and now.

In the same way, authority is real—not just pervasive in any realistic appraisal of the present state of affairs, but real in itself. Someone facing the authoritative does not choose to grant authority—authority is not a matter of choice. One can deny it, because one can deny anything. But one does not deny authority without striking at one's own integrity, one's identity, and one's own reality.

The reality of authority is rather like physical reality, which one also does not deny except at great cost or by a seeming self-delusion to which one is a knowing party. It is not wholly like physical reality, of course. There is a passivity in acknowledgment of physical reality—less passivity perhaps than might once have been thought, for experimental psychology suggests much activity at semiconscious or unconscious levels before the simplest perception, but there is at least a sense of passivity in physical experience, which happens *to* me though I may struggle to evade it. In the experience of authority there is no passivity at all. The authoritative that one recognizes takes work to find. Activity precedes recognition—listening, discarding, and listening again. But there are ample incentives to the work however hard the work may be, in either the Christian community or secular life, and all who work are working toward that which they must acknowledge. There is choice in choosing to work. In the end, those who do the work do not choose whether to hear what they hear.

AUTHORITY AND VALUE

All this has much to do with one further aspect of the phenomenon of authority, with which we will end this sketch of it. That is the internalization of value that accompanies recognition of authority and perception of a person.

The achievement of a sense that someone asking for attention does have the identity or "name" that is initially claimed is an achievement through work, action really, "creation," as we have noted. With it comes a living connection with value that, we assume in all our practices, can be felt within and seen from without. Individuals grow into the world asking, "What should I do or say or think?" and grown individuals wander the world asking the same. They ask the same when moving to speak for the persons they are also. There are responses, voices back, and then responses in turn to those. When what we commonly call "value" animates the response—animates, in a living way—then those asking and those responding are in the world of authority. We have noted that the world of authority is one in which the person, the very notion of a person, can and does exist. The world of authority is marked by that possibility and presence. The line and difference between what is within us and what is outside us also marks the border of the world of authority, and on the question of the internal, Catholics can speak and show and speak and show again.

The person to whom we listen and respond in good faith is not outside our skin but brought within us. That which we of the genuinely puzzled question "What should I do?"—we of the here and now—have a part in creating, is part of us. This is the source of our response in good faith, of our true willingness in what we call "willing obedience" (to the degree we are indeed truly willing to do what we do in our response and in our continued listening): that all this that is beyond our hereness and nowness is *within*, as much within as our hereness and nowness is within.

Authority "commands," it is said. Authority "orders" thought and action. But there are two polar attitudes toward any "command," and the choice to range toward one or the other is always open. One possibility is to take the command into account in good faith in making one's decisions—after, of course, coming to some conclusion about how to read it. The other is not to take the command into account except insofar as we are forced to or it is convenient and good strategy to do so. The one attitude partakes of faith; the language of faith, "good" faith, is found everywhere salting descriptions and prescriptions of secular social and political organization, private and public, local, national, and international.[15] The other attitude turns us to pursue our various ends to gain whatever advantage we can until superior force comes after us and makes us stop. We take the initiative with respect to the purpose and sense of the command, understanding it as having purpose and sense. Or we are begrudging, passive. We shift the burden of initiative to those seeking to affect our behavior, and we use the advantages of delay and congestion—two of the givens of the here and now, real limits of space and of passage of time, always hold those advantages out to us. We externalize the command, keeping it quite at arm's length. Or we internalize it.

If it remains not internalized, that does not mean that someone has not given an order, that a decision has not been made or conveyed by someone, or a statement has not been issued, or that the decision or the statement will have no factual effect, no effect on history. It does mean that the hearer will not be actually guided by it and instead will work against or around it. That will be the reality, whatever the soothing appearances. But it is equally a reality of human life that to the extent the statement or decision is not worked against or around, it is internalized. It is part of one to that extent; it animates and directs one's affirmative seeking. Indeed, an authoritative statement is a piece of the evidence of what oneself believes.

I think I need hardly add, in speaking of authority and internalization, that we don't take poison into ourselves. Nor do we need to add an equation to our earlier set of sentence-propositions about authority to reflect this. Whatever is merely a system may not be a mind at all, but a "mindless system" that spins or grinds on without regard, respect, or care. What is wholly self-aggrandizing, wholly competitive and manipulative, can make no authentic statement about a value that might be internalized, and could not be or speak for a person that is a living connection between us as individuals. This is obviously true in secular law that speaks openly of authority, in the "name of the law," and obviously true in the Church. But it is equally true in the business entities where so much of the experience of secular authority in daily life occurs. They do not, either in legal contemplation or in practice, have the face economic theory paints. The possibility of the authoritarian, that uses you and does you in if it is internalized, always shadows the experience of authority, but authoritative voices are heard often enough and for long enough to make life together possible and sometimes (as we say) absorbing.

In fact, the very way authority comes to be through internalization can serve to nourish the essential equality of individuals to which we alluded earlier, since it may be thought that each must presuppose and come close to concluding that the mind and voice constructed and heard cares about *him* and his own, *her* and her own, not merely him or her as a fungible and dispensable part of a system. There is a mutuality in the way authority comes to be. The listener, as individual, asks and learns, but on the understanding that she is learning something about herself.

Person, understanding, authority, and internalization thus flow together. A claim of authority—and this extends to the secular world in general and secular law in general—is an asking. It is, again, an asking for willingness, or "good will," and good faith. A claim of authority is not asking for obedience based on habit and unthinking reflex, which at the very least would be exasperating and unreliable in a changing world, nor for obedience based on fear, however much fear is in the picture, which would have nothing to do with a sense of obligation and the opening of the imagination that comes with it, the "devoting" of oneself as we say even in secular life. In this asking for willing obedience, and in the fashioning of statements legal or otherwise that when read as a whole over time actually can be willingly obeyed, lies the merger of speaker and listener—the same merger, it may be noted, that has always been at the center of Catholic perception of the world.

An authoritative statement incorporates what is to be done by the one wondering what ought to be done or said or thought in a brief appearance in a vast, complex, and changing world. An authoritative statement is very nearly a responsive definition of the one wondering, a definition at least offered, and what happens when authority appears happens in the mind of the listener quite as much as in the mind of the speaker. The same statement is also a definition of the person speaking the statement—again, not the individual speaking but the person—and as the statement is developed, understood, and internalized, and values that animate the speaker come to animate the listener and be the listener's own, the two are pulled together.

As to value as such, when a decision is being made or a statement written that is to be offered as authoritative, it is often said that "considerations" or "factors" are *weighed* or given *weight*, or are the *grounds* for what is offered. If an end sought or consequence contemplated bears on the decision, it is marked for notice as a factor or consideration, and indeed the particularity of a person speaking or deciding authoritatively is produced by or found in the particular factors or considerations that person is authorized to take into account and does in an authentic way. "Grounds" and "weighing" are geographical and gravity-derived images. But in a human decision cast into human language, "factors" become values for the listener seeking to understand, as much as for the speaker and decider. They are no longer something outside and weighing on one, to which attention is paid because it must be paid as one acknowledges the weight of one's leg and takes it into account because gravity outside oneself requires that one pay attention to its weight. They are warm, because inside, and the authoritative decisionmaker is warm toward them. They are not so much restraining and limiting as animating and feeding thought. Their place is not in past time, with causation in the nature of a push, but in the future, from which they pull like a voice calling. Defined though they may be by the very course of human decision and response, it does not go too far to say that they have something at least like life themselves.

In secular discussion the phrase "living value" comes often and easily to the tongue, and there is no suggestion that it is not at all really meant. In fact, in criminal law analysis, both in the development of a sense of what it is that makes an action criminal, the so-called mental element of the crime that is essential to "true" crime, and in determinations of criminal sanctions based in any degree on retribution with the possibility of remorse and forgiveness, discussion often and quite naturally paints a picture of the value itself as injured, and the object of prosecution, conviction, and punishment as restoration or maintenance of the value as a living force in the human world.

AUTHORITY AND THE SENSE OF LIFE

This leads me to suggest, but only suggest, that the Catholic sense of life, so very far from the sense of anything that is merely a "product" of a system and part of a system, may contribute at the same basic level we have been trying to explore. No confident claim about the nature of the reality of value has to be made here. It is enough to think of the possibility of adding a breath of life into secular discussion of value.

I will illustrate with a contemporary example—the ongoing discussion in the United States of the legal status of torture—where the need for such help seems very clear.

In an "instrumental" vision of the world, there are only systemic costs and systemic benefits. This is axiomatic in the biological sciences and in economics, and there is a push to think the same in all secular social and political affairs. Catholic moral and social thought is very different. There can be and there are some things you just do not do, some considerations that are paramount, some values that are, as is said, "absolute." There are in Judaism, ancient and contemporary—I think of Rabbi Jonathan Sacks's fine book of a decade ago, *Faith in the Future*—"in the entire created universe there is only one thing of absolute value . . . the human individual. *Any* human individual."[16]

But in the modern secular world there is at least one value that has been designated by international treaty and national statute as absolute, its violation unjustifiable in any circumstance and not to be done whatever the cost. It stands against torture of even a single human being by one in a position of authority. There is never authority for torture. The international Convention Against Torture, emerging from the horrors of the twentieth century, is quite explicit, and it is a felony now under federal law for any agent of the United States to torture a human being.

In 2002, eight years after American ratification and implementation of the Convention Against Torture, lawyers in the United States Department of Justice undertook to make statements about the meaning of torture that would have the authority of their offices in government behind them. What they wrote was received with widespread revulsion and eventually disavowed, but most certainly conveys a recognizable cast of mind.[17]

They asked, "If this is a thing you just don't do, what is the *thing*?" and they took a somewhat scientific stance of open-minded ignorance (though it should be said that experimental scientists less and less take such a stance where in question is the torture of animals who are legally protected against it, "it" being "torture" without elaboration). They were in this sense cold, as they went about the business they had set themselves. They dwelt on examples, writing in sentences that might be pasted in a manual for torture and not look out of place. They went to the dictionary looking for a definition. They sought to quantify suffering, and turned to statutes and decisions on flows of quantities of compensatory money or health insurance, looking for a calculus of pain. They sought to fold the question of torture into the likelihood a judge and jury might move against an official accused of torture and make him suffer in some way himself, implying that the question "Am I a torturer?" is not "What will happen to this creature in my hands?" but rather "Will someone stop me?" as in the world imagined by Oliver Wendell Holmes, which his official biographer called "bleak and terrifying,"[18] where that is the only question.

When they did turn to other responsible authorities that might genuinely have wrestled with what is protected by the prohibition against torture—that might have wrestled even in the biblical sense with What protects—they were publicly charged with methodological "incompetence." Incompetent, because they did not do the work necessary to hear, themselves, an authoritative voice—they did not look to the whole but picked out a single statement here or there from statements succeeding one another in ordinary time as the statements of any living voice do. Moreover, as when wondering what sufficiently "rends" a human being's personality in the use of mind-altering drugs as part of modern torture, they picked out statutory terms (such as "profound" from "disrupt profoundly the senses or the personality") as if Congress legislating was approaching torture in the same way they were, setting up rules with which would-be torturers would have to contend. There is more than a suggestion that tax law, with its rules and categorizations and interpretations of it scaled according to their relative "aggressiveness," was the model of law itself they had in mind; and tax law may indeed have edged into the center of secular legal thought today, the more so because it matches law as the purely "economic man" would have it. Distinctively, and explicitly, tax law imposes little or no obligation to seek the ends it seeks. There is no value at its heart meant to be internalized by those to whom it is addressed. It hardly has a heart. That is its peculiarity as law.

Why the official disowning of what they did,[19] and why the widespread fear for ourselves that it was done? Is it not the absence of any sense that they were dealing not with a thing, but a value? They were seeking how close they could get to "it," how close to a line without "crossing the line," when, as in the case of any crime, you are not to go close to the line—if in truth there is any such thing as a "line" in the "definition" of crime. We commonly use instead the language of "respect" and "violation," respecting a value as if it were a person. A value has a glow and indistinct edges. It beckons and is fragile and can be injured like anything alive. What the prohibition of torture speaks of is a value of such a kind that when near it you take off your shoes.

While no doubt there were Catholics involved in the interrogations of terror suspects, Catholics might be particularly expected to see that these statements about torture were untouched and unguided by any sense of the sacred. And while Catholic lawyers too might try to respond to a plea for help from interrogators, they would think as Catholics think, from the beginning, of life and what lives and death and what is dead. They would have in mind not just the mortal individuals whose fates might be in their hands but, in some real way, the fate of that to which they looked for hope. They would, as Catholics, be serious as the authors of these statements were not serious, engaged as these authors were detached, warm as these authors were cold. It would not be beside the point for Catholic lawyers, though it might be for those they could help, that it is a crucifix that might be on their wall at home, and that in reality, and with time as it actually is, Christ's suffering is not only an "event" that occurred but occurs now, all around the world.

Let us end this brief look at the ways in which Catholic thought can serve as something in the nature of a reality check for the secular world by returning to science that plays such a large part in giving the modern world its secular cast. The well-known Cambridge paleobiologist Simon Conway Morris's recent book, *Life's Solution*, reviews the evidence for and against adaptational trajectories and inevitabilities in evolution as it is now understood—as opposed to everything we see now being entirely "accident," happy or unhappy. He ends his preface saying, "Contrary to popular belief, the science of evolution does not belittle us. As I argue, something like ourselves is an evolutionary inevitability, and our existence also reaffirms our one-ness with the rest of Creation." "Nevertheless," what "we are given allows us to make a choice." He then ends the book with the "special dilemma" of modernity, the human possession now of tools that "treat the world as endlessly malleable," open, as he says earlier, to "limitless manipulation."[20]

The place of authority is in Conway Morris's words "we" and "us." Authority resides there. Authority makes it possible to think of an "us" making a choice that has some hope of effect. That to which his "we" and "us" refer is, I think, a reality for Conway Morris and a reality for others throughout science and throughout the secular world. That reality, however, many shy from acknowledging, with consequences they themselves lament. Acknowledgment of reality has its own way of healing, in social and political affairs as much as in personal life. Here Catholic thought, in its conscious affirmation of persons beyond, behind, within, and greater than the individual, can be quite specifically helpful to the secular world. This is only one of the ways.

NOTES

1. James Boyd White, *The Legal Imagination: Studies in the Nature of Legal Thought and Expression* (Boston: Little, Brown and Company, 1973).

2. Charles Taylor, *Modern Social Imaginaries* (Durham, N.C.: Duke University Press, 2004), 49–58, 185–94.

3. Mark S. Massa, *Anti-Catholicism in America: The Last Acceptable Prejudice* (New York: Crossroads, 2003), especially 51–58; Eugene McCarraher, "Some Things Never Change," review of *Anti-Catholicism In America*, by Mark S. Massa, *Commonweal* 130, no. 15 (September 2003): 38–40. See generally John T. McGreevy, *Catholicism and American Freedom: A History* (New York: W. W. Norton, 2003), and its sensitive review and summary in Richard W. Garnett, "American Conversations With(in) Catholicism," 102 *Michigan Law Review* 1191 (2004). On "analogical" imagination, see David Tracy, *The Analogical Imagination: Christian Theology and the Culture of Pluralism* (New York: Crossroads, 1981).

4. Commonweal Foundation, "American Catholics in the Public Square: A Report to the Catholic Community," *Commonweal* 131, no. 13 (July 2004): A1–15.

5. This nice phrase, a variant of "the universe and everything in it," is from Steven Weinberg, *Dreams of a Final Theory: The Search for the Fundamental Laws of Nature* (New York: Pantheon, 1992), 242: "A 'final' or 'total' theory (the offering of imagination and ready to be replaced by it) is 'the book of rules that governs stars and stones and everything else.'" Like the individual offering visions of this kind or the individual listening to one offering them, human imagination is not governed by a "book of rules." Nor is law's authority. Charles Taylor's *Modern Social Imaginaries*, which is offered as a work of intellectual and cultural history, might be read to the contrary, but for Taylor's response (p. 51) to his own question whether "ontically" human response to "some human-transcending spiritual reality" is an "inescapable dimension of human life," or whether instead, in the working of cultural evolution "exclusively within the psyches of human beings," "humans can eventually put [their 'common religious capacity'] behind them." "Obviously," Taylor says, he himself has "strong hunches" on the matter.

6. Free societies do not have easy words for what might be called the second half of the phenomenon of authority. I have used "deference" before, e.g., "Authority and Responsibility: The Jurisprudence of Deference," 43 *Administrative Law Review* 135 (1991). It may have too passive a connotation, but it includes in one term both one's response to a direct order and one's response to an "authority's" action or statement that changes the world without a direct order to oneself. "Deference" also includes respect for responsible decisionmaking, and may operate down a hierarchy, from one above to one below, as well as in the more conventionally imagined direction up. Philip Soper has written recently of the "ethics of deference" in *The Ethics of Deference: Learning from Law's Morals* (Cambridge: Cambridge University Press, 2002).

7. See, e.g., Frank H. Knight, *The Economic Organization* (New York: Augustus M. Kelly, 1951), 28–30.

8. The most perceptive and detailed treatment of relationships of authority between human beings and animals is Vicki Hearne's *Adam's Task: Calling Animals by Name* (New York: Alfred A. Knopf, 1987).

9. There is some further playing with such "equations" in my *The Authoritative and the Authoritarian* (Chicago: University of Chicago Press, 1988), 230–234. For contrast with the terms in which these are cast, see, e.g., Murray Gell-Mann, *The Quark and the Jaguar: Adventures in the Simple and the Complex* (New York: W. H.

Freeman, 1994), 117: "At Caltech, it is mostly the brain that is studied. The mind in neglected, and in some circles even the word is suspect (a friend of mine calls it the M-word)."

There are in fact attempts to use equational or quasi-mathematical notation in a quite serious way in discussion of authority and human law. See, e.g., Joseph Raz, *The Authority of Law: Essays on Law and Morality* (Oxford: Clarendon Press, 1983), 64–65; and John Searle, *The Construction of Social Reality* (New York: Free Press, 1995), 43–51. For my own comments on such reduction and fixing of what speakers have in mind, see "The Gift of Language," 73 *Notre Dame Law Review* 1581, 1582–85, 1594–95, 1597–98 (1998).

10. Steven D. Smith, *Law's Quandary* (Cambridge, Mass.: Harvard University Press, 2004). See also Smith's concluding chapter in this volume and his essay, "Metaphysical Complexity?" 55 *Catholic University Law Review* 639 (2006).

11. Cf. Patrick McKinley Brennan, "Meaning's Edge, Love's Priority," 101 *Michigan Law Review* 2060, 2072–73, 2082 (2003); John E. Coons and Patrick McKinley Brennan, *By Nature Equal: The Anatomy of a Western Insight* (Princeton, N.J.: Princeton University Press, 1999).

12. The life in the individual and in the person of the human world becomes more insistent, in thinking of them, when contrasted with the "individual" and "identity" in scientific thought. See Peter Pesic's interesting account of the latter in *Seeing Double: Shared Identities in Physics, Philosophy, and Literature* (Cambridge, Mass.: MIT Press, 2002).

13. See note 3 supra. My own *The Song Sparrow and The Child: Claims of Science and Humanity* (Notre Dame, Ind.: Notre Dame University Press, 2004) is an exploration of the relation between human law and total or final theories.

14. "Why Are You a Catholic?" in *Living Philosophies: The Reflections of Some Eminent Men and Women of Our Time*, ed. Clifton Fadiman (New York: Doubleday, 1990), reprinted in *Why I Am Still a Catholic*, ed. Kevin Ryan and Marilyn Ryan (New York: Penguin-Riverhead, 1998).

15. As with other aspects and conditions of authority, secular reliance and insistence on "good faith" can be helped. Under increasing pressure from the thrust in Western thought that positively wants to see each of us and each of our institutions as only systems reacting to the actions of other systems, never as responsible and choosing, it just may be that over time the secular language of "good faith" will become too feeble to do its work without aid from its more robust source. Tacit acknowledgment can sometimes be enough—the chemist Michael Polanyi has often referred to the "tacit dimension" of any knowledge, including the scientific. But under such constant pressure, the social and political sensibility may need some more conscious apprehension of the actual faith there is within the secular sense of "good faith."

16. Jonathan Sacks, *Faith in the Future* (London: Darton, Longman and Todd, 1995), 86.

17. Their memorandum to the Counsel to the President remained the official position of the Department of Justice for two years, 2002–2004, before being withdrawn and replaced by a new memorandum of a different tenor, prepared for release to the public as theirs was not. The text can be found at www.washingtonpost.com and other websites, under the title "Standards of Conduct for

Interrogation under 18 U.S.C. §§2340–2340A, August 1, 2002," and in *The Torture Papers: The Road to Abu Ghraib*, ed. Karen J. Greenberg and Joshua L. Dratel (Cambridge: Cambridge University Press, 2005), 172. It is discussed and quoted in its public replacement, "Legal Standards Applicable Under 18 U.S.C. §§2340–2340A, December 30, 2004," at www.usdoj.gov. "This memorandum supersedes the August 1, 2002, Memorandum in its entirety." Ibid. See Adam Liptak, "Legal Scholars Criticize Torture Memos," *New York Times*, 25 June 2004; Kate Zernike, "Defining Torture," and Adam Liptak, "How Far Can a Government Lawyer Go?" *New York Times*, 27 June 2004; Douglas Jehl and David Johnston, "C.I.A. Expands Its Inquiry into Interrogation Tactics," *New York Times*, 29 August 2004; *Confirmation Hearing on the Nomination of Alberto R. Gonzales to Be Attorney General of the United States*, 109th Cong., 1st sess., 6 January 2005, 157–70 (testimony of Harold H. Koh); David Johnston, Neil A. Lewis, and Douglas Jehl, "Nominee Gave Advice To C. I. A. on Torture Law," *New York Times*, 28 January 2005. But see, "Can Torture Ever Be Justified?" *Bulletin of the American Academy of Arts and Sciences* (Summer 2004): 3–4; Michael Ignatieff, *The Lesser Evil: Political Ethics in an Age of Terror* (Princeton, N.J.: Princeton University Press, 2004); and essays in *Torture: A Collection*, ed. Sanford Levinson (New York: Oxford University Press, 2004). For a discussion of the historical and international background see Rod Morgan, "The Utilitarian Justification of Torture," *Punishment & Society* 2, no. 2 (April 2000): 181–96.

18. Holmes's official biographers fell away from their encounter with Holmes's imagined world, one by one. In the words of one of them, Holmes himself was "savage, harsh, and cruel." But cruelty was in fact meaningless in the world in which Holmes tried to live or thought he lived, since it was without persons, or indeed individuals. Law, for Holmes, was "like everything else" in the universe and "[t]he postulate on which we think about the universe is that there is a fixed quantitative relation between every phenomenon and its antecedents and consequents." Oliver Wendell Holmes Jr., "The Path of the Law," 10 *Harvard Law Review* 457, 478 (1897). See Grant Gilmore, *The Ages of American Law* (New Haven, Conn.: Yale University Press, 1977), 48–49; Albert W. Alschuler, *Law Without Values: The Life, Work, and Legacy of Justice Holmes* (Chicago: The University of Chicago Press, 2000), 31–33; and my "The Cosmological Question," 94 *Michigan Law Review* 2024–25 (1996).

19. What they wrote was replaced "in its entirety"; see note 17. Public argument then shifted to treatment that current language separates from torture—the "cruel," the "degrading," the "inhuman," "outrages against personal dignity," in the words of the Geneva Conventions or the Universal Declaration of Human Rights. The same pursuit of quantification and self-executing "definition" occurred, as if law were present or absent to the degree of mathematical clarity in its expression—though all knew that neither murder nor manslaughter is definable apart from regard for the value of individual life. The galvanizing problem was, again, not fear of committing a crime against humanity but fear of suffering for doing so. For a sampling of contemporaneous description of the debate see, e.g., Tim Golden, "Senior Lawyer at Pentagon Broke Ranks on Detainees," *New York Times*, 20 February 2006; Jane Mayer, "The Memo," *New Yorker*, 27 February 2006, 32–41; Jim Rutenberg and Sheryl Gay Stolberg, "Bush Says G.O.P. Rebels Are

Putting Nation at Risk," *New York Times*, 16 September 2006; Scott Shane, "The Question of Liability Stirs Concern at the C.I.A.," *New York Times*, 16 September 2006; and Kate Zernike, "Top Republicans Reach an Accord on a Detainee Bill," *New York Times*, 22 September 2006.

20. Simon Conway Morris, *Life's Solution: Inevitable Humans in a Lonely Universe* (Cambridge: Cambridge University Press, 2003), xv–xvi, 2, 328–29. See also Conway Morris, The Gifford Lectures, 2007: "What Organic Evolution Tells Us about Our Place in the Universe."

2

The Disappearance of Natural Authority and the Elusiveness of Nonnatural Authority

Michael J. White

INTRODUCTION

As a philosopher who was partly trained in the tradition of so-called ordinary-language philosophy, I perhaps find the unabridged version of the *Oxford English Dictionary* more interesting reading than do many persons. On consulting its entry for "authority" (ultimately derived from the Latin abstract noun *auctoritas*, as the English "author" is derived from the Latin concrete noun *auctor*), I find as the first definition the following: "1. Power or right to enforce obedience; moral or legal supremacy; the right to command, or give an ultimate decision." In view of the fact that the definitions in the *OED* are given in chronological order—from oldest to more recent historical usages—I draw an inference from this entry that seems to me to be relevant to my remarks today: even in early English usage there seems to have been some ambivalence about whether authority is a matter of power or of right. Most of us tend to believe, I think, that there is some difference between the two. Jean-Jacques Rousseau certainly believed that there is a difference, writing in the *Social Contract* that "[f]orce is a physical power; I fail to see what morality can result from its effects. To give in to force is an act of necessity, not of will. At most, it is an act of prudence. In what sense could it be a duty? . . . Obey the powers that be. If that means giving in to force, the precept is sound but superfluous."[1]

Thomas Hobbes, on the other hand, has problems with the distinction. There are, he says in the *De Cive*, two species of *natural obligation*.

> One, when liberty is taken away by corporal impediments, according to which we say that heaven and earth, and all creatures, do obey the common laws of their creation. The other, when it is taken away by hope or fear, according to which the weaker, despairing of his own power to resist, cannot but yield to the stronger. From this last kind of obligation, that is to say, from fear or conscience of our own weakness in respect of the divine power, it comes to pass that we are obliged to obey God in his natural kingdom; reason dictating to all, acknowledging the divine power and providence, *that there is no kicking against the pricks*.[2]

These passages from Rousseau and Hobbes point the way to a distinctively modern problem concerning authority. The problem can be characterized as that of the disappearance of *natural* authority. In speaking of "natural obligation," Hobbes is referring to the correlate of what I mean by "natural authority." If there is any such thing as a natural authority, that authority will impose some natural obligation, at least on some persons in some circumstances. Hobbes is claiming that any natural obligation must derive either from the irresistible causal action, in terms of which he conceives the "laws of nature," or from the fear generated from our consciousness of our weakness relative to an agent who is much more powerful than we are and who, so to speak, takes an interest in our business. Hence, Hobbes locates the source of any natural obligation that we may owe to God (if indeed God exists) in God's immensely great power and in His supposed propensity to meddle with our affairs. Indeed, in a note to the above text, Hobbes interprets St. Paul's conversion as a matter of our Savior's "requir[ing] obedience from him for this cause, because he had not power enough to resist."[3]

Rousseau responds, in the best ordinary-language analysis tradition, that obligation (and the correlative notion of authority) are irreducibly *moral* concepts, which cannot be reduced to force—either to the force of causal necessitation or to the force that generates consciousness of the futility of attempting to resist overwhelming power that is brought to bear on us as agents. "Let us then agree," Rousseau concludes, "that force does not bring about right, and that one is obliged to obey only legitimate powers."[4] It would seem to follow that any natural authority, where we are talking about "right" rather than mere "power," could not be reduced to force in the manner of Hobbes. An enduring problem concerning authority for us post-Enlightenment moderns, it seems to me, is that natural authority has largely disappeared from our most common worldviews. The only sort of "natural" authority that might remain, according to such views, is brute force or power. But, with a few exceptions (such as Hobbes), most of us have been inclined to accept Rousseau's claim that such brute force cannot in itself really constitute authority. Must it be the case, then, that we moderns are always afflicted with the tendency to regard authority as authoritarian, in the sense of not being really *legitimate* authority (that is, not really *authority*, in the proper sense) at all?

The great Enlightenment hope—one of many such hopes—has been to develop an adequate account of *nonnatural* authority—that is, an account of authority as a human, social construct. In the case of the *moral* legitimacy of authority, the relevant convention that has typically been taken to underwrite authority is some sort of consent, assent, or agreement. I should mention that I am aware of those forms of legal positivism that locate the *legal* legitimacy of authority in forms of social convention other than consent or agreement. But here I am concerned with the moral dimension of authority rather than the legal one, in terms of a positivistic distinction between these notions—should one be inclined to apply such a distinction here.

The notion of *natural* authority may, in fact, be sharpened by defining it as a sort of authority that imposes obligations that are *not* the consequence of social conventions—that is, in the moral sense, not the consequence of some sort of consent, agreement, or promise on the part of those so obligated. Natural authority, then, is not the result of social convention but, rather, is in some sense a consequence of the nature of human beings and the relations in which human beings stand to God and to the rest of reality. Natural authority often involves the idea that God or our own human nature or features of the wider universe possess some authority (in the sense of *rightful* power) over us human beings. This is *not*, I emphasize, simply the brute force of causal necessitation to which Hobbes refers when he speaks of "heaven and earth, and all creatures, [as obeying] the laws of their creation." I think that it is not unfair to characterize modern thought, beginning in about the seventeenth century, as exhibiting a profound skepticism concerning the classical idea of natural authority. The consequent tendency has been to limit authority to the nonnatural sort—i.e., to that grounded in social convention, particularly the consent of human wills.

Of course, it is the path of nonnatural authority that both Hobbes and Rousseau pursue, in rather different ways and with very different results. So have most contemporary social-political theorists within the so-called liberal tradition. My own view is that modern and contemporary attempts to develop the idea of nonnatural authority, at least with respect to its moral dimension, have not been very successful. And if the idea of natural authority is suspect to the modern mind, the result is a pervasive modern suspicion that the emperor has no clothes—that, while authority may claim to dress itself with the mantle of moral legitimacy, it is ultimately nothing more than a matter of the assertion of one will, or group of wills, over others. In this sense, all authority is authoritarian, even though it may be to the advantage of those who claim to possess it to pretend otherwise. In his description of the civil society wrought by the social contract toward the end of his *Discourse on the Origin of Inequality*, Rousseau expresses with greater candor and less inhibited cynicism this more-or-less common (but sometimes repressed) modern suspicion:

> The uprising that ends in the strangulation or the dethronement of a sultan is as lawful an act as those by which he disposed of the lives and goods of his subjects the day before. Force alone maintained him; force alone brings him down. Thus everything happens in accordance with the natural order, and whatever the outcome of these brief and frequent upheavals may be, no one can complain about someone else's injustice, but only of his own imprudence or his misfortune.[5]

If I am at least approximately correct about the status of authority in the modern world and if this situation constitutes—as I believe it does—a moral and social "problem," I doubt that the problem has any obvious, let alone quick and easy, fix. What I propose to do in the remainder of this chapter is to begin to take measure of the dimensions of the problem, so to speak, by considering two issues that seem to me to be intimately related to it and to which I have already alluded. The first is the disappearance of the concept of natural authority. The second is the elusiveness of an adequate notion of nonnatural authority.

THE DISAPPEARANCE OF NATURAL AUTHORITY

A thesis that I shall propose, but cannot really argue here, is that the notion of "power the exercise of which is rationally directed toward a/the objective good" is crucial to the concept of natural authority (although I do not propose this notion as a *definiens* or even as a sufficient condition for the concept of natural authority). Perhaps one of the few areas of modern life where most persons are still (sometimes) willing to countenance the idea of natural authority pertains to the relation between parents and children. And here, I think, we pretty clearly find connected to the idea of parental authority the idea of authority exercised rationally and for the objective good of children. We also find the idea of a kind of authority that is grounded in our objective human (social) nature. And, finally, we find the idea that claims of natural authority can be defeasible—particularly where a case can be made that such authority is *not*, in fact, exercised rationally or for the objective good of a child.

Since parental authority is such a (relatively) clear and uncontroversial example of natural authority, it is perhaps understandable but unfortunate that Sir Robert Filmer attempted to derive *political* natural authority—in particular, the authority of "legitimate" monarchs (such as the Stuarts)—

from the parental authority of the *primus parens* Adam. Of course, the idea of natural authority has now been so completely banished from the political realm that contemporary teachers of political philosophy do not take Filmer's doctrine seriously enough to assign (or usually to read) John Locke's demolition of it in his *First Treatise of Government*. Also, the idea of natural authority in religion (in the sense of authority not grounded in human social conventions)—for example, with respect to the office of the episcopacy or the papacy, or with respect to the magisterial office, in general, within the Roman Catholic Church—is widely regarded with suspicion, as is the once-common idea of some sort of relation of natural authority between those who are more wise or virtuous and those who are less wise or virtuous (e.g., teacher and student, master and apprentice, etc.).

Even with respect to what may seem to be the last bastion of natural authority, the parent-child relation, I think there may be signs of erosion. The recent idea of children "divorcing" parents or vice versa is not really coherent unless one thinks of the relation in quasi-contractual terms; there we appear to encounter nonnatural authority, the ultimate foundation of which must lie in social convention and that is typically thought to depend on the continuing explicit consent of those who are a party to the relation.[6]

The idea of parental authority as natural authority seems to me to represent a sort of vestigial idea that is not comfortably at home within the wider modern *Zeitgeist*. The idea of natural parental authority presupposes that the parent possesses a degree of wisdom that he or she is prepared to exercise on behalf of the child. It implies that, whatever the child's subjective preferences may be, the parent possesses knowledge about the child's objective good and what the most effective means are for procuring that good. One sense of the term "wisdom"—the relevant one here, I think—is a kind of practical rationality (rationality directed toward action) that includes a correct grasp of the objective human good or goods attainable by action. This "broad" sort of practical rationality is not merely what Aristotle calls "cleverness" or *deinotês*[7]: the skill in finding the necessary or the most efficient means for advancing one's ends, whatever those ends may be. Rather, it also comprises the ability to ascertain the proper ends of action—the objective good or goods of something.

While the classical idea of practical rationality included the idea of the ability to ascertain the objective good, more modern conceptions of practical rationality typically do not. St. Thomas Aquinas and David Hume starkly illustrate the contrast. For St. Thomas, "good is the first thing that falls under the apprehension of the practical reason" and "whatever the practical reason naturally apprehends as man's good (or evil) belongs to the precepts of the natural law as something to be done or avoided."[8] The will (*voluntas*) just is an intellective or rational appetite, according to

Thomas: "[c]onsequently, in order that the will tend to anything, it is requisite not that this be good in very truth, but that it be apprehended as good."[9] There certainly is an objective "good in very truth" for human beings, according to Thomas, but he does not ignore the obvious fact that we can be mistaken, both individually and as a society, about the nature of that objective good. Nonetheless, he holds the following two doctrines: (1) practical rationality has the capacity for discerning the objective human good; (2) the will, or faculty of choice, is a *rational* appetite naturally directed toward that good.

By way of contrast, consider the following famous passages from David Hume's *A Treatise of Human Nature*:

> Since reason alone can never produce any action, or give rise to volition, I infer, that the same faculty is as incapable of preventing volition, or of disputing the preference with any passion or emotion. . . . Reason is, and ought only to be the slave of the passions, and can never pretend to any other office than to serve and obey them.

> 'Tis not contrary to reason to prefer the destruction of the whole world than to the scratching of my finger. 'Tis not contrary to reason for me to chuse my total ruin, to prevent the least uneasiness of an *Indian* or a person wholly unknown to me. 'Tis as little contrary to reason to prefer even my own acknowledg'd lesser good to my greater, and have a more ardent affection for the former than the latter.[10]

Although Hume expresses the view in his characteristically provocative style, his view seems to me to have become, in its essence, a very common modern one. St. Thomas's human goods—whether the true human goods or only some apparent and mistaken ones does not really matter—have become subjective personal preferences. So long as one's individual system of preferences is not internally inconsistent (and, perhaps, not inconsistent with nonmoral facts about the agent's environment), practical rationality must maintain a respectful silence concerning them. They are neither correctly described as rational or as irrational, but as a-rational—in the sense of having nothing to do with reason, as being beyond its purview.

This constriction of the concept of practical rationality has much to do with the demise of a teleological conception of the universe, and of human nature, more particularly. If there is no objective *telos* of human beings (or of the rest of nature)—which practical reason is fitted to ascertain—in what could a person's good consist *except* in his or her subjective preferences? And as long as these preferences are internally consistent, and consistent with limitations imposed on human endeavors by nonmoral facts about the rest of the natural world, what has reason to do with them? The biological and social sciences may perhaps aspire to give some *causal* account of an agent's possession of some particular structure of preferences; but, at least if minimal requirements of consistency are met, reason can say nothing with respect to the worthiness of that structure of preferences.

Once practical rationality is conceptualized as directed toward the satisfaction of subjective preferences, there is little room for natural authority. For who has a fuller knowledge of and more intimate acquaintance with his preferences than the agent who possesses those preferences? Consequently, the exercise of natural authority as essentially involving practical rationality directed toward someone else's good (read: subjective preferences) scarcely makes sense without the explicit agreement on the part of the person on whose behalf the authority is exercised.

Witness the comment of Jeff Wunrow, deputy campaign manager for the Constitution Defense League, a group that was founded (and exceptionally well funded) to fight a Missouri constitutional amendment banning homosexual marriage. In expressing his deep disappointment that the amendment was supported by about seventy percent of the voters, Mr. Wunrow was quoted by the *New York Times* as follows: "I guess what this says is that 7 out of 10 people here think they know better how I should live my life than I do."[11] From a common contemporary perspective, Mr. Wunrow is right to be upset. If the human good is reducible to subjective preferences, then any exercise of natural authority—in particular, authority that does *not* have the explicit endorsement of those over whom it is exercised—is going to appear to be (and, in reality, to be) simply the attempt by those who can garner sufficient power to impose their own preferences on those who do not happen to share those preferences. The exercise of authority not explicitly endorsed by those over whom it is exercised, in other words, must needs be authoritarian.

One exception may be parental authority, with respect to which, as I suggested earlier, we seem not yet to be quite ready to dismiss the idea of natural authority. But, as I also suggested, parental authority fits uncomfortably within the intellectual milieu I have been describing. It makes little sense, I believe, to think of parental authority as nonnatural—in particular, as grounded in the consent of children over whom it is exercised. But we may, some of us, be inclined to think that it is still being exercised in behalf of a child's pursuit of his or her own subjective preferences. It is just that children, particularly young children, do not yet *have* what could plausibly be described as a structure of preferences that orders their behavior. So the parent is acting in a "fiduciary" capacity until such time as a child really "knows his own mind," in the sense of being sufficiently mature to possess a structure of preferences.

Such a perspective, which is at least implicit in much contemporary culture, yields what I suspect is a distinctively modern form of parental *angst*. Particularly with respect to rebellious behavior of adolescent children, the conscientious and thoughtful modern parent will typically find himself troubled by certain vexatious questions. Am I not *really* simply imposing my preferences on the kid? Insofar as I take myself to be exercising (currently resented) authority on behalf of what I judge will be the kid's mature, considered preferences, how can I be sure that the kid will/would actually *have* those particular preferences—apart from my parental "interference"? In other words, isn't the exercise of my parental authority likely to be a causal influence on the kid's formation of a particular structure of preferences (to the exclusion of some other preference structures), and can *that* sort of influence of one autonomous will over another ever be justifiable?

It seems that we may have arrived back at what I shall call modern thought's "basic picture" of natural (i.e., unauthorized or "nonconsensual") authority: The picture is that of the imposition of subjective preferences by one will on some other will that happens not to share those preferences. So isn't the exercise of the authority that is an apparently necessary constituent of parenting (at least when it comes to the exercise of authority that has anything to do with "values") always authoritarian? Parental worry and concern—including a parent's conscientious concern about whether he or she is actually doing what is best for his/her children—is no doubt a pervasive, cross-cultural feature of the institution. And I certainly do not mean to suggest that a parent is not sometimes right to worry about whether he or she is exercising authority in pursuit of the child's good or is merely trying to impose subjective preferences, which are not a part of that good, on the child. But the particular *kind* of worry I have been describing as well as its forcefulness—which come with the modern *Zeitgeist*, I think—are due to the implicit or explicit assumption that the good of the child is just to be *identified* with the satisfaction of the child's yet-to-be-developed "mature" structure of subjective preferences. This conception of the thoroughly subjective, idiosyncratic, and not-yet-actual "good" of the child creates a special kind of problem for someone, like a parent, who regards himself as standing *in loco agentis* for the child. I hope that I shall not scandalize anyone by suggesting that I doubt that St. Thomas, had he been a parent, would have shared this particular kind of anxiety.

Since we seem not to be able to get along very well without authority altogether, the "answer," according to the modern *Zeitgeist*, is rather obvious. It is to conceptualize all authority, to the greatest extent that we can, as nonnatural—that is, as a matter of convention grounded in the agreement or consent of those over whom authority is to be exercised. In the following section, I attempt to sketch my reasons for thinking that this move does not work.

THE ELUSIVENESS OF NONNATURAL AUTHORITY

First of all, I certainly do not deny that *some* instances of authority are best explained as devolving from social conventions and that one sort of convention that may ground authority is agreement, consent, contract, or promise (which, incidentally, do not always amount to exactly the same thing). However, there is an extremely influential tradition within what I have referred to as the "modern *Zeitgeist*" that seems to be committed to the enterprise of attempting to analyze all *moral* authority (or as much of it as possible) as nonnatural, in the sense of grounded in the consent of the wills of those over whom it is exercised. (Again, I realize that there are forms of legal positivism that ground *legal* authority—or, perhaps better, the legal dimension of authority—in conventions that are not a matter of consent or agreement.) In the particular case of political authority, the assumption that it must be nonnatural is now standard. As Rousseau puts it:

> A people, says Grotius, can give itself to a king. . . . This gift itself is a civil act; it presupposes a public deliberation. Thus, before examining the act whereby a people chooses a king, it would be well to examine the act whereby a people is a people. For since this act is necessarily prior to the other, it is the true foundation of society.
>
> In fact, if there were no prior convention, then, unless the vote were unanimous, what would become of the minority's obligation to submit to the majority's choice, and where do one hundred who want a master get the right to vote for ten who do not? The law of majority rule is itself an established convention, and presupposes unanimity on at least the one occasion.[12]

I have maintained that obligation and authority are correlative notions. More particularly, authority implies the obligation of some persons (at some times and in some circumstances) to accede to that authority. Rousseau believes that it is morally necessary that political obligation, and hence political authority, rest upon a "*première convention*," which would appear to be the *explicit* consent or agreement of all those over whom the authority is to be exercised. In fact, however, Rousseau seems to backtrack on this point in the *Social Contract*: The general will (*la volonté générale*) is not to be identified with "sum of private wills" or "the will of all" (*la volonté de tous*). Indeed, in a famous (or infamous) passage, Rousseau asserts that "whoever refuses to obey the general will be forced to do so by the entire body. This means merely that he will be forced to be free."[13]

Rousseau's discussion, in fact, leads to my criticism of the attempt of the modern *Zeitgeist*, or at least of one influential tradition within modern thought, to render all authority nonnatural. I have suggested that this attempt is ultimately grounded in the assumption that the *raison d'être* of authority is to advance the subjective preferences of human persons over whom it is exercised. Consequently, the exercise of power that contravenes the voluntary choices of a human agent cannot contribute to the advancement of that agent's preferences and cannot really be an exercise of authority—that is, an exercise of *legitimate* power. A sort of paradox results. Morally legitimate authority exists only if those over whom it is exercised explicitly consent to it; and this consent, according to the modern view I have sketched, must ultimately be an expression of their preferences. The "paradox" to which I allude is that while we normally think of authority as morally constraining, as entailing certain obligations, it appears that, according to the present view, this is false—my preferences certainly do not obligate me (I am free simply to change them). So, without my explicit consent, which will ultimately be a manifestation of those preferences, there is no (legitimate) authority to which I am subject.

The result would seem to be, at the very least, a very diminished notion of authority. It appears that the exercise of authority is transformed into something like giving technical advice or counsel, counsel that will help the person to whom it is given better to satisfy his or her preferences. But there is no obligation on the part of the recipient to take advice—it can be either accepted or ignored as the recipient sees fit—while this does not seem to be the case with respect to the exercise of authority, as we understand the meaning of the term "authority." So, if something remains within this worldview that we wish to call "authority," it must be quite different from authority as we usually conceive of it. This is an "authority" that does not impose any obligation to accede to in the absence of its conformity with one's preferences.

In the face of such an unpalatable consequence, a standard modern attempt to "save" authority (in the more standard sense of the term) has been to rely on some concept of *initial* or *fundamental* consent, actual or ideal, which is required for the moral legitimacy of authority and apparently should be regarded as being directed toward satisfying the preferences of those giving the consent. Thereafter, however, obligation and authority are traced back to that initial or fundamental consent. The actual consent of those over whom authority is exercised is not morally required in *each individual instance* of its exercise. Thus, to consider Rousseau's concrete employment of this line of reasoning, the majority can gain authority over the minority because of the unanimous consent of the *première convention*.

There seems to me to be two main problems with this picture. The first pertains to the picture's conception of "vested authority." It is no doubt socially useful, probably even socially imperative, for forms of authority to exist each exercise of which does not require the explicit ratification by every person over whom it is exercised. This is what I mean by "vested authority." Vested authority may even in some cases be a useful means for best satisfying the preferences, by and large and for the most part, of those over whom it is exercised. But the modern assumptions with which we are dealing really derive obligation from the will's agreement, rather than from practical rationality directed toward the objective good. So I fail to see what obligation an agent has *not* to revoke, as it were, a more "fundamental" or "prior" grant of authority, on any occasion when his or her current preferences come into conflict with the exercise of that authority. It might be foolish or practically unwise, in terms of his long-term preference/satisfaction, for an agent not to submit to such vested authority in a particular instance. But is it morally wrong for the agent not to do so? Well, if the *ultimate* moral *raison d'être* of authority is to be found in its contribution to preference/satisfaction and if one assumes that the "criterion" of morally legitimate authority is one's judgment that some institution or general principles of authority is likely to satisfy one's preferences and one's consequent assent to that institution or those principles, I see no obvious reason why this same line of thought should not apply to any *particular instance* of the exercise of authority. If my voluntary choice, as an expression of my current preferences, is opposed to a particular exercise of authority, can the particular exercise of that authority in the face of the opposition of my will be anything more than the imposition upon me of preferences that I do not *currently* share? And can such an imposition be anything other than the exercise of force—illegitimate power that cannot, in the absence of the consent of my will, be correctly characterized as authority?

In the light of such a conundrum, the modern strategy has been to move to a form of nonnatural authority that purports to rest on the *idealized* rather than explicit, actual consent of the wills of those over whom it is exercised. This strategy yields Rousseau's general will, which has very little to do with the actual wills and preferences of citizens. It also yields the universal "affirmation" of John Rawls's basic principles of justice by his highly idealized representatives in the highly idealized epistemic circumstances of the "original position."[14]

This strategy is also the focus of what seems to me to be the second problem with the modern attempt to analyze all authority as nonnatural authority. If one is committed to this attempt, which involves grounding all authority in the consent of those over whom the authority is exercised, the pragmatic rationale for moving to idealized consent is obvious. At least according to the modern, human conception of it, the will can be an extremely capricious faculty. People consent to or withhold consent from all kinds of things for all kinds of reasons (or for no reason at all). If the existence of authority were to require the continuing, actual consent of those over whom it is exercised, there would exist very little authority. Hence the desirability of grounding authority in some form of idealized consent—which is to say, not grounding authority in actual consent at all.

Indeed, the fact that idealized consent is not really consent *is* the "second problem" to which I alluded. As I have argued, the modern nonnatural conception of authority that I have been considering is strongly voluntaristic. According to this conception, it is the consent of the wills over whom power is exercised that is essential to that power's being *authority*, as opposed to merely brute force. Idealized consent, however, is not the actual consent of any will. Rousseau's *volunté générale* is not any actual will. Nor is the "affirmation" of Rawls's principles of justice by representatives in the original position the assent of any actual wills. What is important, what "does the work," in theories of idealized consent is not the voluntaristic window-dressing, but the particular substantive conditions constraining the idealization. I submit that these conditions are usually best understood as expressing some conception of an objective human good and/or the rational means for attaining that good. But, in *that* case, it appears that the idealized-consent theorist is appealing—perhaps surreptitiously and perhaps unwittingly and perhaps incoherently—to a concept of *natural* authority—that is, authority that is *not* grounded in the actual consent of those over whom it is exercised but, rather, essentially involves practical reason exercised on behalf of others and directed toward the objective human good(s).

CONCLUSION

My principal conclusion is that the modern, voluntaristic nonnatural conception of authority that I have been considering almost inevitably is transformed into some idealized-consent conception. This transformation appears to be "inevitable" insofar as one who is attracted to the voluntaristic conception wishes to preserve the very idea of authority. However, I have suggested that the result is a rather roundabout reintroduction of some idea of natural authority, which is not grounded in the actual consent of those over whom it is exercised, but *is* directed toward what is taken to be their objective good. Modern antipathy toward the idea of natural authority, however, produces considerable resistance to this sort of reconceptualization of idealized-consent doctrines of authority. Hence, the voluntaristic terminology remains popular—even though, so I have claimed, it is really only a verbal husk.

My very programmatic proposal, which I certainly cannot pursue here, is that the notion of *natural* authority needs to be further analyzed and developed. I myself am quite uncertain to what degree such a conception might be rendered consistent with a broad range of contemporary moral, social, and political thought. My suspicion is that a coherent conception of natural authority may prove to be possible only within the context of some "teleological" conception of the universe and of human nature. That is, I suspect that a conception of human beings that is consistently and thoroughly antiteleological, in the sense of insisting that whatever "meaning" or "value" there may be to human existence (or in the universe, more broadly) is the result of human choice and social construction, may not be able to accommodate a notion of natural authority. For someone like Bertrand Russell or Professor Richard Dawkins, who holds that "Science [note the capitalization] presents for our belief" a world that is "purposeless" and "void of meaning,"[15] I suspect that the notion of natural authority can have little, if any, purchase. If this suspicion is correct, whether some thoroughly nonnatural conception of authority can be resuscitated is certainly a major issue for folk with such antiteleological commitments. They have my sympathy. But I am disinclined to join in the enterprise—and not merely because I am skeptical concerning the possibility of its success.

NOTES

1. Jean-Jacques Rousseau, "On the Social Contract," in *The Basic Political Writings*, trans. Donald A. Cress, bk. 1, chap. 3 (Indianapolis: Hackett, 1987), 143.
2. Thomas Hobbes, *De Cive*, in *Man and Citizen*, ed. Bernard Gert (Garden City, N.J.: Doubleday, 1972), no. 7, 294.
3. Ibid.
4. Rousseau, "Social Contract," 144.
5. Jean Jacques Rousseau, "Discourse on the Origin of Inequality," in *The Basic Political Writings*, trans. Donald A. Cress, pt. 2 (Indianapolis: Hackett, 1987), 79–80.
6. Law-school colleagues have suggested to me, however, that most legal issues surrounding the parent-child relation are still framed in terms of a "paternalistic" rather than a contractual model.
7. See Aristotle, *Nicomachean Ethics*, bk. 6, ch. 12, 1144a23ff and ch. 9, 1142b18ff.
8. Thomas Aquinas, *Summa Theologica*, trans. Fathers of the English Dominican Province (1948; reprint, Wheaton, Md.: Christian Classics, 1981), Ia IIae, q. 94, a. 2.
9. Ibid., Ia IIae, q. 8, a. 1.
10. David Hume, *A Treatise of Human Nature*, ed. L. A. Selby-Bigge, second ed., rev. P. H. Nidditch (Oxford: Clarendon Press, 1978), bk. II, pt iii, sec. 3, 414–16.
11. Monica Davey, "Sharp Reactions to Missouri's Decisive Vote against Gay Marriage," *New York Times*, August 5, 2004, national edition.
12. Rousseau, "On the Social Contract," I, v, 147.
13. Ibid., I, vii, 150.
14. See John Rawls, *A Theory of Justice* (Cambridge, Mass.: Harvard University Press, 1999), especially ch. 3.
15. Bertrand Russell, "A Free Man's Worship," in *Mysticism and Logic and Other Essays* (1917; reprint, Totowa, N.J.: Barnes & Noble Books, 1981), 41.

3

Authority in the Church

Avery Cardinal Dulles, S.J.

The question of authority in the Church has been much discussed since the Second Vatican Council. On the eve of the council, John M. Todd edited under the title *Problems of Authority* a valuable collection of papers from an Anglo-French symposium.[1] In 1966 John L. McKenzie published his challenging study, *Authority in the Church*, based chiefly on the New Testament.[2] Since that time there has been a steady stream of books bearing titles such as *Authority in a Changing Church*,[3] *Authority and Leadership in the Church*,[4] *Authority in the Church*,[5] and *Authority in the Roman Catholic Church*.[6] In 1999 the Common Ground Initiative published a symposium on *Church Authority in American Culture*.[7] In addition, there have been many specialized studies dealing respectively with the powers of teaching, sanctifying, and governance. The sexual abuse crisis has prompted still another volley of books, some of which advocate a firmer exercise of hierarchical authority while others plead for a wider distribution of decisionmaking in the Church. It would be impossible for me, in a single brief chapter, to do justice to all aspects of this complex question.

The complexity of the problem is due in part to the nature of the Church that is, in the language of Vatican II, a *realitas complexa*: "one complex reality comprising a human and a divine element" (LG 8). On the one hand, it is a supernatural society, established by divine initiative for the sake of human salvation. On the other hand, it is a human community existing in the world. Under the first aspect ecclesiastical authority has to be studied theologically, in light of faith; under the second, such authority is subject to social and historical conditions and is capable of being analyzed from a sociological perspective.

THE NOTION OF AUTHORITY

The term "authority" is fluid and is used by different authors in different senses. As we all know, the word is derived from the Latin word *auctor*, which is connected with the verb *augere*, meaning to grow or to increase. The *auctor*, according to Lewis and Short's *New Latin Dictionary*, is one who "brings about the existence of any object, or promotes the increase and prosperity of it, whether he originates it, or by his efforts gives greater permanence or continuance to it."[8] But efforts to regulate current usage by referring back to the etymology of the word would scarcely be helpful. For better or for worse, the term has taken on a modern meaning, which might be summarized as rightful influence or rightful power over the minds and behavior of persons. When we speak of authority in a society, we generally have in mind something more than influence. Authority in the strict and formal sense means rightful power to perform certain official acts, such as the issuance of laws and commands that require obedience or the formulation of doctrines that require assent. Authority implies dominion over free human agents.

In this chapter I shall approach the theme from a theological point of view, making use of Holy Scripture and documents that count as authoritative in the Catholic Church.

BIBLICAL DATA

The first point to be noted is that all authority comes from God, as Paul explicitly teaches in his letter to the Romans (Rom 13:1). In the Old and New Testaments it is axiomatic that God, who created the world from nothing by his own unaided power, is the rightful ruler to whom everyone and everything is necessarily subject. In the first article of the creed we proclaim our faith in God the Father Almighty, who made heaven and earth. In producing free and rational creatures, God relinquishes none of his sovereignty. Creatures can do nothing without his approval or at least his toleration (which theologians have called his "permissive will"). Even when creatures rebel, God retains his authority over them.

The authority of God is absolute and supreme, but it is not the only authority. By God's will, authority exists in natural institutions such as the family and civil society. In the family parents have authority to educate their children and bring them to maturity. In civil society duly constituted rulers have authority to govern for the sake of the common good. The powers of government are often divided into the legislative, the administrative, and the judicial.

Authority is sacred to the extent that it is connected with the holiness proper to God. In contradistinction to the secular, the sacred is something in which God is present in a special way or something specially set apart for religious uses, such as a temple. Israel, by reason of its election, was "a chosen race, a royal priesthood, a holy nation, God's own people" (1 Pt 2:9). The nation was formed by God's special action in history. God governed it through prophets, priests, and kings, who were sometimes anointed as a sign of their sacred office. In the Old Testament we read of revelations by which God calls individuals to be prophets, priests, judges, or kings.

Under the New Testament a sharper distinction is made between the secular and the sacred. Although sacral practices such as the anointing of kings have at times been revived in Christian societies, it has become increasingly apparent that civil society is and ought to be secular. In the political sphere, each people has the freedom to adopt its own form of government and determine the processes by which its rulers will be selected, provided only that common good be served. Once appointed, the rulers obtain their authority from God (Rom 13:1–7) and are to be obeyed in their own sphere of competence (Mk 12:13–17; 1 Pt 2:13–14). But the rulers have no authority to act unjustly. When human governments command anything contrary to God's precepts, God is to be obeyed rather than they (cf. Acts 4:19).

Jesus Christ, as the anointed Son of God, exercised the fullness of sacred authority as prophet, priest, and king. As prophet, he amazed his hearers by the majesty with which he spoke (Lk 4:32). As priest, he forgave sins, expelled demons, and instituted the sacraments. And as king, he established the pastoral government of the Church. One aspect of his royal power he keeps in reserve. Only at the end of history will he appear as judge to demand a full accounting from the living and the dead, and to pronounce fitting sentence on each individual.

During his earthly ministry and risen life, Jesus, making use of his plenary authority, equipped the Twelve to carry on his work. Promising them his continued assistance to the end of the age, he commissioned them to make disciples of all nations, to baptize, and to teach all peoples to observe his commandments (Mt 28:18–20). The New Testament, read within the Catholic tradition, enables us to understand the threefold mission of the apostles as a prolongation of the threefold office of Christ himself.

In their prophetic role, the apostles are called to preach and to teach. In sending them forth on mission, Jesus endows their teaching with obligatory force. "He who receives you receives me, and he who receives me receives him who sent me" (Mt 10:40; cf. Lk 10:16; Jn 13:20). With the help of the Holy Spirit, who descends upon the apostles at the Pentecost, they are to be Christ's witnesses "in Jerusalem and in all Judaea and in Samaria and to the end of the earth" (Acts 1:8).

The priestly ministry of the apostles includes, among other things, their power to baptize (Mt 28:19), forgive sins (Jn 20:23), and celebrate the Eucharist (Lk 22:19; cf. 1 Cor 11:24). Their ministry of government is implied in the power to bind and to loose (Mt 18:18), which would seem to involve the ability to make and interpret laws and to impose penalties for wrongful conduct. To Peter alone, as chief of the apostles, is given the power of the keys (Mt 16:19), which signifies being made a kind of majordomo, the manager of the household of God.

After praying that Peter will be constant in the faith, Jesus commissions him to strengthen the faith of the brothers (Lk 22:32). Finally, the risen Jesus appoints Peter to be pastor of his whole flock (Jn 21:15–17). The title of "shepherd" is a common designation of kings in the Old Testament and in the ancient Near East.

The later books of the New Testament depict the group of apostles—gradually expanded to include figures such as Matthias, Paul, and Barnabas—exercising the mandates given to them by the Lord. Although we have a very incomplete record of their activities, we have historical grounds for a number of essential points. We see Peter speaking with authority for the apostolic body, we see the apostles with some presbyters coming into council to make doctrinal decisions, and we see Paul exercising his office as an apostle to found churches, ordain ministers, teach, command, correct, and punish. The letter to the Hebrews instructs the faithful to obey their leaders and submit to them as men who will have to give an account of their souls to God (Heb 13:17).

SACRED AUTHORITY IN THE CHURCH

According to established Catholic teaching, the threefold charge of teaching, sanctifying, and ruling that Jesus gave to the twelve apostles, with and under Peter, is an abiding feature of the Church and continues without a break to the present day. Passed on to the successive popes and bishops, this authority resides in the episcopate as a collegial body, with and under the successor of Peter. The Second Vatican Council teaches with great emphasis "that by divine institution the bishops have succeeded to the place of the apostles as shepherds of the Church, and that he who hears them, hears Christ, while he who rejects them rejects Christ and him who sent Christ" (LG 20). The bishops, with the pope as their head, preside by divine right over the People of God, holding the threefold office "as teachers of sacred doctrine, priests of sacred worship, and ministers of government" (LG 20).

The authority of bishops is sacred because it is exercised in the name of God, with his authorization, and with the intention of passing on the sacred deposit and leading the faithful to eternal life. Going beyond previous Church teaching, the Second Vatican Council declares in solemn language that episcopal ordination is a sacrament conferred through the imposition of hands by bishops who have themselves been ordained in the apostolic succession (LG 21). The council also states that the functions (*munera*) of teaching and ruling are conferred by the sacrament itself, rather than being received subsequently by canonical mission. But the text goes on to say that bishops cannot exercise their *munera* of teaching and governing except in hierarchical communion with the pope and the members of the college (LG 21). For any particular office in the Church, bishops must receive an appointment from the competent ecclesiastical authority, normally the Holy See.

In favoring the threefold division of hierarchical functions, Vatican II largely displaced an earlier schematization that recognized only two powers: those of order and jurisdiction. The twofold schema failed to do justice to the function of teaching, which cannot be easily fitted into order or jurisdiction. Unlike the power of order, which derives from ordination alone, hierarchical teaching authority requires that one be in communion with the see of Peter, and is forfeited by heresy or schism. Unlike jurisdiction, teaching is directed to the intelligence and calls for internal assent. Jurisdiction, as an act of governance, is directed rather to the will and calls for external obedience.

By grounding the powers to teach and govern in the sacrament of episcopal ordination, the Dogmatic Constitution *Lumen gentium* (and the *Nota praevia* appended to it) overcame a tendency in some preconciliar theology to expound ecclesiastical governance in overly political terms, drawn from the analogy of the civil state. Teaching and governance in the Church are sacred actions, to be carried out in a pastoral spirit. The authority to teach or govern ordinarily presupposes sacramental ordination, which brings with it special graces. According to the Code of Canon Law, "[o]nly clerics can obtain offices for whose exercise the power of orders or the power of ecclesiastical governance is required" (canon 274 §2). But as we shall see, the unordained may have a share in these sacred functions.

The three *munera* of sanctifying, teaching, and governing should not be isolated from one another, but should be clearly distinguished. The authority to sanctify consists primarily in the offering of the sacramental sacrifice of the Eucharist and in administration of sacraments, especially those reserved to the ordained. Priests and bishops alone can confirm, confer ordinations, forgive sins in the sacrament of penance, and anoint the sick. As public acts of Christ in the Church, these sacraments must be performed by sacred ministers. Matrimony, however, is performed by the spouses themselves, who administer the sacrament to one another, with the priest being present as the official witness of the Church who pronounces on the validity of the union and blesses it in the name of God. Baptism is ordinarily administered by a priest, but in a situation of urgency can be administered by anyone at all.

In teaching, the pastors transmit the revelation of Christ in an authoritative manner, requiring assent on the part of the faithful. Bound to the word of God as transmitted in scripture and tradition, they have no authority to alter or supplement it with their own ideas. They are expected to instruct the people committed to their care, explaining the doctrine of the Church in such a way that its meaning and credibility can be seen. The hierarchy, and they alone, have the power and obligation to issue binding doctrinal declarations.

In governing, the pope and the bishops regulate the corporate life of the People of God. They do so, for example, by designating feasts and fasts, issuing liturgical norms, and enacting ecclesiastical laws and penalties. In performing these governmental acts, the pastors act in their own name and use their own discretion. While it is desirable that all should accept the regulations, the faithful are not bound to hold that their pastors are always prudent. They are, however, normally required to obey.

Authority in the Church differs in many ways from political authority in secular societies, especially those that are democratic. In a representative democracy the people are sovereign, and the elected officials, as their servants, are accountable to them. In this sense, authority comes from below. But in the Church authority comes from God through Jesus Christ, who instituted the Church as a hierarchical society. By divine right, the pope and the college of bishops enjoy the fullness of sacred power.

THE MORAL AUTHORITY OF PASTORS

A valid command or teaching issued by competent authority requires the response of obedience or assent. Even when ignored or rejected, an authoritative act retains its juridical force.

For authoritative decrees to be effective, it is not sufficient that they be juridically authentic. They must be perceived as prudent and timely. Superiors must prepare their subjects to understand and appreciate what they are being told to accept. Above all, it seems necessary that the decisions be palpably motivated by love and respect for the dignity of the persons affected. The fulfillment of these conditions makes the decrees not only juridically authentic but also, we may say, personally and pastorally authentic.

Pope John Paul II, in his Apostolic Exhortation *Pastores gregis* (2003), declares that the bishop cannot be a good teacher unless he lives the gospel. The testimony of a good life, he says, adds weight (*gravitas*) to his authority. Over and above the objective demands arising from the office he has received, the bishop inspires trust in his message by giving an example of evangelical behavior. It is necessary but not sufficient for the bishop to profess sound doctrine. For his teaching to commend itself to his subjects, he must have the moral authority bestowed by an irreproachable life.[9]

It is often said that pastors should be servants of their flocks and should be accountable to them. These statements can be true if rightly understood. Authority is given for service, as the Gospels insistently proclaim (Mt 20:25–28; Mk 10:42–45; Lk 22:24–27; Jn 13:14–16; cf. 1 Pt 5:1–5). The pastors are servants primarily of Christ the chief shepherd, who is Lord. Christ obliges them to work for the good of the Church, especially the people under their charge. But they are not servants in the sense that they are to do the bidding of the faithful entrusted to their care. Their specific service is to exercise authority in a conscientious and responsible way.

Accountability is unproblematic if it means that the pastors should practice openness and transparency while observing the proper requirements of discretion and confidentiality. The Pontifical Commission on the Means of Social Communication wisely pointed out in 1971:

> The normal flow of life and the smooth functioning of government within the Church require a steady two-way flow of information between the ecclesiastical authorities at all levels and the faithful as individuals and as organized groups. . . .
>
> When ecclesiastical authorities are unwilling to give information or are unable to do so, then rumor is unloosed, and rumor is not a bearer of truth but carries dangerous half-truths. Secrecy should therefore be restricted to matters that involve the good name of individuals and that touch upon the rights of people whether singly or collectively.[10]

To maintain goodwill and guard against suspicions of waste or misappropriation, pastors will want to explain, for example, how they are using their financial and other resources. The U.S. Conference of Catholic Bishops in November 2002 enacted binding norms to govern fund-raising drives. These norms call for annual reports that set forth the amount collected, the cost of the fund-raising effort, and the amount and use of the funds that were disbursed.[11] Candor on issues such as these is to be expected. Bishops, however, are not accountable to the faithful in the sense that the lay faithful are their judges or could have a right to depose them.[12] The faithful can properly use persuasion to influence the decisions of their pastors, but should not attempt to exercise coercion by threats or economic pressures.

Pope John Paul II in *Pastores gregis* reminds bishops that all the faithful are called to cooperate in building up the Body of Christ. The bishop will do everything possible to win the consent of the faithful, but in the end he will have to take personal responsibility before God for decisions that he considers necessary (PG 44). The *Directory for the Pastoral Ministry of Bishops* (2004), following up on this admonition, instructs bishops to make every effort to enlist the collaboration of the laity in councils and diocesan agencies, but admonishes bishops not to abdicate their personal responsibility as pastors: "The weight of responsibility to govern the diocese falls squarely on the shoulders of the Bishop."[13]

Generally speaking, Catholics will be disposed to accept determinations that come from the pope and their bishops. In exceptional cases they may be inclined to dissent or disobey. I cannot go into all the distinctions that would be necessary to say when or whether such negative responses might be justified. I shall content myself with saying that disobedience and dissent, if they occur at all, should be rare, reluctant, and respectful. Even though believers may have difficulties in understanding the rationale for the command or doctrinal pronouncement, they should try to feel and think with the Church, overcoming individualistic or separatist tendencies. In general, their docility and obedience will bring them into closer union with Christ and a deeper appreciation of the riches of revelation. It is never objectively justifiable to reject a doctrine infallibly taught by the magisterium or to separate oneself from the Church by schism.

PARTICIPATORY STRUCTURES

The pope and the bishops are not the exclusive holders of authority in the Church. They associate many others with themselves in such a way that the exercise of hierarchical authority may be called participatory.[14] Among their associates are presbyters (commonly called priests) and deacons. Presbyters have priestly powers and, if they remain in hierarchical communion, participate likewise in the offices of Christ as prophet and king. But they have no authority over popes and bishops. They are ordained by bishops and depend on bishops for their faculties to perform priestly ministry. Deacons, likewise, are authorized to perform certain liturgical and charitable ministries, but only under the direction of pastors.

In some circles there is an opinion that the Second Vatican Council transformed the Church in a democratic direction, introducing constitutional checks and balances.[15] This opinion is in my judgment a misreading of the council documents. The doctrine of collegiality, while it was a new and important development, was framed with great care not to lessen in any way the authority of the pope, who has primacy over all members of the Church, including bishops. In the words of the council: "In virtue of his office, that is, as Vicar of Christ and pastor of the whole Church, the Roman Pontiff has full, supreme, and universal power over the Church. And he can always exercise that power freely" (LG 22).

What the Second Vatican Council did was to strengthen the authority of bishops without weakening that of the pope. The body of bishops, together with the pope as its head, is recognized as "the subject of supreme and full power over the universal Church" (LG 22). These words clearly imply that no one in the Church holds authority over the pope and the body of bishops.

The council and subsequent directives have mandated presbyteral councils and pastoral councils, but these agencies are merely consultative. Since they have no power to reach binding decisions, they are not authoritative in the strict or juridical sense of the word. The bishop ought to have these consultative organs in his diocese and make use of them as helps in reaching his own decisions.

Vatican II had many encouraging words for the laity but it refrained from assigning them any teaching or ruling authority. The Constitution on the Church recognizes that the laity have the right to receive from their pastors the word of God and the sacraments. They are, moreover, always free to reveal their needs and desires to the pastors and, in the measure of their competence, to express their opinions about matters pertaining to the good of the Church. But they cannot enforce their rights without support from the hierarchical authorities. In the end they "should accept whatever their sacred pastors, as representatives of Christ, decree in their role as teachers and rulers in the Church" (LG 37).

Over and above the functions that belong to laypersons in their own right, the council acknowledged that they may on occasion be called to a more direct participation in the apostolate of the hierarchy (LG 33). The hierarchy may entrust to them certain functions closely connected with pastoral duties, "such as the teaching of Christian doctrine, certain liturgical actions, and the care of souls." But after stating this, the council added, "[b]y virtue of this mission the laity are fully subject to the direction of higher ecclesiastical authority in the performance of such work" (AA 24).

Some forty years after the council, the Catholic Church is still seeking to clarify the extent to which laypersons can be involved in offices of sanctification, teaching, and governance that have traditionally been reserved for the clergy. Paul VI in *Ministeria quaedam* (1972) instituted the "installed ministries" of lector and acolyte, no longer as minor orders but as lay ministries, but these ministries confer little or no authority. In cases of need, laypersons are designated to serve as extraordinary ministers of Holy Communion. In addition to these liturgical ministries, the laity may by exception perform acts of government normally reserved for the ordained. They may, for example, be appointed to serve as a judge on tribunals, as diocesan chancellors, or as members of diocesan finance committees with consultative vote. All these developments are relatively new.

In the exercise of the prophetic or teaching office, unordained scholars can receive a "canonical mission," which entitles them to teach "not on their own authority but by virtue of the mission they have received from the Church."[16] Laypersons may be summoned as experts to assist in drawing up papal or conciliar documents, but they do not take responsibility for the documents produced. In cases such as these, selected laypersons may be said to participate in the authority proper to the ordained. But that is not a right that they can claim. They serve in these capacities only when the clergy call them to do so.

To summarize the findings of our exploration thus far, we may conclude that authority, in the sense of capacity to issue commands, enact laws, and make binding doctrinal pronouncements, belongs normally to the pope and the bishops. They alone are entitled and obliged by their office to formulate official teaching, regulate public worship, and govern the People of God. Qualified priests and nonclerics may be called to participate to some degree in the apostolate of the hierarchy according to the needs of the Church.

LIMITS OF ECCLESIASTICAL AUTHORITY

Although the pope and the bishops have full and supreme authority in the Church, they do not have absolute or unlimited authority. They are bound by divine law, which requires them to observe the natural law and likewise to respect the constitution of the Church with its doctrinal, sacramental, and ministerial structures. The Theological Commission at Vatican II, rejecting a proposed amendment to the Constitution on the Church to the effect that the pope is accountable to God alone, stated that "the Roman Pontiff is also bound to revelation itself, to the fundamental structure of the Church, to the sacraments, to the definitions of earlier councils, and other obligations too numerous to mention."[17] The pope cannot dissolve the college of bishops or deprive bishops or priests of their power to exercise their power of orders. Nor does he have authority to dissolve sacramental, consummated marriages (CIC, canon 1141). If a pope or bishop attempted to perform actions such as these, his acts would be null and void.

In their capacity as teachers, popes and bishops are bound to the revelation of Christ. They are authorized to proclaim only truths that belong to the deposit of faith and morals, or truths necessary for the correct understanding of the deposit. Individual bishops are in a way held in check by their need to keep in communion with the whole college of bishops and by its head, the bishop of Rome, who can overrule or depose them if they fall into error.

Members of the hierarchy are bound likewise by the ethical precepts of natural law and the gospel. If they were to command sinful acts such as torture or mutilation, or if they were to wage an unjust war, they could and should be resisted. The pope and bishops, moreover, are bound to respect civil governments. The Church as a sacred or supernatural society does not supplant or absorb the powers of the state, nor does she attempt to organize the secular life of citizens, except in the miniscule Vatican city-state. She does, however, urge temporal rulers to live up to their moral responsibilities.

The Church must likewise respect the family as a natural society. Sometimes the family is called, by analogy, a "domestic church." But this analogy should not be pressed too far. Unlike the diocese or the parish, the family is a natural unit, not a mere part of the Church. It is not equipped with the hierarchical powers.

Canon law, which derives its force from the approval of the pope, prevents bishops and pastors from acting as absolute monarchs within the dioceses and parishes. On the diocesan level, cathedral chapters, parish councils, and other such bodies, although "consultative" in character, have certain statutory rights that bishops must respect. According to canon law, moreover, all parishes are "juridic persons" and in that capacity they themselves own and administer the property they have legitimately acquired (CIC, canon 1256). The bishop cannot dispose of the assets of a parish as if they belonged to the diocese.[18]

Although all the factors here mentioned, and many others, limit the authority of the hierarchical leaders, there is no office in the Church juridically empowered to prevent the supreme authority from acting irresponsibly. For if there were such an office, the question would have to be asked how it, in turn, could be prevented from transgressing the norms. In the end, the Catholic has to rely on the Holy Spirit to prevent the hierarchy from falsifying the faith of the Church. There is no way in which any earthly power could guarantee the validity of the decisions of popes and bishops. As Karl Rahner has written:

> Catholic theology sees and affirms that the institutional element in the Church does not ultimately function on its own. The assurance comes only from the Spirit, who is never simply identified with any institution, and this is the reason why one can rely with confidence on the permanent maintenance of the institution. There is no point, therefore, in arguing against the

> primacy and against the doctrine given in the Constitution [on the Church] on the synodal structure of the Church that it leaves it open to the Pope to do everything autocratically in the end and to exclude the college of bishops in practice. The simple answer is that he "can" do so, but he will not. The Catholic does not demand a juridical norm by which the Pope could be impeached, he relies on the power of the grace of God and of the Holy Spirit in the Church.[19]

THE "SENSE OF THE FAITHFUL"

As a counterpoise to the hierarchy, some have looked to the "sense of the faithful." The Second Vatican Council taught that whenever the pope and bishops use their supreme authority to define matters of doctrine, the assent of the Church will never be wanting (LG 25). Could one therefore conclude that magisterial definitions would not be valid if the assent of the faithful were not forthcoming? Could the lack of assent serve as a criterion by which to judge that in certain instances teachings proposed as definitive were not binding?

From the context in the conciliar documents it seems clear that an affirmative answer to these questions would be contrary to the intent of the council. The First Vatican Council, in its definition of papal infallibility, had already condemned the doctrine that papal definitions of doctrine were not valid without the "consent of the Church" (DS 3074). Vatican II, in its reference to the assent of the Church, intended to make it clear that the hypothesis of a lack of assent rested on a false premise: namely, that the Holy Spirit would allow the magisterium to proclaim error by a definitive act. The same Holy Spirit, it taught, is at work in the magisterium and in the body of the faithful. Although it may take some time and effort for the faithful to elicit an affirmative response, the Holy Spirit will not allow the Church as a whole to fall into dissent.

The sense of the faithful is a valuable auxiliary criterion in arriving at the truth in matters of faith. Pius IX, before he defined the Immaculate Conception of the Blessed Virgin, and Pius XII, before defining the Assumption, both polled the bishops of the world and asked them, among other things, whether the clergy and people of their dioceses accepted these doctrines as revealed truths and considered it opportune that they be proclaimed as dogmas.[20] Together with a number of other indications, the sense of the faithful functioned to clear the way for these two dogmatic definitions.

The consensus of the faithful does not by itself suffice to give full assurance that a given doctrine should be proclaimed as true or condemned as false. Before any such proclamation Church authorities will consult scripture and tradition in their full amplitude. The dogmatic pronouncement, issued by the hierarchical magisterium, serves as a touchstone by which to identify those who deserve to be reckoned among the faithful. Whenever a heresy is condemned, the heretical party, while claiming to uphold the faith, is officially judged to have strayed from orthodoxy. The Holy Spirit will move those who are truly faithful to give their assent. The Spirit impels the faithful to defer to the authority of the sacred magisterium (LG 12).

When the magisterium is not teaching infallibly, its pronouncements may be corrected in certain respects by negative feedback coming from faithful Catholics. In a careful study of this phenomenon, Father J. Robert Dionne argued that in five cases the Second Vatican Council corrected, or at least gave a new modality to, noninfallible teachings of the magisterium that had been negatively received by large segments of the Church.[21] His five cases are: the relation of the Catholic Church to non-Christian religions, religious freedom, the ideal of Church-state relations, the identification of the Mystical Body of Christ with the Catholic Church, and the theology of Church membership. In none of these cases is it evident that the council contradicted the earlier teaching of the magisterium, rightly understood. But Dionne's study does tend to show that critical reception on the part of scholars may motivate the hierarchical teachers to reformulate their positions in a more nuanced and accurate manner.

The question of whether the sense of the lay faithful counts as authority in the Church became critical in 1859 with the publication of John Henry Newman's article "On Consulting the Faithful in Matters of Doctrine." Newman's critics understood him as contending that the laity was a second authoritative source of doctrine, alongside the magisterium. As they read the essay, he was suggesting that the laity had a kind of veto power over the official teaching. Newman explained himself as intending to say only that "the sense of the faithful is not left out of the question by the Holy See among the preliminary acts of defining a doctrine."[22] Newman's position is actually rather complex and difficult to summarize. Thus, it is easy to understand why his adversaries were able to stir up suspicions about his orthodoxy among Roman authorities. The laity clearly has no mandate to establish Catholic doctrine, nor did Newman intend to teach that they had. The *sensus fidelium* has no juridical standing; it cannot overrule the teaching of the hierarchy, but it can stimulate the hierarchy to formulate new doctrines or reformulate older doctrines.

SUBSIDIARITY AND COMMUNION

The supreme authority of the pope and the college of bishops, some might argue, is held in check by the principle of subsidiarity.[23] The idea of subsidiarity was introduced in Catholic teaching by the encyclical *Quadragesimo anno* published by Pius XI in 1931. In this encyclical the pope was speaking only of secular society. Against totalitarian ideologies, he contended that the state should do only what it alone could do, leaving lower-level agencies free to accomplish what they could by their own powers. According to the pope:

> It is a fundamental principle of social philosophy, fixed and immutable, that one should not withdraw from individuals and commit to the community what the individuals can accomplish by their own enterprise and industry. So, too, it is an injustice and at the same time a grave social evil and a disturbance of right order to transfer to the larger and higher collectivity functions that can be performed and provided for by lesser and subordinate bodies.[24]

The authority of the sovereign state, therefore, was "subsidiary" in the sense of supplementary.

Pius XII, in a consistorial allocution of February 20, 1946, mentioned in passing that the principle of subsidiarity was applicable in the Church "without prejudice to her hierarchical structure." Since that time it has been much debated whether and how subsidiarity applies to the Church. All admit that local and inferior agencies should be allowed to function without undue interference from above, but many deny that this principle of sound government amounts to "subsidiarity" in the technical sense. At least it is not true that authority first arises in the local church and accrues to the universal Church only in matters that exceed the competence of local or regional churches.

The Synod of Bishops in its assemblies of 1969, 1985, and 2001 took up the question of subsidiarity but failed to reach any consensus. After the assembly of 2001, Pope John Paul II in *Pastores gregis* concluded that "the Synod Fathers considered that, as far as the exercise of episcopal authority is concerned, the concept of subsidiarity has proved ambiguous, and they called for a deeper theological investigation of the nature of episcopal authority in the light of the principle of communion" (PG 56). The pope then referred back to his Apostolic Letter *Novo Millennio Ineunte* (2001) for a fuller exposition of the principle of communion. In this letter he spoke extensively of a "spirituality of communion," which would enable the members of the Church to see the light of the Trinity shining on the faces of all their brothers and sisters and to offer them deep and genuine friendship. Bishops, priests, deacons, religious, and laypersons should be united by a lively sense of communion, speaking and listening to one another with trust and openness (NMI 43–45).

In a recent *ad limina* address to some American bishops, the pope elaborated further on the application of the ecclesiology of communion to the ministry of bishops. "While the bishop himself," he said, "remains responsible for the authoritative decisions which he is called to make in the exercise of his pastoral governance, ecclesial communion also 'presupposes the participation of every category of the faithful, inasmuch as they share responsibility for the church which they themselves form'" (quoting PG 44). Then he added:

> Within a sound ecclesiology of communion, a commitment to creating better structures of participation, consultation, and shared responsibility should not be misunderstood as a concession to a secular "democratic" model of governance but as an intrinsic requirement of the exercise of episcopal authority and a necessary means of strengthening that authority.[25]

Whether or not one speaks of "subsidiarity," it seems clear that, for the sake of prudent government, local and regional bodies should ordinarily be permitted to take care of purely local and regional matters that fall within their competence. Consultation with interested parties should be the rule. But these prudential norms cannot be used to limit the power of higher agencies to intervene when they judge necessary. The Holy See or an ecumenical council has the "ordinary" power to perform the actions that a local bishop or local council could also perform. A bishop or pastor may use his authority to decide a question that could in theory be settled on a lower level.

In this connection questions could be raised about Catholic churches of Eastern rites, which have been concerned about protecting their own traditions against the Latin rite majority. Eastern churches are undoubtedly under the supreme authority of the pope and the college of bishops, but the Church as a whole has committed itself to respect their autonomy. Vatican II, in its Decree on the Eastern Catholic Churches, declared: "It is the mind of the Catholic Church that each individual Church or rite retain its traditions whole and entire, while adjusting its way of life to the various needs of time and place" (OE 2). After asserting that the universal Church looks upon the Eastern churches with esteem, the decree went on to say: "The Churches of the East, as much as those of the West, fully enjoy the right, and are in duty bound, to rule themselves" (OE 5). It then assured members of these churches that they would always be allowed to preserve their lawful liturgical rites and their established way of life (OE 6). The prerogatives of Eastern Catholic churches, therefore, are guaranteed by the pope and the universal college of bishops. The supreme authorities have not surrendered their powers but rather have used those powers to protect the relative autonomy of the Eastern Catholic churches.

Similar statements could be made about institutes of the consecrated life. As juridical persons they enjoy the right to live according to their own constitutions and statutes, which have been approved by the Holy See. But all such institutes are subject to the supreme authority of the Church, and must obey the pope "as their highest superior by reason of the sacred bond of obedience" (CIC, canon 590 §2). In principle, the Holy See could suspend or alter their constitutions, but in practice it will generally leave them untouched. In some cases popes have acted to make sure that the essentials of the institute of a particular order are preserved. Paul VI, for example, instructed the thirty-second General Congregation of the Society of Jesus in March 1975:

> Some of you, perhaps in order to inject new vigor into the life of your Society, thought that it would be necessary to introduce substantially new elements into the Formula of the Institute, that is, into its primary norms or into its adaptation to the present social milieu. For our part, we cannot allow changes based on such reasoning to enter into your religious institute, which is of its very nature so special and so fully approved, not only by historical experience but also by hardly doubtful indications of divine protection.[26]

In a longer chapter, it would be necessary to examine the status of church-related organizations, such as universities and hospitals, which are civilly incorporated according to their own statutes. Because they are church-related, the Church can take the measures needed to safeguard her own concerns, but she must respect the proper autonomy of these institutions to function according to their own principles and finality. The exact limits of proper autonomy have to be carefully examined in particular cases, taking into consideration the statutes and history of the institution in question.

INFORMAL AUTHORITY

Up to this point I have focused on authority in the strict and formal sense of the term. Such authority, I have tried to show, belongs primarily to the pope and the bishops as successors of the apostles, even though they may delegate a limited share of their powers to other clerics and even, by exception, to laypersons.

This approach could give the impression that priests, religious, and laity are in an inferior position and can do little or nothing on their own initiative. But if one begins from the baptismal dignity of all Christians and from the access of all to the Holy Spirit, a different impression arises. All the baptized are empowered to carry out the distinctive functions that pertain to them. They enjoy varying degrees of "rightful influence" even without being empowered to issue commands or binding doctrinal pronouncements.

In their priestly role, baptized members of the congregation offer the Holy Sacrifice of the Mass through the hands of the priest-celebrant and in union with him. The powers of the faithful to confer the sacraments of matrimony and baptism have been mentioned above. In general, members of the congregation are expected to participate actively in liturgical celebrations. Devotions of many kinds, including certain major feasts in the liturgy, have arisen in the Church through the zeal and initiatives of unordained religious and laypersons.

Priests, religious, and laity participate in many ways in the prophetic office. Under the vigilance of bishops, they are expected to conduct religious education and catechesis. Parents bear the primary responsibility for the education of their children. Highly educated laypersons can achieve great prominence as teachers and writers without holding any office in the Church. St. Ephrem was only a deacon, but is a doctor of the Church. And three religious women—Catherine of Siena, Teresa of Avila, and Thérèse of Lisieux—are also doctors of the Church. Their writings are approved as orthodox and edifying, even though their opinions are not of themselves obligatory. The spiritual life of the faithful, including popes and bishops, is sustained far more by the writings and lives of holy believers than by the bare bones of official doctrine.

A word needs to be said here about the authority of theologians.[27] If they hold positions as professors or editors, they exercise a measure of formal authority within the academy or the publishing industry. The hierarchy may enhance their prestige by giving them a canonical mission, by appointing them to ecclesiastical faculties, or by awarding them degrees. They may be consulted by the hierarchy; they may be asked to participate in some hierarchical function—for example, by voting on a decree, though ordinarily their vote would be only consultative. By their opinions they prepare the way for magisterial decrees and shape the interpretation of decrees already made. Theologians such as Augustine and Thomas Aquinas have had incalculable influence over the magisterium itself throughout the centuries. But theologians do not have the power of issuing binding declarations as to what doctrines may or must be held or to impose canonical sanctions for doctrinal deviations. In other words, theologians as such do not possess what I have called formal authority in the Church.

Vatican II encouraged many forms of the lay apostolate, including Catholic Action, adding the caution that such associations are subject to the authority of the hierarchy (AA 20). Many of the great religious orders and movements that have energized the Church owe their origin to the initiative of priests, religious, and laypersons, using their talents and inspirations without waiting for bishops to tell them what to do. The founders have, however, been careful not to go against the orders of prelates, and have sought formal ecclesiastical approval for their institutes when a certain maturity has been achieved. Instead of complaining that the pastors are not doing enough, priests and laypeople would often do better to take it upon themselves to bring a remedy. If they show a spirit of cooperation rather than contention, the pastors may be expected to welcome their zeal.

The primary role of the laity, according to Vatican II and John Paul II, is to sanctify the temporal order. Their distinctive field of responsibility extends to the worlds of family, community, commerce, communications, government, the arts, and the professions. These worlds have been far too little touched by the gospel. For them to be evangelized, the laity who dwell in these spheres must act as a leaven from within. While requiring faith and spiritual gifts, this apostolate rarely requires ecclesiastical authority in the strict sense of the term.

THE VALUE OF AUTHORITY

In some circles the very idea of authority provokes negative feelings. People wrongly imagine that authority is the enemy of freedom. Normally, however, the very opposite is the case. Authoritative direction makes for order in society, which is a condition for freedom. Authoritative teaching, based on the word of God, clarifies the path of truth, without which freedom would be empty and meaningless. Whenever freedom is cultivated at the expense of good order or truth, freedom itself diminishes.

In the Church, whose very existence depends on the faithful transmission of the word of God, authority is particularly important. Unless held in check by firm authoritative structures, human willfulness and ignorance could easily corrupt or distort the deposit of faith, sacraments, and ministry. The vagaries of public opinion beat against the Church like storms. It is not difficult, therefore, to see why the Lord equipped the Church with a hierarchical form of government, perpetuating itself by co-option.

Ecclesiastical authority can be abused, and sometimes has been. Popes and bishops, in their hunger for power or their anxiety to protect what they perceived as sacred, have on occasion acted tyrannically. They have sometimes issued arbitrary commands and imposed excessive punishments without adverting to the negative consequences of their actions. But the opposite failing is no less common. Often ecclesiastical authorities have been too timid or indolent to correct manifest errors and scandalous misconduct. They have delayed too long before taking firm action. If the Church had engaged in serious self-reform at the beginning of the sixteenth century, the tragedy of the Reformation might well have been averted. The recent scandals regarding clerical sexual abuse evoke similar reflections. Perhaps the antiauthoritarian climate of the nation in the 1960s and early 1970s was partly responsible for the failure of some bishops to act decisively.

However that may be, recent experience gives no grounds for rejecting or seeking to overthrow what councils have affirmed as the divinely given constitution of the Church. The Church is, and will remain, a hierarchical society. The bishops, with and under the pope, possess the full authority to teach, to govern, and to preside over the life of worship. The hierarchical leaders will be acutely conscious that they need the collaboration of the whole people of God to be successful in their own mission. In dialogue with the rest of the Church, and making use of consultative structures, they will draw on the vast reservoirs of wisdom, talent, and energy that are available in the community. It is vitally important that all Catholics work in solidarity to fulfill the corporate mission of the Church and that struggles for power among competing factions be avoided. Only in this way can the Church be what God intends it to be, a sign and instrument of union with God and unity among the whole human family (LG 1).

ABBREVIATIONS

AA – Vatican II, Decree on the Apostolate of the Laity, *Apostolicam actuositatem*
AAS – *Acta Apostolicae Sedis*, Rome, 1909ff.
CIC – *Codex Iuris Canonici*, Code of Canon Law for the Latin Church, 1983
OE – Vatican II, Decree on Eastern Catholic Churches, *Orientalium Ecclesiarum*
PG – John Paul II, Apostolic Exhortation *Pastores gregis*, 2003
DS – Heinrich Denzinger and Adolfus Schönmetzer, eds., *Enchiridion Symbolorum definitionum et declarationum*, thirty-fourth ed., 1967
LG – *Lumen gentium*
NMI – John Paul II Apostolic Letter *Novo Millennio Ineuente*

NOTES

1. John M. Todd, ed., *Problems of Authority* (Baltimore: Helicon, 1962).
2. John L. McKenzie, S.J., *Authority in the Church* (New York: Sheed & Ward, 1966).
3. John Dalrymple and others, *Authority in a Changing Church* (London: Sheed & Ward, 1968).

4. Thomas P. Rausch, S.J., *Authority and Leadership in the Church* (Wilmington, Del.: Michael Glazier, 1989).

5. David J. Stagaman, S.J. *Authority in the Church* (Collegeville, Minn.: Liturgical Press, 1999).

6. Bernard Hoose, ed., *Authority in the Roman Catholic Church: Theory and Practice* (Burlington, Vt.: Ashgate, 2002).

7. Catholic Common Ground Initiative, ed., *Church Authority in American Culture* (New York: Herder and Herder, 1999).

8. Charlton Lewis and Charles Short, *A New Latin Dictionary* (New York: American Book Co., 1907), 198.

9. See John Paul II, Post-synodal Apostolic Exhortation *Pastores gregis*, 31 and 43. The term *gravitas* in PG 31 is translated "authoritativeness" in the official English translation.

10. *Pontifical Commission for the Means of Social Communication, Pastoral Instruction Communio et Progressio* (Washington, D.C.: United States Catholic Conference, 1971), §§120–21.

11. For a summary of this document, see John Beal, "Weathering 'The Perfect Storm': The Contribution of Canon Law," in *Common Calling: the Laity and Governance of the Catholic Church*, ed. Stephen J. Pope (Washington, D.C.: Georgetown University Press, 2004), 173.

12. The questions of service and accountability require much more discussion than I can give them here. For a variety of views, see Francis Oakley and Bruce Russett, eds., *Governance, Accountability, and the Future of the Catholic Church* (New York: Continuum, 2004).

13. Congregation for Bishops, *Directory for the Pastoral Ministry of Bishops* (Vatican City: Libreria Editrice Vaticana, 2004), §160, 177. See also Pope John Paul II, *Pastores gregis*, 44.

14. Terence L. Nichols in his book *That All May Be One: Hierarchy and Participation in the Church* (Collegeville, Minn.: Liturgical Press, 1997) contrasts two styles or models of hierarchy: the dominative and the participatory. He recognizes that neither exists in pure form. The main thrust of his book, as I understand it, is to encourage consultation and coresponsibility. He does not deny that popes and bishops sometimes have to demand obedient submission, but he sees such cases as very rare.

15. Eugene C. Bianchi and Rosemary Radford Ruether write, "Vatican II enunciated themes from the New Testament and from later theology that undergird the fashioning of a multifaceted democratic church. Collegiality, people of God, pilgrim people, and many other terms from the council denote an egalitarian and communal church." Bianchi and Radford, eds., *A Democratic Catholic Church: The Reconstruction of Roman Catholicism* (New York: Crossroad, 1992), 248. The discussion of the Church as pilgrim people of God in chapter 2 of *Lumen gentium* (LG) does not encourage egalitarianism. It insists that the difference between the common priesthood of the faithful and the ministerial priesthood of the ordained is, and always was, essential. This is not to deny, of course, the teaching of LG 32 that "if by the will of Christ some are made teachers, dispensers of mysteries, and shepherds on behalf of others, yet all share a true equality with regard to the dignity and to the activity common to all in building up the body of Christ."

16. John Paul II, Apostolic Constitution *Sapientia christiana* (1979), Part I, Article 27 §1.

17. See comments on the Draft of the Constitution on the Church of July 3, 1964, 93; quoted by Karl Rahner in Herbert Vorgrimler, ed., *Commentary on the Documents of Vatican II*, vol. 1 (New York: Herder and Herder, 1967), 202.

18. I cannot here enter into the question of the status of parishes in civil law in the United States. John Beal argues in favor of the "parish corporation model," illustrating this by a statute in the State of New York that provides for the separate incorporation of each parish in the diocese with five trustees: the bishop, the vicar general, the pastor, and two laypersons. See Beal, "Weathering 'The Perfect Storm,'" 168–69.

19. Rahner, *Commentary*, 203.

20. J. Robert Dionne surveys the evidence and concludes that for the Immaculate Conception the consensus was 90 percent or more; for the Assumption, "the consensus among Catholic bishops clearly approached 100 percent." *The Papacy and the Church: A Study of Praxis and Reception in Ecumenical Perspective* (New York: Philosophical Library, 1987), 317, 335–36. The majority of those who expressed opposition to the definitions of these two dogmas did so on the grounds that the definitions would not be timely, not because they considered them erroneous.

21. Ibid., 83–282.

22. John Henry Newman, *On Consulting the Faithful in Matters of Doctrine*, ed. John Coulson (New York: Sheed & Ward, 1961), 56.

23. I have treated the question of subsidiarity in my book *The Reshaping of Catholicism* (San Francisco: Harper & Row, 1988), 201–5, and in my article "The Universal and the Particular Church," in Proceedings of the 65th Annual Convention (October 13–16, 2003), *Canon Law Society of America*, ed. (Washington, D.C., 2004), 36–37. See also the chapter by Russell Hittinger in the present volume.

24. Pius XI, Encyclical *Quadragesimo anno*, AAS 23 (1931): 2–3; cf. DS 3738.

25. John Paul II, "Address to Bishops from Pennsylvania and New Jersey," September 11, 2004; *Origins* 34 (September 30, 2004), 254.

26. Pope Paul VI, "Address of Pope Paul VI in the Presence of Father General and the General Assistants, March 7, 1975," in *Documents of the 31st and 32nd General Congregations of the Society of Jesus* (St. Louis: Institute of Jesuit Sources, 1977), 543.

27. I have written on this topic in many places; for example, in *A Church to Believe In* (New York: Crossroad, 1982), chapters 7 and 8.

II

PHILOSOPHIES OF AUTHORITY

4

Authority and Liberty

Glenn Tinder

That the Western nations today are in the midst of a crisis of authority is sensed very widely. But neither the nature nor the cause of crisis is clear. Nor is it clear even whether it is altogether a bad thing, since it presumably consists of a weakening of authority and that, given the evils of "authoritarianism," may be desirable. My aim in the following pages is to examine this crisis with particular attention to the relationship between authority and liberty. This relationship is, I believe, at the source of the crisis. Moreover, the relationship is paradoxical, in that liberty is at once indispensable and threatening to authority. The situation thus challenges our understanding.

Contrary to the connotations of "authoritarianism," authority and liberty belong together. Neither can be healthy without the other. And neither can be fully understood apart from the other. Authority only exists where it is freely accepted, and for this reason liberty is a primary condition of authority. A sharp line needs to be drawn between authority and power. Authority is, in essence, without calculation. It does not—so far as it is pure, as perhaps it rarely or never is in the world—seek obedience or even credence, but simply speaks the truth. Its defining characteristic is veracity, untainted by any manipulative intent. "Authoritarianism" is a perversion of authority, not its full realization.

While authority cannot exist without liberty, the converse is not the case. Liberty can exist without authority. Indeed it must, given the present crisis of authority. But it can exist only precariously, in a state of moral fragility and peril. Again a sharp line, like that between authority and power, needs to be drawn between liberty understood as moral responsibility and liberty understood as personal autonomy. Moral responsibility is the heart and soul of liberty; if there were no moral law and no true values, liberty would be pointless. And moral responsibility, as I shall try to show, cannot be effectively borne without authority. An individual stands in need of guidance in the discernment of moral standards and values. Autonomy, on the other hand, is not simply the personal independence that is inherent in moral responsibility. It is living in accordance with self-created and self-given laws and values. At its core, it is simply self-will. It is therefore in no need of authority and is by its nature intolerant of authority. It is, however, the end of significant liberty.

Authority has existed, of course, in times and places where there was little liberty in the modern sense of the word—in the Middle Ages, for example. For it to be in any degree authentic, however, its acceptance had to be unconstrained, and so far as it depended on constraint it ceased to be true authority. By "constraint" I mean not only coercion by threat of violence, but subjection to conditions of any kind, like absence of alternatives or deep ignorance, which stand in the way of reasoned choices. In the period between the fall of the Greek democracies and late modern times, authority has depended on considerable constraint, but not, most of the time, on violence. It can be said, accordingly, that the rise of modern liberty, in the last two or three centuries, has opened up the possibility, for virtually the first time in history, of complete and pure authority. As everyone knows, however, the possibility has not been realized. This great fact lies behind the present crisis of authority, and we must try to understand it.

The main paradox marking the relationship of authority and liberty is that the rise of modern liberty, in spite of laying the foundations of true authority, has undermined it. The plight of authority in the modern world is closely connected with modern liberty. Seen from a Christian vantage point there is little mystery in this fact. Liberty for a fallen species means that evil is enfranchised. Liberty is meant to release what is good in men and women. But in doing this, it inevitably releases at the same time what is evil in them, and the doctrine of original sin tells us that there is a great deal of such evil. Hence, liberty leads to the rejection of worthy authorities and the acceptance of unworthy ones. It leads also to the rejection of all authority. It is not hard to understand how this happens.

Among the diverse human sins—greed, lust, envy, and so forth—there is some reason for giving primacy to the sin of pride. Many common sins are only different ways of putting the self at the center of the universe—which is pride. The accumulation of wealth or power are perhaps the most common and conspicuous expressions of pride. The allure of pride owes in large part to the deep insecurity of a finite and morally fallible creature in the world. Inherent in finitude are physical vulnerability and the certainty of eventual death. Inherent in moral fallibility is the impossibility of establishing one's own worth, once and for all, either in one's own eyes or in the eyes of others. Strenuous efforts to rise above these conditions are virtually inevitable and they are apt to take the form of magnifying the self by cultivating—through money, fame, or power—feelings of omnipotence and immortality. The seductiveness of pride bears closely on our attitudes toward authority. To accept genuine authority depends on a quality at the opposite pole from pride—humility. It acknowledges superiority of some sort in another person. One might, this suggests, describe human fallenness in terms of a pervasive reluctance to grant authority.

Why, then, do we see so many apparent instances of exaggerated and overbearing authority, such as the fascist and communist tyrannies of the twentieth century? These were not instances of true authority, let us remember, since liberty was entirely lacking. Nonetheless, phenomena such as Hitlerism and Stalinism suggest that some terrible motive—some sin—other than pride was at work among the masses that threw themselves into states of fervent self-abandonment, and, in many cases, into death at the behest of a tyrant. I believe there was, and that the motive might appropriately be called "diversion." Pride often fails. Thus, most people who aspire to riches gain only modest means, and most of those who dream of power and fame remain weak and obscure. Hence the threatening face of finitude and moral fallibility is still there. Moreover, it may still be there even for some who satisfy the impulses of pride. Death and guilt sometimes break through the thickest walls. When pride fails in such ways, it is tempting, not to magnify, but to try to forget the self and all of its physical and moral weaknesses. Every society provides ways of doing this—in the ancient world, for example, the arena and its bloody spectacles, in the modern world television and sports. These are ways of diverting oneself from the central task of a human being in the world, that of taking on the responsibilities of mortal and fallible selfhood.

The crucial point is that diversion is as hostile to authority as pride. It draws people toward immersion in physical pleasures and mindless entertainment, or into deification of a tyrant who will help them dissipate the miseries of solitary and responsible selfhood. In one way or another, it incapacitates people for the thinking, critical assent that establishes true authority. The concept of authority is bipolar; it implies not only an authority, who speaks (which can be done in diverse ways), but also another, who hears and freely assents. The capacity for hearing and assenting is possessed only by one who accepts his finite and erring selfhood, a selfhood often falsified through pride, but oftener, perhaps, forsaken through diversion.

Granted, this is a simplified picture. There is an in-between area. Some allegiances and actions may serve either pride or diversion, and to an outside observer it might be hard to say which it is. For example, membership in a totalitarian party might be a way either of magnifying, or of forgetting, the self. Much or all of this in-between area consists of various ways of practicing what might be called "idolatry." This is bowing down to, and placing absolute reliance on, a finite and man-made entity, such as a nation, leader, or party. There is apparently a proud idolatry, in which by exalting a finite entity, like one's nation, one exalts the self. And there is an idolatry of diversion, in which the deified entity provides a way of escaping from selfhood. Everything depends on inner mood. Here it must suffice merely to note this middle area while keeping our attention focused on the principle that there are two main ways in which finite and responsible self is betrayed, and both are antithetical to authority.

The present crisis of authority, then, is not to be wondered at. A species plagued by pride and diversion is unlikely ever, on this earth, to give securely under worthy and universally recognized authorities. Some periods of history are better than others. For example, at the time of its revolution and founding, America was led by men of exceptional intelligence and courage. But that period lasted for only about a generation, and in the succeeding two centuries there has not been another period quite matching it, although there have been one or two great leaders. One may infer that the present crisis of authority is only the human condition become pronounced and conspicuous. And it is especially noteworthy because it arises from the very circumstance—general liberty—that for the first time in the history of the world makes true authority possible.

The signs of this situation are all about us and are familiar subjects of comment. The widespread fascination with celebrities is an example. Scanning *People* magazine is an easy way of gaining vivid awareness of the disappearance of true authority from many minds. Celebrities, as someone has said, are famous merely for being famous. Another example is the general run of politicians. There are a few quite intelligent and admirable people among elected officials in America at the turn of the millennium. But most of them, from my observation, deserve the disdain in which they are commonly held. They are taken seriously mainly as experts in eliciting governmental support for various group interests, and have little to say that deserves public attention. They shed little light. As a final example of authority in ruins I might point to corporate executives. Many of course are both astute and honest, but we picture them most readily as they proceed, shackled, into a courtroom.

These, however, are mere random phenomena. What is underneath them? What are the basic consequences of the fading of authority? Alexis de Tocqueville provided a highly plausible answer to this question. In a democracy—that is, a society in which all possess liberty—everyone behaves and thinks as does everyone else. Moral responsibility is transferred from the singular, thinking self to a collective, unthinking self. In other words, the failure of authority calls forth mass society. But mass society is a form of diversion, and I have maintained that diversion is a major cause of the crisis of authority. It may seem that I am arguing in a circle. What we see, however, is simply that sin exacerbates sin. Deepening the chasm between the sinning person and the good, it enhances the power of sin. How this works in the circumstances we are examining is easily seen. Authority is a precondition of righteousness. It is not surprising, then, that the unrighteousness that weakens authority exacerbates the unrighteousness.

Fundamentally, it is a matter of sin throwing off restraint. What makes Tocqueville's emphasis on conformity and mass society plausible is the impossibility, not merely for average people but for everyone without exception, of an altogether independent moral and spiritual life. Even the most profound and inspired individuals follow trails that have been in some part blazed. The ordinary and extraordinary alike need authorities, living or dead, to help them know what they should think and how they should live. Without authorities, they do not become independent centers of creativity, for a single human being is incapable of that. They usually flee from their singular humanity—that is, they seek diversion. They look about to see what others are thinking and doing, and in most cases they follow the others. Hence arises the phenomenon of "the masses."

Pride, of course, does not die out. Those who are extraordinary by virtue of ambition or ability may satisfy the impulses of pride through economic and professional success. They may win a tawdry renown by catering in some way to mass taste. I emphasize diversion because, in the form of mass society, it has taken on new power to the modern world—to the extent, arguably, of becoming the predominant form of sin. Given industrial abundance and the ethos of equality, diversion has become a way of living that is readily available to everyone and conspicuous on the global scene. Even the proud—the wealthy, famous, and powerful—ordinarily gain their preeminence by serving the masses. And they are, for the most part, notably ordinary people. They gain a kind of ascendancy by descending, in ways cleverly calculated to redound to their own power, renown, and profit.

Mass dominance is enhanced by what can appropriately be called "the culture of diversion." Here we can see more clearly the meaning of diversion. The pursuit of serious human ends, such as truth, is difficult. It is far easier to let oneself be diverted—by physical pleasure, say, or by entertainment. Modern industry provides unprecedented opportunities for diversion. These include manifold possibilities of "physical gratification" (Tocqueville's label for a kind of diversion he observed in America); the mass media of communication, making entertainment available at every hour; and equipment and mobility enabling multitudes to indulge themselves without stint in various sports and recreational activities. Technological development, not only continually enhancing industrial productivity but also providing a constant stream of novel ways in which people may indulge themselves in mechanical trivia, plays a key role in the modern culture of diversion.

The love of money, the New Testament declares, is the root of all evil (I Timothy 6:10). A culture of diversion stirs this love, for the facilities of diversion have to be imagined, manufactured, and made attractive to the general public. Hence the ascendancy in late modern times not only of entrepreneurs of various kinds but of advertisers, who are skilled at luring people into lives of diversion. Entertainers and athletes become among the most prominent of celebrities. In these ways the culture of diversion serves pride. Next to money, perhaps only power more effectively incites and sustains illusions of a godly self—a self superior to guilt, finitude, and morality. But money also serves the masses. Great numbers can possess money enough to sustain lives of diversion. The degree to which the economy and popular culture in the Western nations rests on the deliberate cultivation of qualities that have traditionally been deplored testifies to the confusion and decline of authority.

It is obvious that liberty is subtly subverted both by mass society and by the culture of diversion. It may continue to exist as a formality, but it lacks all serious human purpose and may not be needed even as a formality. Hence the anomaly so eloquently noted by Tocqueville: that democracy, a regime of equal liberty, is a near neighbor to despotism. Tocqueville's insight has been confirmed by subsequent history. The mass character of modern dictatorship is a commonplace of sociology and political science. The diversionary character of such dictatorship is evident in omnipresent uniforms and banners, spectacular mass rallies, and the impassioned propaganda that fills the air. Thus, when authority disappears, the figure that eventually steps forward to take its place may be the tyrant. Now what we might call "old-fashioned pride," the kind of pride that was considerably suppressed by mass society, returns to the scene. Godly pretensions are nakedly thrust forward in the public world. Liberty, eviscerated by the fading of authority, dies. This is not surprising. If authority and liberty belong together, then when one of them falls into ruins, the other will not long remain standing. In undermining authority, liberty inflicts a fatal injury on itself.

It becomes clear at this point that the crisis of authority is a crisis of liberty. One way, accordingly, of probing more deeply into the whole matter is that of rethinking liberty, and setting out on this project with a clear understanding that liberty is not antithetical to authority but dependent on it. Liberty must be thought of as bound to authority by necessities rooted in human finitude and moral perversity. If we think through this relationship successfully, I believe it will provide us with a better understanding not only of liberty but of authority as well.

Thinking about liberty cannot be fruitful unless it begins with one very simple proposition. I am tempted to call it an obvious proposition, except that it is often unseen and uncomprehended, at least in popular talk of liberty. The proposition is merely that liberty cannot be justified unless it has a moral purpose, such as conformity with the moral law or adherence to authentic values. Justification as such is moral. To deny that liberty has a moral purpose, and then to ascribe value to it is logically incoherent. It follows that the popular idea that liberty is good simply because it allows people to do what they want to do is entirely baseless. Everything depends, as Edmund Burke observed, on what it is they want to do. Liberty in itself is worthless. Its worth is determined by how it is used—that is, on whether it serves a moral purpose. In short, liberty cannot be justified unless it aims, in some sense of the word, at righteousness. There is no more deadly confusion in the public mind than the notion that liberty presupposes moral relativism. If moral relativism were true, liberty would be trivial.

The next step in thinking about liberty, however, brings us to a point that is not quite so simple. It helps explain why so many people misunderstand liberty. While the purpose of liberty is moral life, any effort to enforce such a life would be self-defeating. It would destroy both liberty and moral life. The standard of liberty rests on the assumption that doing what you ought to do is morally insignificant unless you do it freely. The concept of coerced righteousness is self-contradictory. It follows from this that allowing people to do what they ought to do is impossible unless you allow them to do what they ought not to do. And this is equivalent to allowing them to do what they want to do even if what they want to do is morally wrong. We cannot enfranchise righteousness without enfranchising unrighteousness at the same time.

Here the doctrine of original sin sounds its alarm. If human character in the world is affected by a primal moral disorientation, liberty is bound to have some harsh consequences. It is unlikely to eventuate in happiness and harmony. That this indeed is the case is manifest in the multitudinous social ills infesting America today. I can only note in passing that this circumstance brings proponents of liberty face-to-face with that ancient problem of political theory: the proper extent and the moral justification of coercion. Allowing members of a fallen species to do—without limit—everything they want to do would result in chaos. All order would disappear, and with order liberty likewise would disappear. But how can liberty be limited without denying the very principle of liberty? That is, assuming that granting liberty is a way of recognizing personal dignity, how can someone's liberty be limited without making the person so limited a mere means in relation to the welfare of others? Needless to say, I cannot take up this problem here. The problem does, however, direct our attention back to our central concern, that of authority. People who are fallen but free obviously are in need of authority.

Still reflecting on liberty, one more step will bring us very near to authority. I have said that liberty must aim at righteousness if it is to be justified and, moreover, that righteousness is authentic only if it is freely practiced. But what is the freedom that righteousness presupposes? Surely it does not consist in sheer choice, made without understanding of what is chosen. The concept of freedom as a leap seems to be unfortunate. It suggests that will is prior to intellect, and that choice therefore can be responsible even when made with little or no thought concerning what deserves to be chosen. But to choose blindly and willfully—for example, to choose to be a Christian simply from a recoil against death (a choice powerfully described by Kierkegaard and Unamuno)—seems hardly to be a morally significant act.

It follows, I believe, that the freedom righteousness calls for is exercised first of all in moral inquiry. Will, to be moral, presupposes intellect. Freedom does involve choice, and this is because it involves personal responsibility. But choice is the final stage, and is preceded by an earnest effort—an intellectual effort—to discover what is worth choosing. Freedom begins in a search for understanding. It is a quest for light and to find the light is to know what ought to be chosen.

It may be asked, however, how much light mortals can find. Surely the light, here on earth, is always dim and uncertain. We are never in a Socratic position; virtue can never be simply equated with knowledge. Choice must always occur in partial darkness. And if this is so, it must have some of the characteristics of a leap. In response, I would simply argue that we never choose in absolute darkness. The Israelites in the wilderness were always accompanied at night by a pillar of fire. The light is no doubt at times distant and scarcely discernible. And there are usually other seeming lights on the horizon, which cause confusion in our minds. There is even, Christian doctrine implies, within us a perverse will to turn away from the light and live in darkness. I do not mean to deny these things in speaking of intellect as prior to will but rather to say that the first use of will is pursuit of light—discrimination between false and true lights, and efforts to draw nearer to the latter. Freedom does not consist of mad forays into the darkness but, first of all, of efforts to dispel the darkness. Don Quixote is not a good model.

It may clarify my argument to note that relying on intellect does not mean excluding revelation. Nor does it mean excluding those immediate insights into truth and value that are often called simply "intuitions." But revelation and intuition do not gain a place in human life unless they grasp, and are grasped by, intellect. The Bible is not only spiritual; it is also thoroughly intellectual. The letters of Paul, for example, are magisterial works of intellect and only thereby do they convey revelation. As for intuition, the works of great artists, composers, and novelists presuppose not only insight, but also painstaking intellectual operations.

On these grounds, I suggest that we have our eyes on the central issue of liberty if we see it as focused on the struggle to know the truth in order, to paraphrase John, that the truth may make us free (John 8:32). I began this chapter by asserting the interdependence of liberty and authority. Liberty may be understood as the state of someone enjoying the legal and constitutional arrangements that allow people to choose freely. Liberty derives its importance from the fact that the freedom of choice it safeguards is indispensable to moral life. If moral life depends in turn on understanding, warrant is thereby given to the statement above that freedom must be focused on the struggle to know the truth. Liberty has to do with light.

How does authority come into this? In a rather simple way, I believe. Light is not equally distributed among humans. Most people have little of it and in searching for it must look to a few who are, so to speak, transcendentally privileged. Indeed, even the greatest visionaries, philosophers, or theologians cannot gain comprehensive understanding without looking to others. Creative philosophers progress in understanding only by consulting great philosophers of their own and past times. Major painters and composers work by responding to other painters and composers. Theologians could accomplish little without consulting Scripture and other theologians, and most of them consult philosophers as well. As for ordinary, unintellectual men and women, gaining understanding comes down in large part to deciding whom to believe—that is, in aligning themselves with one or several authorities.

Here it becomes apparent that authority is primarily spiritual. It is made up of those who see, and speak, or in other ways communicate. Authority is light in the world. More precisely, it is a diversity of lights, some of them bright, some dim, and many of them, given human fallenness, false—darkness in disguise. Light may be found in a tradition or in a person, in someone living or in someone dead, in a source that is grounded in revelation or in one that is grounded, at least ostensibly, in reason alone. Light also may be found in someone whose life is noteworthy for deeds as well as for words. A moral exemplar, such as George Washington or Dietrich Bonhoeffer, sheds light by his character and conduct apart from anything said. Most people, of course, will find light in numerous and diverse sources.

If we now can perceive the nature of authority more clearly, we also can better apprehend the nature of liberty. Where there is liberty, you have two fundamental rights. The first is to live in a critical relationship with every possible authority. Doing this plays a key role in deciding what to believe and how to live, so a serious person will exercise the right carefully and continuously. Many of the most familiar rights under constitutional governments, such as those of speech, press, and religion, derive from the fundamental right of living critically in relationship to every seeming source of light.

Fruitful freedom, however, consists not simply in critically evaluating but in choosing among these sources, and the second basic right you have where there is liberty is that of making this choice for yourself. As an independent moral inquirer, you may align yourself with your own authorities. You may follow such light as you consider revealing and true. Thus a Christian is someone for whom Christ—again paraphrasing John—is light shining in the darkness of the world and therefore the ultimate authority. A protagonist of reason may be an Aristotelian, an Epicurean, a Kantian, or perhaps a follower merely of a scientific figure such as Newton, Darwin, or Freud. Choosing an authority, however, does not mean that one ceases to reason. Since humans are reasoning beings, choosing the authorities one will follow should be choosing interlocutors in dialogue. An authority should be a source of reflection. And this is true no less of authorities relying on revelation than of those relying on reason alone.

It is true in particular of those claiming Christian authority. Even Christ, to say nothing of the multitudinous theologians, saints, and prelates in his train, should not be the end of moral and spiritual inquiry. Christ is, in a sense, the beginning of inquiry, as is implied by the ancient apothegm that faith seeks understanding. To follow Christ is not to follow one who is perfectly known. Christ's question to Peter, "Who do you say that I am?" is addressed again and again to every Christian. Following Christ can be likened to pursuing, and drawing ever closer, to a pillar of fire by night. This is presumably true as well of following Buddha, Muhammad, or the ancient prophets of Israel. We see again the close connection between authority and liberty.

It is worth noting that if liberty involves critical reflection on all possible authorities, then liberty is an engagement with history. Most possible authorities belong to the past. A literate person, seeking light in thinkers, scientists, writers, artists, and others who have attained and expressed visions of human life, must cast his mind, so far as possible, depending on various conditions like personal temperament and educational background, over the whole human past. Indeed, a rough sketch of the pattern and meaning of past history is a task inherent in assessing possible authorities and thus in liberty. Is primacy to be accorded to Jerusalem or to Athens? Must the Reformation be counted as a great liberating event or a tragedy? How heavily should science weigh? Even people ignorant of history must deal implicitly with questions such as these. And in doing so they are in their own fashion philosophers of history.

If authority is primarily spiritual, however, one naturally asks about that other authority, recognized at least since the time of Pope Gelasius I as a second sword. What is the nature and role of political authority? In raising this question we encounter something quite different from spiritual authority. The latter, it might be said, can do nothing but speak. Political authority can act. Action, indeed, is the primary responsibility of political authority. This responsibility casts political authority in a quite distinctive mold.

To begin with, the prerogative of action presupposes a distinctive purpose. The main aim of political authority is not to shed light but to found and maintain the kind of order in which light can be freely shed and freely perceived and followed. Above all, such an order must be liberal. There must be as much liberty as possible for potential authorities to develop whatever light they find within them and put it before a people. And there must be room for the critical examination of such light. Summarily, it might be said that political authority, as the second sword, is meant to serve spiritual authority, with the latter ideally not just one commanding light but a shifting variety of lights.

Responsibility for action presupposes, however, not just a distinctive end but also the distinctive means. Authority to act must be accompanied by the prerogative of using violence in support of action. That prerogative, moreover, must be exclusive. One is reminded of Max Weber's famous definition of the state as the organization that possesses a monopoly of violence. The reasons political authority must have these characteristics are obvious. "Authority to act" is a general phrase that means, more precisely, authority to act in behalf of society or even to marshal society for the accomplishment of an action. The action of a political authority is in one way or another collective, and collective action could not be effectively carried out except by an authority possessing an exclusive right of coercion. The contrast with spiritual authority, at least in modern nations of the West, is pronounced. Implicit in the ancient doctrine of the two swords, and quite explicit in the modern doctrine of the separation of church and state, is the principle that spiritual authorities must be without coercive power. They must be grounded, in some sense, on free assent. This principle, indeed, is presupposed in my initial proposition that authority depends on liberty.

Once we have perceived the distinctive purpose and powers of political authority, then we can see another distinctive characteristic of such authority. To put political authority in place requires a clear and commonly accepted definition of such matters as how the authority is to be chosen, the range of its powers, and its relationship to other powers and entities in the society. In short, it requires a constitution. And it follows from this that the prerogative of actions must be primarily official rather than personal. It must derive primarily from the office rather than the person of the authority. Political authority is always partly personal, of course, in that a highly respected official has a wider sphere of action than one who is held in disdain. But only in the worst of governments—tyrannies—is political authority primarily personal rather than official. Spiritual authority, in contrast, although sometimes connected with an office, like that of pope or priest, is more often personal rather than official.

Political authority, then, is in basic ways different from spiritual authority: concerned primarily with action rather than communication; vested with the right of violent coercion; and essentially official rather than personal. These differences are so fundamental that one is bound to ask whether, if authority is primarily spiritual, political authority deserves the name. The question is of interest because the answer to it sheds light on the nature of authority. What warrants the application to both spiritual and political ascendancy of the term "authority"? The answer, I believe, is contained in the concept of deference. A spiritual authority is someone to whom others defer by paying attention; a political authority receives the deference inherent in normal obedience. The concept of deference is useful partly because it is not logically antithetical to the concept of liberty. It connotes respect rather than unconditional and unthinking submission.

Defining political authority in terms of action, coercion, and office, however, contains implications more disturbing than any concerning the nature of authority. It indicates that politics must in some degree be a realm of darkness. Not that the darkness is usually total. One of the main purposes of such institutions as parliamentary debate and court hearings is that of shining light into political corners and hiding places. But no earthly light can completely dissipate the shadows within the political realm. Darkness is inherent in the very function of political authority, that of action. Action seeks specific ends and therefore looks on persons as means to those ends. Persons are used as means—sometimes very ruthlessly—even when the end being sought is their own welfare. This is a way of saying that action entails power, and the power of the state, as already noted, must extend to the use of violence. The dependence of action on power can be seen even in small private actions, such as those of parents on children. Concern for the welfare of the children, and utmost reliance on persuasion, may reduce power to a small element. That element, however, always is present. In the case of political authority, power is a very large element. Every political authority must continually look on people as potential means in relation to political ends, and must be ready at times to use violence. No responsible political leader can say something merely because it seems true. There must always be a calculation of consequences. And sometimes such calculation mandates deliberate deception. Power must sometimes resort to darkness deliberately.

These necessities do not only spread darkness. They also affect the character of political leaders. Such leaders are, to restate in mild terms the commonplace that "power tends to corrupt," not ordinarily made morally better or spiritually more discerning by the deeds they must accomplish. Hence, by virtue not only of function but also of effect on character, political authority ordinarily obscures the light. Occasionally, as shown in instances like Nazi Germany, it almost completely extinguishes the light.

Yet the situation is not utterly simple. It is obvious from numerous historical examples that the necessities and consequences of political action do not rob political leaders of all opportunity for voicing, or all capacity for perceiving, the truth. Moreover, their very immersion in the stringencies of history can give them a sense of reality, and thus a clarity of mind, that may be lacking in purely spiritual leaders. It is doubtful that any spiritual leaders at the time of the American Civil War spoke about the American situation with Lincoln's profundity and eloquence. It is only absolute power, according to Lord Acton, that corrupts absolutely. Indeed, political leaders cannot be effective—aside from cases in which a populace is completely demoralized—unless they are thought to have some respect for truth. And finally it must be noted that political authority is volatile, occasionally descending into nearly total darkness but occasionally ascending to a light that shines over a nation's whole history.

The political realm is therefore ambiguous, containing both darkness and light. This is to say that political authorities ordinarily possess, along with their political authority, a degree of spiritual authority. Their very responsibility for action requires them to speak and assures that attention will be paid to the things they say. Only in exceptional cases will they be so degenerate that their words cast no light at all. Political power remains, however, a disturbing presence on the spiritual scene in any society. Such power is, of course, indispensable. Our inability to live without it is one of the primary signs of our fallenness. And it is bound to be spiritually impure. The situation is worsened by the fact that spiritual authority likewise is bound to be impure, since it is necessarily possessed by flawed and finite creatures. For spiritual authorities, in all their spiritual frailty, to have always standing alongside them, or over them, political authorities, assures that every society will be threatened by an encroaching darkness. And in even the most enlightened societies, like Germany before 1914, there is an ever-present danger that the surrounding darkness will engulf the whole society.

The present crisis of authority is certainly caused in part by the degradation of politics in our time. The dim light shed by political authority is dimmer than usual. The reasons for this are various. Democracy is one of them. It must be granted that the fact of Abraham Lincoln, the most luminous of American presidents as well as the most democratic in origin, manner, and character, shows that democracy is not necessarily degrading. But in the absence of exceptional personalities among political leaders, democracy ordinarily lowers the level of public life. It turns elected officials into mirrors of popular prejudice. In the modern world, political discourse merges with public relations and advertising. Also among the causes of political degradation in recent times are organizational and technological habits of mind, these linked by the depersonalization inherent in both. Political campaigns come to be dominated by professional managers and "communications" experts. Finally, the brutality of international relations has to be counted among these factors in current political degradation. Political leaders in nations where civilized discourse is encouraged become habituated to the use of deception and violence. For all of these reasons, political authority has in the twentieth century been bent toward domination, power, and sway from discourse and reason.

More important for understanding our situation, however, is the state of spiritual authority. Not only is this the primary kind of authority; were it altogether sound, the light it sheds would illuminate the political realm and contribute to the restoration of true political authority. But it is not altogether sound. This collapse is evident in diverse current phenomena in the multitudes of people, especially in Europe, who have lost all interest in Christianity; in the readiness of numerous professed and fervent Christians to identify Christianity with particular political ideologies and programs; in the sexual scandals in the Catholic hierarchy in America and other Western nations, and the consequent decline of public respect for priests and bishops; and finally in the state of Christian writing, which attracts little public attention except in the form of fictional eschatologies, highly sensational and of doubtful Christian provenance. Altogether, few Christian voices manifest the purity and power which Bonhoeffer felt modern Christianity was in urgent need of recovering. And even if pure and powerful Christian voices existed, one can doubt that they would be heard by people so diverted by pleasures and amusements as are the populations of the industrial nations today.

My subject is dual, that of authority and liberty. It is appropriate in concluding, therefore, to note the impact of the crisis of authority on liberty. It can be summarily characterized in a word: liberty becomes an ordeal. Darkness is all about, and such lights as remain are dim and confusing. And there are numerous false lights luring one toward ostensible values that are only disguised forms of darkness. Hence it is difficult to know how one should live. Personal responsibility becomes burdensome and guilt inevitable. This is the situation, I submit, in the Western nations today.

The result is a flight from freedom. In its more benign form, this flight is manifest merely in mass society. Creativity is dissolved in routine and fashion. The lives of people enjoying liberty testify less to the potential grandeur of humanity than to its potential banality and degradation. In its more sinister form, liberal institutions and habits are wantonly overthrown. The allure of totalitarianism in our time is surely owing in some part to the strong desire of many to have someone compellingly prescribe a great cause to which they can subordinate every detail of their daily lives.

Thinking and writing as a Christian, I scarcely need to say that our situation is not hopeless. There may come a renewal of authority. This would come as a brightening and multiplying of the lights available to free men and women. These lights might appear in any of various places—in literature, in philosophy, in religion, or even in politics. They might, needless to say, appear in Christian places. But the appearance of new light is beyond human contrivance. In secular terms, it depends on inspiration; in religious terms, on grace. This implies that no human program of action will bring us out of the present crisis. We can only, in accordance with repeated injunctions in both the Old and New Testaments, wait.

It must immediately be added, however, that Christian hope is not mainly for what can happen in our mortal lives. No renewal of authority, on this earth, would dissipate the darkness completely or last for long. A crisis of authority, of greater or lesser magnitude, is an abiding feature of the earthly city. This is incontestable in view of the two main roots of the crisis as noted at the outset of this essay—the radical evil in man, which Christians know as "original sin," and the liberty without which authority in its plenitude and power cannot exist, but with which authority is continually threatened by the human evil that liberty releases. So it is inappropriate to speak of the present state of authority as a condition that may in time disappear. Rather, it is among the earthly adversities that must in some form and in some degree of intensity simply be endured.

Reflecting on the present crisis of authority, then, brings us face-to-face with two necessities—waiting (for a possible renewal of authority) and enduring (the absence of authority). These are so closely allied as to be almost identical. It is true that waiting suggests expectancy while enduring suggests suffering. But for Christians both involve suffering, for they presuppose the absence of something very much wanted—in the present case, light. And both entail expectancy—that what is needed will eventually, within or beyond the sphere of earthly life, appear. This is not in spite of the suffering but because of the suffering, for Christians see in the Crucifixion divine warrant for the principle that suffering is not, in the long run, useless or destructive. It plays an essential role in washing human beings clean of the unrighteousness into which the whole human race has fallen.

Hence our present state, however unsatisfactory, is bearable. We can live in freedom, even though doing so is an ordeal. And we can endure the ordeal of freedom, and bear its strains in a posture of waiting, because we can live with hope. Enduring and waiting alike fall under Paul's assurance (Romans 5:3–5) that suffering produces endurance, and endurance character, and character hope—hope for the kingdom of God, where all crises of authority will have been left behind—and, moreover, that such hope will not be in vain. It will be fulfilled by the love that the Holy Spirit pours into our hearts.

5

Does Authority Invite or Command?

John E. Coons

> Authority is a power or right . . . to issue commands and to punish for violations.
>
> *Webster's Collegiate Dictionary*

> [T]he command of love of neighbour is inscribed by the Creator in man's very nature.
>
> Pope Benedict XVI, Encyclical *Deus Est Caritas*, 2005

Authority is a relation between persons that entitles the one to command and obliges the other to obey or merit punishment. So thinks *Webster*. This is a plausible interpretation of authority's part when it rules our affairs through positive law; by easy extension, this alliance of an entitlement to command with sanctioned obedience can appear, unalloyed, to be the manner of the authority that is exercised by God and by nature as God's instrument. This chapter will suggest a more mixed interpretation. Whether any particular relation of authority originates with God, nature, or the Berkeley City Council, the spirit of its work may be less that of command and sanction than of invitation. This shift in our apprehension might have significance.

As it unfolds here this claim may seem a song addressed to the choir—that is, to religious believers who lodge the ultimate capacity to create moral obligation outside the human ego and, indeed, outside human institutions. Most of these faithful will add nature as a locus of authority, but only so long as this is a nature already pregnant with design and subject to the continuing and plenary authority of the Designer. Nor are we humans who receive freedom as our portion an exception to this unqualified dominion; in fact, it is our freedom that makes the work of authority so interesting a subject and understandable, perhaps, as an agency of love.

All this the choir accepts. Still, the effort to attenuate the element of command will not pass without challenge. For the propositions that I will need to invoke constitute a particular theological and legal account of the human moral condition; some of these premises are contested and unlikely to convince every mind that credits revelation and a created nature. What I can promise is to affirm the dependence of human authority of every kind upon these same transcendental sources. And, for that occasional and welcome reader who stands outside the choir, I would add this reason to continue: to the extent that individual Christians, Jews, and their diverse neighbors share the account of authority offered here, this convergence of mind might deserve political respect simply as a social fact that helps sustain the rule of law and the prospect of peace.

Two technical points should be noted. First, I will avoid the usage that makes authority an example of a "right."[1] The term right does not easily fit authority of a sort that is not only prior to positive human law, but that renders judgment upon its content. To say that God exercises authority because he has a right to do so reverses the real order of things in which God institutes forms of authority that either create rights or delegate their creation to human agency. Further, in respect of all authority invested in humans, there exists some corresponding responsibility regarding its use. To speak of any such limited commission as a right without observing this qualification is grossly misleading and may well encourage the "command" fixation. Second, regarding *Webster's* other notion that authority can be reduced to "power," I shall have but little to say. Only the resolute secular determinist could believe this, and I have already lost his attention.[2]

AUTHORITY AS RELATION

I am committed to a particular solution of an ancient puzzle that neither believing nor secular minds have in our time cared much to probe but that will matter here. The philosophers would label this the question about ontology: if authority exists, what is it? Is it more than the name for a notion lodged in individual minds? I am not able to settle the matter, but the reader needs to know my premise,[3] as I proceed toward a definition of our subject.

The term authority can denote either of two rather different existential objects. First, it can be the report of a purely subjective phenomenon;

specifically, in this view it is a perception by some necessary fraction of some community that a relation conventionally called authority holds between particular persons. Authority then consists exactly in the sufficiently widespread belief in its existence; and the test of sufficiency is satisfied to the degree that this belief is concurrent with obedient behavior. If people generally stop at red lights, the evidence is strong for authority understood as a notion widely entertained; but only as such does it exist. Interpretations of this sort thrive, at least implicitly, among theories of social contract that invoke the radical autonomy of the human will. In these conceptions authority comes into existence when enough of us have both given free internal consent that it do so and perceived this necessary consensus to be in place. This subjective state of affairs becomes an empirical reality insofar as it can be inferred from conduct.

The second usage of the term authority (my own) also denotes a relation, but one that can hold independently of its perception by any consensus of human minds. For me the word "relation," in some circumstances, can denote what is a distinct and important form of reality. When this exists, it does so as something added to the sum of the properties of those persons whom it relates. To say that Mary has the authority to forbid Susie to smoke is to identify some third thing—a relation—that constitutes these two persons respectively an "authority" and a "subject."

It is not surprising that modern thought on authority habitually avoids this question, but I cannot; I am stuck with the "realistic" second usage, being unable to conceive any moral obligation to obey another that consists merely in the subjective perception that it does so. Consider an easy example. A consensus that one community is related to another by an authority to enslave it does not make it so. In fact the opposite is the case. There is a relation among humans—and God and humans—that makes slavery truly wrong. An authority that is real has here created rights and responsibilities that are also real.

Realism regarding both the relation that is authority (and the specific obligations that any particular authority imposes) does not deny the potential of human agreement to produce genuine moral effect; free consent often contributes to the creation of real obligations. Indeed, consensus of a political sort can often be necessary in order to establish the authority of positive law.[4] Consensus is not, however, sufficient by itself to transform an ordinance that by nature or revelation is evil into one that obliges. No purely human compact carries such ultimate authority. But this does not forbid our enthusiastic embrace of social contract as one instrument with which to carry out our responsibility as subjects of authentic preexisting authority; we humans, indeed, are obliged to seek the common good by encouraging general consent to reasonable rules of positive law. For many contemporaries any such resort to a source of moral responsibility that is prior to the ego is exactly the problem. But at least these critics now have my assumptions; and we may hope for common ground when we come to practical judgments. In the meantime I will, in an abstract and very preliminary way, offer definitions for the two forms of "authority" that I apprehend.

AUTHORITY IN A NUTSHELL

Definition starts by exclusion; here it promptly reduces the subject matter to that company of moral agents who are capable of relating as subject and authority.[5] From these I next exclude the angels as beyond my ken. What remain are humans and their creator. Authority can hold by relation either between God and man, man and man—or both. And beware, since it is a relation, the term "authority" can denote either: (1) the role that is by definition complementary to the role of "subject"; (2) the living person in that role of authority; or (3) the relation itself. Care and context should make the specific meaning reasonably clear as we proceed.

Because it presupposes two free persons, authority appears to be a post-creational reality. God preexisted us in solitude, and hence "lacked" authority except in potential. Still, God's nature is disputed, and one wonders whether, in some plausible view, divinity might allow authority within itself. The Trinitarian understands God as eternally active community, rich in every relationship that emerges from its mutualities of knowledge and love. Might authority be possible here? There is a daunting impediment. The three persons are infinite and equal; none is plausible as a subject. Authority would seem ungodly.

Or would it? History may have altered this perception, at least for the Christian, as he contemplates the self-subordination that begins in the Incarnation. This event occurs in time and long after creation has introduced authority both between God and man and between man and man. By the time of Christ the world was long used to it—sometimes sick of it. In the unique case of the Jews, authority had come as the work of a God who is singular in person, hence inconceivable as subject. The intensity and intelligence of this belief may have contributed to the conventional view. Jehovah's occasional anger and vengeance in response to disobedience probably helped to give all authority the aura of command that it retains even in Christian culture. And that perception is plausible, so long as it allows the second and invitational element that is obscured within a monotheism singular in person.

For Trinitarians the Incarnation and Calvary so completely reframe the message about authority as to urge reassessment of its entire motif within the doctrines of love. Indeed, Jesus's latter-day acts of "kenosis" could make the metaphor of "invitation" seem a feeble understatement. Is the Father's will for his Beloved best understood as a command? Or, in spite of his evident reluctance in the role of subject, can the Son be seen as coauthor of this divine will for the unthinkable sacrifice? The gospels speak of Christ as Servant, but in what does his obedience consist other than a love that waives its own infinity? The Christian, of course, can turn Jesus's dual nature to conceptual advantage, explaining his subordination solely in terms of his human side. In any case, as we confront our own human responsibilities, whether as authority or subject, the implication of this story of all stories seems evident. Authority and obedience in pursuit of the good must accommodate love as well as command.[6]

How would love design the architecture of authority to serve the divine purpose? This would depend on the sorts of self-perfection and works to which a benign creator calls this free and beloved creature. That inquiry will reopen classic questions, first about the nature of human good, then about the conditions that the free actor must meet in order to realize that good. We will find disagreement among believers regarding the capacity of every human to achieve these outcomes that each of us is obliged to seek. Here two principal theories compete, and they imply different conceptions of authority. One leaves far greater room for command; the other centers in love, making the invitational understanding of authority more transparent and urgent. The latter view has been underemphasized by the professional, hence this effort.

All authority obliges the subject to seek some possible good; that is its point. Below I will at some length distinguish the two forms of human good. Briefly and roughly, one is the good to be realized in the perfection of the immortal self or soul; shortly, I will call this "First Good." Every other good consists in some possible state of the contingent world that would be right for the self to pursue in the particular circumstances. I will label all these benign contingencies "Second Good." God calls us to quest for both forms of good, but we seek each within its own distinctive regime of authority. Here are preliminary definitions of these two discrete relations; I will call them "primary" and "secondary" authority, according to the form of the good for which each respectively is the instrument.

"Primary authority" is that relation of God to man that is initiated by God's effective disclosure to the subject human self of his or her obligation freely to seek the right in its contingent forms. This will be the theme to which I repeatedly return below. I will claim, first, that the self's free commitment to the diligent search for the contingent, or "second," good is the act of cooperation that is invited by a loving God, as he discloses the authority relation to the person; I will conclude that this search is sufficient to realize the self's own goodness, or First Good. We are to strive diligently for the right, and that commitment works our self-perfection regardless of inevitable errors.

"Secondary authority" is every other moral relation, whether arising from revelation, created nature, or positive law, within which a person becomes a subject bound to value a contingent outcome identified by his or her reason as correct. This contingent outcome—whether it be sharing food, doing homework, or calling 911—is the course of action identified by the actor's honest and diligent reason as consonant with the authority of revelation, created nature, or positive law, with the former trumping the latter where the actor perceives conflict. His reason may err but it is to be followed as the best available understanding of authority.

These definitions together make every moral relation an instance of authority. The divine source fixes the conditions that govern and limit the subordinate orders; any jurisdiction of man over man is justified and judged according to the imperative addressed to every rational person to seek the terms of a just order.[7] Either directly or indirectly revelation and created nature are the criteria of every possible use of freedom. Thus, even in the world of positive law, it remains God who addresses the person of man, though here through authorities that utter reasoned conventions, identifying specific choices they judge that we ought (and ought not) make. But, of course, authority in all its forms presents correct choices without determining that we make them. We are free, and this bears upon the interpretation of the manner of authority's exercise.

The implication of this freedom is not that authority lacks the power to enforce by sanction (though a particular authority might). But freedom does make the language of sanction awkward. Is there a right way to characterize the response that authority gives to the specific choices that are actually made by persons? Are we limited to descriptions of reward and punishment? When we flout duty, are we truly lashed for our sin? Or, since choices do have automatic consequences for the chooser, do we in some way simply become the corruption that we have decided to pursue—and, if so, is "punishment" really anything apart from this freely elected effect? Correctly or not, the idea of authority can be separated conceptually from that of sanction; the former can be intelligible apart from the latter and seems the larger for the distinction. With sanction held at arm's length, authority can emerge more plainly as a distinctive office that renders particular choices important precisely by giving them moral implication in the mind of the subject.

AUTHORITY AND THE FORMS OF HUMAN GOOD

I will begin now to elaborate further distinctions between the two forms of good to be sought. The self is the one human element that believers typically suppose to be invulnerable or noncontingent. Whatever time, fortune, and prior choices may do to an individual's wealth, health, knowledge, habits, and happiness, the self survives, and, in this life, its perfection remains imaginable apart from such contingencies. The self, or soul, perdures beyond the reach of chance; it is the locus of a cosmic guarantee that we are never alone, unless we choose to be. In obscure ways even philosophers who claim no access to revelation have affirmed the reality of such a self.[8] And certain contemporary Catholic writers call the perfection of this ineradicable capacity simply "the Good." Because I intend to elaborate the twofold distinction between forms of human goods, I will use various other terms and have already referred to this good that is unique to the self as First Good,[9] "self-perfection"—and simply, "goodness." The manner of its achievement is disputed and shortly will play a role in our deciding between "command" and "invitation" as the motif of authority.

Second Good comprises every possible moral perfection of the world of humans other than the perfection of the self. Second Goods, when realized, are morally desirable states of affairs that, unlike the self, remain vulnerable to forces we cannot always control; they are contingent and ephemeral. They may consist in a just decision, a piece of knowledge gained, a child fed, or a valid positive law observed. Their continuation over time is subject to both choice and chance. We should seek these particular contingent states instead of others, either because we are directed by revelation to do so, or because this would be reasonable for creatures of our nature in the particular circumstances—or because valid positive law requires it. The use of means that would be reasonable and appropriate to achieve these ideal possibilities constitutes the behavior that would be "correct."

For this essay I will identify Second Good specifically as conduct. I could instead have identified it as the outcome of correct conduct that has actually achieved its well-intended goal. Any realized possibility—any outcome—is distinct from the conduct that affects it. Honoring my mother is a good deed; her being honored is a good outcome. If I were to speak of Second Goods as outcomes, I would, indeed, be adopting the manner of certain modern natural lawyers who emphasize the actual achievement of various "Human Goods,"[10] even tending to conflate these goods that consist of right outcomes with the perfection of the self.[11] I do not make this extension of their theory. As a consequence I see possible differences arising between us in the meaning of such categories as "attempts," "conduct," "outcome," and "achievement"; rather than elaborate all these concepts I limit the meaning of my own preferred term, Second Good, to the free activity—intellectual or other—that one undertakes in response to specific moral questions. I focus on conduct undertaken in the quest for right outcomes rather than upon the outcomes themselves. The distinction may be useful, as well as convenient, if it turns out that the manner of choosing conduct affects the self (for good or ill) independently of the outcome.

Let Second Good, then, be behavior that, given all the circumstances, would be the reasonable means to enhance some "human good." Today at least one important school of Catholic writers tends to call such conduct the "Right" in order to distinguish it from the "Good."[12] It is the human person whom they see as potentially good or bad; it is his or her conduct that is right or wrong. This distinctive conception of "right" is exactly what I call "Second Good," and I aim to serve the hope of these writers to maintain its integrity. On occasion, they have let the "right" itself seem a function of the actor's good intent.[13] I will understand the correctness of any potential conduct as a reality that is strictly independent of the actor's belief and intention, and this difference might be important.

THE MISSION OF AUTHORITY

One distinguishing function of authority, then, is declaratory. It enters the human self first in its primary form as the consciousness of our general vocation to seek Second Good; in its secondary form—employing the voices of nature, revelation, and positive law—it then assists imperfect reason in the search for the behavioral content of the right in specific cases. The effect is transformative, delivering the human will from what is otherwise a repertoire of unmeaning possibilities for choice. When authority confers consciousness of good and evil, it allows the capacity for choice to become a real actor in a real story in which decisions cease to be arbitrary preferences. Its first gift is the news that there is a point to this freedom.

The maintenance of this general moral consciousness of the self continues through rational life—in the naked insight that conduct can be correct or not and that we are supposed to care about this. Here is primary authority. Such, I suppose, is an early state of the typical infant intellect; all he or she knows is the obligation to seek and learn about the yet unknown good. By contrast, as the child matures, secondary authority identifies concrete dos and don'ts. Parts of the Decalogue come to us in this manner as specific obligations; the same is true of positive law. And, by our knowledge (or what fallible reason tells us is knowledge) we are morally bound. The defining act of authority—its signature—is that of instruction regarding duty. The lawless bully can move me with sheer power; it is authority alone that can prepare me to move myself with the insight that I have a vocation to the good.

THE MANNER OF AUTHORITY

To the extent that teaching is its identifying function, it is no stretch to understand authority as pure invitation. Its deliverance of insight empowers us. Here, it whispers, is my sustaining secret; now choose to live it. In this mode authority verges upon the manner of love. Of course, it can also arrive via the exercise of power; but unlike the bully, it employs power only in pursuit of some good. All of us experience a great deal of authority exercised in this mixed manner, starting with our mothers.

I think the two strains can be separated, at least in degree. When issued by authority, invitation is an act distinct from command in two important ways. First, when authority invites, it tends to apprehend its subject as a unique person. Offers addressed to crowds of strangers do sometimes get labeled "invitation," but only by gross extension. The host who invites Susie knows her precisely as Susie and nobody else. She may, at the same time, be a member of various abstract classes—women, farm workers, and ecologists—but, insofar as she is an invitee, she is addressed as the only one of her kind. That is what invitation pure and simple is about—thou and I.

Command, by contrast, is typically a way of encountering classes or sets of responsible subjects. The individual receives the message exactly as a member of a collective. Even if the commander learns that the specific subject he addresses is the unique Susie, this does not alter the nature of his intention, which is the performance of some proper function of his office. Her fungible status as one mechanic or medic among a larger class is sufficient to justify his assigning her to the particular responsibility: "Here, you are a nurse, and this must be done; do it."

The second distinction is related. In any act of invitation, the subject—the invitee—is apprehended as a potential beneficiary of her own correct choice. To accept would be in Susie's own interest; it would be good for her to know and perform her duty. By contrast, in the mode of command, authority's concern is indiscriminate; it wills the objective outcome for which this conduct would be the reasonable means. Its hope is, first, for correctness and then, perhaps, for Susie as well, but only as she shares in the good generated by a correct outcome.

Obviously, command and invitation may cohabit the same authoritative message. The lieutenant who tells Private Zwicker that it is his duty to stand firm in the face of hostile fire may cherish him as a brother with a deep concern for both his body and soul; he thus invites even as he commands. This sort of admixture is so common as to be the rule in everyday life. I will later argue, nonetheless, that authority exercised by God can be understood simply as invitation; its call to responsibility is a constant act of unmixed love for the specific person. In this it is distinguishable from derivative forms (such as law) that tend to meld invitation with command.

THE MYSTERY OF AUTHORITY

To its human student the voice of primary authority unequivocally—and prior to all specifics about behavior—declares both the theoretical possibility and the practical hope for good. It (somehow) discloses to each rational person the basic human vocation freely to seek the correct way. It is a calling, first, to commit to the voyage of discovery, then to set reason to the helm. Primary authority never ceases to preach. Over the course of every lifetime it broadcasts the constant imperative—look for the good. Its voice delivers the one who seeks to the secondary authorities who specify details of the correct path. Exactly there, they tell us, lies the right way; do this and avoid the other.

Insight of the right conduct may come from secondary authority as a rule of positive law (for example, you owe this tax); on the other hand it can come as a hard-earned personal judgment drawn in bits from a long moral harvest, as questing reason, over time, probes both revelation and its own experience of nature. In one way or another, by the time we are fifteen, so many rules of behavior have become evident and assimilated that the discovery of a particular duty can almost seem a clear and simple enterprise. Kant supposed it so, even—or especially—for ordinary folk who live undistracted by moral philosophy.[14]

I want to pour a bit of cold water on such celebration of our moral acumen. I can agree that the first stage of moral experience is utterly plain. Primary authority proclaims, then sustains, in every mind the one necessary truth; every sane person has been designed to recognize the vocation to seek.[15] Even at this first stage, however, the deliberate act (or art) of self-delusion is possible. We can decide to fool ourselves. Perhaps this strange capacity is necessary to our freedom. If all were involuntarily clear, we could never make that destructive negative choice. In real life we are able to prefer and to seek freely a world designed, not as the true and right, but to our own preference. I can say no to the calling of primary authority and do it my way.

But, if this extravagant mutiny is possible as a response to our basic vocation to seek, how much easier is it in one's daily judgments of specific conduct—decisions made, often in a rush, while hordes of distracting possibilities crowd our consciousness and obscure the message of secondary authority. The constantly shifting wilderness of sensation and language inflates the opportunity for error in the quest for Second Good. Nor is this vulnerability confined to those who are already half-inclined to self-delude. In the smoke and clatter of specific judgments, even the most committed pilgrim can lose his way and wonder whether in some particular decision he is correct, wrong—or even successfully self-deluding! We experience our own fallibility so vividly that we can only trudge on, maybe learning from mistakes, always worrying and ever seeking our salvation in fear and trembling.

An example: I sit in a faculty meeting considering an appointment. I happen to know a strange story about the candidate—it doesn't make him crooked or criminal, just weird. Is this report germane? I am in equilibrium. Should I disclose this hearsay, or is my duty to remain discretely silent? Is it relevant that I am itching to tell this juicy tale? The reader could supply a dozen versions of this story from her own experience. Nor does it matter whether you, the reader, are a truck driver, an academic, a housewife, or a nun. We all know at first hand these cases of moral indeterminacy. They come more seldom for some; but they come. And we make decisions. Even for the mind of a self deeply committed to the search for the good and the true, there are mistakes; we do not need to be self-deluders in order to reach incorrect judgments. It is a problem that has vexed moral realists,[16] and it seems to threaten my thesis. Whatever happened to the pure voices of authority that I have pictured as showing us the correct way?

Again, the answer must be that this same authority whom we encounter in our created nature, the one who announces our vocation and on occasion identifies specific responsibilities, has also willed our fallibility. Our judgments are vulnerable with respect both to correct conduct and even the authenticity of our own commitment to search for it. In specific cases we can be honestly blind; and, in all cases, we can be willfully blind. Patrick Brennan and I have argued elsewhere and at length that God's providence here can only be understood as part of his gift of freedom.[17] The tenuous and shifting images of the true and the good that frustrate the seeker are a way of avoiding the servitude to certainty that Plato and even Augustine so desired.[18] Plato seems right about the psychology; if you see the good with sufficient clarity, you cease to choose. Even Milton's angels required a measure of intellectual suspension, leaving them "sufficient to have stood, though free to fall."[19] The possibility of such obscurity may be necessary to the uncommanded love that primary authority wills possible to its human creatures. Maybe its declarations of both First and Second Good are sufficiently muted and muffled precisely to allow freedom.

I recognize that such an emphasis upon human freedom can seem *lese majesty*. Augustine and even Aquinas were uncomfortable that a man would have an active role in his own salvation; and the cautionary views of Luther and Calvin on the subject are well known. The crime of this "pelagian" idea was that somehow it worked a diminishment of God. Doubtless I need wisdom on this touchy point; but, despite my reverence for these sources, their conclusion appears a non sequitur—and their impulse to protect God remains a paradox. Surely the insult would consist rather in supposing God incapable of creating a being so graced in nature as to be able to choose to love, or not to love, his Creator in return. If God wants this, he gets it. If it entails giving man the capacity to defect, God still gets what he wills. To be sure, one has to deal with scriptural signals that God simultaneously wills the salvation of all. But universal salvation can easily be understood as a possibility that is subordinate to God's more basic "preference" for a human friendship freely joined. Love is first, and love is free—or it is nothing. Now, whether God so designed human nature could be a question of fact, but it is not a question of power.

To restate these points: (1) In the relation of primary authority God creates and communicates to every person the basic vocation to seek the correct way; (2) nevertheless, (somehow) we are free deliberately to delude ourselves and to reject the call to seek; and (3) with respect to the content of correct conduct we lack the sort of knowledge that coerces the will—we can be either honestly mistaken or self-deluding.

TERMS COMMON TO COMPETING THEORIES

I hope it is evident where I am bound. The interpretation of primary authority as an inviting host assumes a world of human invitees who are free to RSVP; authority seeks their chosen communion, and that ideal outcome follows from God's offer and man's acceptance. But, of course, the offer includes terms; to clinch the connection the response must comply. The world's first recorded invitation was of this sort. It called for an RSVP that included a simple act of dietary self-restraint. The offerees both declined, favoring instead their own trivial preference. Things thereafter grew complex, as authority presented new and more exacting terms to future invitees.

Viewing the ensuing ages before Christianity, it is very difficult—at least for this amateur—to speculate plausibly about the specific terms of communion between mankind and primary authority that remained possible to the fallen race. Still, it would not surprise me that some economy of salvation remained in which God and the free subject could bond. Lot and Abraham had their moments—and even Dante and Aquinas declined to close that door.[20] For the latter, of course, it was Christianity that had already flung it wide—and, in our own time, would draw it wider yet. It is risky today to try to recast the centuries of anxiety about this subject that preceded the advent of the "anonymous Christian."[21] Nor do I suggest that there is today one official Christian blueprint of salvation. Still, it does seem that the intellectual competition has narrowed to two identifiable stories; the choice between them might affect one's interpretation of authority's central office either as command or as invitation.

These two competing accounts seem to agree to this extent: any person can be saved, even without the gift of specific faith in the Christian vision. The atheist himself has access, if, with benign intent and reason, he pursues Second Good, doing what many medievals described as "what is in him." *Facienti quod in se est*.[22]

AT LAST, THE ISSUE

But this is ambiguous, and a conflict remains at the heart of Christian moral theory and its application to the problem of salvation. Granting the universality of primary authority's call to the human self to seek the right way, what exactly is the significance, if any, of successful rightness—of getting truly correct answers to moral questions? Even if I do not self-delude, I can make practical moral mistakes—big ones. I can with clear and enthusiastic conscience demonstrate for abortion rights or gay marriage; I can kill as a volunteer in a war that I wrongly suppose to be just; I can benignly and conscientiously lie to my terminally ill patient—or, if I am a Dutch doctor, even help her along. What becomes of sweet guys like me who make such honest mistakes? If you like, you can imagine me a Wahabi fanatic. Not only am I a dedicated polygamist, but an enthusiastic and self-sacrificing murderer of Christians and Jews. Am I saved? What kind of authority would that imply?

Please note that the issue is not whether the honest bungler is reaching some Aristotelian or Stoic version of natural perfection. If I perform wrong acts, even in the best of good faith, I automatically corrupt my repertoire of "habits."[23] Though I am ardently seeking Second Good, I am, in objective terms, becoming a locus of Second Bads. This aspect of the person I will here locate in what I call the "persona," defining that term more fully in a footnote; put very simply, persona denotes the totality of my capacities to identify specific correct choices.[24] Given this distinction between self and persona, the question becomes whether the mistakes and failures attributable to my imperfect persona are relevant to my salvation. Can the vocation that I receive from primary authority be answered effectively by doing the best I can; will this attain the one prize that will never cease to matter?

The ever-hesitant—and embarrassed—answer of tradition has, for the most part, been "no." Salvation has required what I will call a gnostic component. One has to get correct answers. The customary reliance on Aquinas for this conclusion is proper and does justice to an intellectualist tradition. To be sure, I have wise friends who would set St. Thomas outside this circle; and I agree that, were he with us today, he would, with relief, sign on for those scattered passages from Vatican II that exalt good conscience as not only necessary but, somehow, as sufficient. But, so far as I can tell, Aquinas never was able in his own work to shed this condition of correctness.[25] One's ignorance of fact might excuse; but excuse from a particular error—even if one is diligent—does not suffice for salvation. And, where knowledge of right behavior is in theory accessible in one's own culture, honest ignorance, though of the very sort that would seem to make the act in effect involuntary, does not even excuse. In any case, to merit the grace necessary to salvation, one needs more than excuse; he is simultaneously bound, not merely to follow conscience, but also "bound to know" the right answer.

For several generations, theology—Catholic in particular—has witnessed a serious effort by certain Europeans and Americans to shed this old view, and, in its place, to empower good conscience as the sufficient condition of salvation. This project may prove one of the few enduring gifts of the twentieth century. The various moves in this intellectual drama are well known; I need not replay them or the relevant ripostes from Rome, including the delicately balanced—even ambivalent—declarations of principle in *Veritatis Splendor*.[26] This commotion over the criterion of correctness continues today even at the deepest levels of Catholic culture, including the schools (the issue is carefully elided in the new *Catechism*).[27]

I suspect that, by misadventure, an ancient misunderstanding has survived to confuse the basic issue—at least for dabblers like me. The most professional of scholarship on this subject has on occasion lapsed ambiguous regarding the nature of the distinction between First and Second Good. Specifically, good intention, love, and best effort sometimes seem permitted, by themselves, to transform, not only the person, but even the conduct itself from bad to good.[28] Quite clearly this was not the intended meaning of the authors of those contemporary works that I know; a full, fair reading seals this conclusion. Still, the vocabulary of the discourse about the two distinct forms of human good remains to be perfected. As they labor in charity to secure the bungler's hope to see God, the theologian and the moral philosopher must take more care not to denature Second Good. Indeed, the "right" way must remain an independent reality precisely that one may authentically seek it and thereby attain his own goodness.

This latter view, comfortable with Vatican II, represents the most straightforward competitor to the intellectualist or gnostic tradition. In a moment I shall give it a distinctive name. Its substance is already plain and can be tersely restated: We are saved by doing our best to discover this true and correct order of conduct that is ordained by secondary authority and holds independent of our intention or, indeed, our charity. We become good by striving to find this path, not by finding it. Our mistakes do matter very much for the practical realization of the many important possibilities of Second Good—justice, civil order, and truth—as each is represented in an actual situation. Each blunder also weakens our own capacity to discover the right way. However, for salvation it is irrelevant; for that, indeed, is a matter of the heart. The conclusion: the inclusive kingdom of conscience and love that lures the modern mind can be achieved while maintaining the integrity of Second Good and the hope that it represents for both the individual and the social order. This latter point is crucial. Any retreat from the reality of Second Good is deadly to moral discourse and the common good.[29] Gladly, then, I return to the familiar world in which red-blooded gnostics still warn against wrong answers, while trimmers like myself are content to preach the duty to seek the right ones.

NAMES FOR THE OPPOSING PROTOCOLS: GNOSTIC AND OBTENSIONAL

Do the two opposing protocols of salvation imply different answers to our question whether authority invites or commands? For that inquiry it will be convenient to have specific labels for each. The more traditional intellectualist view I have already christened the "gnostic" protocol. Again, to be clear, this usage is broader than the historical convention, which would limit the term to antique cults.[30] Modern English badly needs this word in order to characterize the conviction—still common among religious (and even secular) worldviews—that two of the conditions of salvation are cognitive in character.[31] We must know that we are to seek, and our answers must be right.

We must be able to distinguish this intellectualism from the non-gnostic protocol, for which Brennan and I have revived and adapted the archaic noun "obtension."[32] This word in its verb form means to give a reason for belief or action, presumably a reason that honestly is thought to justify. The person who "obtends" is one on the lookout for the correct way, whether or not he gets it right. The *Oxford English Dictionary*'s vivid example of this usage is Origen, who "did geld himself for the obtente of chastity." The obtensional protocol, like that of the gnostics, would declare Origen's act incorrect and a substantial injury to Second Good, including Origen's own persona; however, unlike the gnostic interpretation, it would declare Origen himself a step closer to self-perfection for acting upon his loving misconception of the right way.

How might this distinction between the gnostic and obtensional protocols for salvation bear upon authority as being either invitational or commanding in the manner of its exercise? An answer might begin this way: Invitation would be hard to discover wherever authority rejects and reprobates the honest bungler as unfit for salvation. Such a judgment passed on the self identifies the material content of the misunderstood truth or rule of conduct as the decisive concern; God as authority would thus elevate what is a contingent good above the salvation of the eternal soul who has sought it. The benign possibility that went unrealized—the insight or the right action that was never in fact accessible to the mind of this actor—weighs in to condemn him, however much he had longed to find it. But, in that event, the subject person is not even the primary object of the authority's concern, and we seem to have left the world of invitation altogether. If the God of the gnostic has an interest in Susie, it appears to consist, before all else, in the instrumental value she bears for the maximization of correctness; her fate instructs others who also seek Second Good and the perfection of creation. Her exile is, for the rest of us, an insight and a deterrent. Authority, when exercised exclusively in this manner, commands rather than invites, and—true to its nature—the command is directed prophylactically to those whom it may concern. Others out there may hear what Susie could not. Second Good may thus be increased.

So it is that the exercise of authority bears a rather different interpretation under the gnostic as opposed to the obtensional protocol of salvation. I will now inquire briefly whether—and how—this difference is confirmed in the exercise of authority in and through positive law. I will then conclude with a similar snapshot of moral obligation in the case where it is not regulated by positive law, but by the secondary authority of God exercised in revelation or nature.

POSITIVE LAW AND GNOSTIC SUFFERANCE

Both the "gnostic" and "obtensional" protagonists are believers. And each views the ordinances of human lawmakers as being subject in the same important way to revelation and natural law; that is, so long as human law respects divine law and reason it can create real moral obligation. The legitimate state has the capacity to create moral duty where none would obtain by the deliverance of nature. As Yves Simon has taught us, while specific choices of conduct often are a matter of indifference, the making of some choice among them is often crucial.[33] For the sake of Second Good some course must be taken and can be taken only in common. Human communities survive by anointing "essential authority" to make the decision to drive on the right side of the road or to settle upon one military strategy or taxation policy upon those familiar occasions where we face reasonable but inconsistent options. Some form of political consensus ordinarily constitutes this essential authority, but its capacity to bind the subject morally is a function of its implicit ratification by the source of all authority. In this manner the most accidental details of law (at least in serious matters) become instances of correctness to be sought and respected, and so human law can implicate salvation. The Hound of Heaven deputizes the hounds of the IRS, and real authority informs the application of these all-too-human rules. To reject reasonable positive law is to reject God.

Are all valid rules of the positive law, then, occasions to fear the gnostic concern for correctness? If we are bound on penalty of sin to get right moral answers, and law is one form of these, would the gnostic moralist invoke Aquinas's sad conclusion that in search of salvation we are "bound to know"? I have never heard any such claim. Far from disputing the consequences of ignorance, in the case of positive law the gnostic and obtensionalist appear to be in rough agreement. All of us are obliged to direct reason toward the discovery of the content of this artificial legal correctness. We are responsible, in short, to obtend. But if Section 49x.q of the code—important though it be—should escape your sedulous search, not to worry. You may, of course, go to jail, but there is no injury to your self; to the contrary, you enjoy the benign effect of your obtension, even though the Second Good you intended has been botched.

Thus, the gnostic is in this milieu a believing and practicing obtensionalist. In the realm of positive law he invites and values the honest search for correctness independently of its success. It does not follow, however, that he will take the same view of mistakes respecting acts proposed to reason by the authority of nature or revelation. We must, then, pursue the distinction between invitation and command in the moral world outside law. Before we leave the legislators, however, I wonder that their parochial ways might have something more to teach us about our question.

A PARENTHESIS ON THE POSITIVE LAW

Observing the positive legal system in operation, do we come away with a uniform impression of Austinian command?[34] It would be hard to interpret the Internal Revenue Code as an invitation. Rules of this sort are not personal notes to Susie reminding her that, by sending a check, she can simultaneously do Second Good and perfect herself. Yet even here "essential authority" intends a flourishing and authentic community, of which every Susie is conceived abstractly as a beneficiary. One could say that the code to this extent resembles an invitation to a barn raising. All together now!—for your own individual good.

But if this faint whisper of sweet petition lurks even in remote and abstract codes, how much more evident is it where authority is literally embodied in a specific person by the positive law? I refer specifically to the *corpus juris* of childhood and parenting, and my initial point is simply that here too lies the regime of positive law. The informality and warm mythology that characterize much of family law should not deceive. The sovereign adult—generally the parent—in her or his own person constitutes a legislative, executive, and judicial authority independent of that lodged in any officer of the state. No agent of government can force or forbid Susie to pray, eat her vegetables, or visit the art museum. But Mother can. Without possibility of appellate review, she conscripts the child for enterprises of the most eccentric sort. She may employ physical restraints and penalties. She can even invoke the resources of the state as her subordinate to enforce specific obligations that she has herself created, such as curfew and travel restrictions. Though he thinks her clumsy and absurd, the sheriff will cooperate. Outside the narrow restraints of abuse, Mother is law.

I have smuggled this family business into the discussion to forestall any implication that human law is easy to characterize as authority that exercises pure command. Given the IRS at one end of the legal spectrum and Mother at the other, I would not try to make the case either way. Wherever personal authority in the parental style endures as positive law, John Austin loses his voice. True, Mother does often command, and this too is both law and an exercise of authority. But the whole point of command in her case becomes the encouragement of the child to full personhood. Be good for goodness's sake. The relation of secondary authority and subject here is centered in the uniqueness of Susie. It merges affection with the practical imperative that this child in due course become independent. At least in this one wide province within the world of the positive law, the very architecture is that of invitation.[35]

INVITATION AS THEODICY

In contrast to its lenience for unintended breaches of human law, the gnostic protocol often has denied eternal happiness to those who are invincibly ignorant of important revealed truths or ordinances of reason that are drawn from nature. There are plausible justifications for this firmness of standards, and I must deal with them, if only at the most general and superficial level.[36]

Gnostic strictness here may owe much to the Greek and Thomistic insight that serious departures from authentic correctness work an automatic injury to the actor. I suppose that few disagree with this at the natural level. Every such intellectual or behavioral error has the tendency to become (or to harden) some bad habit. I believe this; however, it does not settle the relevance of honest errors to what we call salvation. This is an event that may be determined quite apart from habits.

I suspect that—right or wrong—the gnostic condemnation of the bungler is in part an inference from a certain model of the individual human person in which the moral substance of each of us is seen as simple, in the fullest sense of that word. The moral actor is a thing uniform, utterly monadic. The individual can experience moral change for the better or worse—but only as a whole. Thus, if my mistaken judgment drives me to volunteer for an unjust war, my consequent behavior corrupts the whole of my integrity as a moral actor. As John Finnis puts it, "my blunders . . . are essentially self-determining—i.e., internal to and constitutive of an individual's character."[37] My habits are me—period. There is no distinction between the good of my self and what is "right." The damage to the persona also suffuses the self.

At the natural level there is much to be said for this view. Most of us have been raised to fear the Cartesian disaggregations of the person into dualisms or something worse. When this healthy fear gets applied at the level of ordinary ethics, it is not surprising that so many of us resolutely identify the person with his evil act. We observe the failure of this human unit to realize its potential. My moral gaffe speaks for me, and nature requires the disinterested judgment that this specimen is a flop. Nor will reason permit a personified caricature of nature in which it petitions its own sovereign creator for a gentler and less monadic view of the sinner. Hence, the specimen that we call Susie either succeeds or fails as a whole. She cannot simultaneously be wrong and saved.

It is paradoxical that the religious gnostic should typify this more naturalistic outlook. In principle his mind would seem the sort most open to irruptions of the temporal order by invasions of grace that disqualify natural considerations. Yet, so sensitive is he to the need for unity of body and soul that he confers a kind of moral sovereignty upon sheer behavior at the expense of the person. I suspect he is the intellectual descendant of Aristotle and St. Thomas; in this great tradition he is uncommonly wary of slighting nature. Should that be the case, I can admire his caution while I deny that there is any real danger of fracturing the human person.

For the obtensional view is in full accord with that of the gnostic on the essential point; the human person is an integrated unity. But this principle does not require us to conceive him as a homogeneous mass of moral jello, which is perfected or compromised either as an entirety or not at all. I see no Cartesian threat in a human nature comprising two capacities that are suited respectively to the pursuit of related but discrete goods. Indeed, such a person is integrated in the very manner of those mistaken actors whom St. Thomas was happy to excuse for their correct intention. Aquinas had no difficulty recognizing the essential unity of the person whose nature includes these two distinct capacities—the one to will the search, the other to conduct it. And he carefully distinguished the respective effects of their proper exercise. For him the choice to will the search—to obtend—can excuse, even if it cannot by itself complete the human side of the event called salvation. That was the narrow and specific issue before him. But (right or wrong) this solution to the problem of the moral bungler only confirms Aquinas's comfort with the coexistence of these discrete powers in the same unified personality. His hesitation about the sufficiency of obtension for salvation was not grounded in any uneasiness about a dualism exposed by recognizing thc independent effect of a good intention.

For one final time let us recall the complementary relationship of these powers. One is the simple and invulnerable capacity to commit to seek Second Good of whose general existence as a set of possibilities one is (somehow) made aware. The other is the diverse and contingent capacity to discover and achieve these same possibilities. At any given time, this second capacity consists in whatever it is that chance, choice, and the grace of God have so far made it in this person and thereafter will transform it. I have called this aggregate of qualities the "persona"; it is the plastic bundle of brains, body, grace, and luck that, at any point in time, the self can freely set in search either of Second Good or the satisfaction of its own egoistic preferences. Insofar as the issue is the essential unity of such a person, I see no conflict with Aquinas; the human person so conceived remains an integrated whole. What I do sense is that this distinction between self and persona might aid us in understanding the exercise of ultimate authority as pure invitation. Its message to the human person would not arrive as a general advertisement: "Wanted, correct answers." It is, instead, utterly personal: "Wanted—you, Susie—as a free seeker of correct answers."

I realize that this conceit of mine might be more convincing were it delivered in the figured language of Christian love. Unhappily, my own persona is barren of the literary gift necessary to such an effort. I can commit only "what is in me."

SO WHAT?

Of this I confess that little more is left, but I did promise one practical application. Brennan and I have attempted several of the sort elsewhere. The most ambitious of these involved equality; we showed (I hope) that the obtensional (now also "invitational") interpretation of the human self is the sole available support for theories of a descriptive human equality—whether natural or supernatural.[38] Individual humans are simply quite disparate in every capacity for insight and for conduct that together constitute the persona. If, nevertheless, we are somehow equal, it must be in our access to God through accepting his authoritative vocation to seek as best we can. That RSVP must suffice (with his grace) for salvation.

Here I would extend that rescue of the obtending self in another direction. This plain and simple equality of access to God is in turn crucial to every version of human dignity. If, instead, one's repertory of right answers were the measure of his worth, dignity would stand wholly relative; and some would, by definition, be relatively impoverished. But to have less or more of dignity is a contradiction. And seeing this drives the Christian, as a matter of common prudence and sound politics, to reexamine this fundamental question about access to God and how we talk about it to others.

Glenn Tinder tells us what is at stake here in the quest for community at every level: "[W]e cannot love . . . those we cannot see as fitted and destined for life in the presence of God."[39] The implication of this is disturbing enough in our own private lives. But consider its application in that universe of strangers who observe us and who fear the gnostic remnant in the Christian vision. Our exclusionary formulas tell upon the minds of those with whom we must share the world and who perceive our assessments of their worth as humans. Weigh the political implications of those triumphal blips that still survive in our religious discourse. Start with this from the recent joint Evangelical-Roman Catholic statement on "The Gift of Salvation": "Many are in grave peril of being eternally lost because they do not know the way."[40]

Obviously, one is bound to teach the truth he knows. We must, with profound respect, confront the minds of intellectual enemies. If they make it necessary, we must go on to confront their physical threats. But, before we do either, it might be well to let them know (if we really believe this) that the invitation to divine love comes to everyone from the same primary authority and on the same terms—onerous but uniform. All share the same hope and are given the same instrument with which to seek it. The least gifted among us is fully responsible—as best he can—to seek, think, judge, and choose the right. But fidelity to this search constitutes the wedding garment; and all are invited to wear it.

NOTES

1. The phrase "power or right" appears repeatedly in the source quoted to introduce this essay. *Webster's Collegiate Dictionary*, s.v. "Right." See also Cass R. Sunstein, "Beyond the Republican Revival," *Yale Law Journal* 97 (1988), 1572.

2. "A common mistake is to identify authority with coercion, which is but the most conspicuous of its instruments." Yves R. Simon, *Philosophy of Democratic Government* (Notre Dame, Ind.: University of Notre Dame Press, 1993), 7.

3. I pretend no technical mastery of the issue. The classics that I have consulted are cited in John E. Coons and Patrick M. Brennan, *By Nature Equal: The Anatomy of a Western Insight* (Princeton, N.J.: Princeton University Press, 1999), 6–10.

4. Yves Simon well describes the authority he calls "essential"; it is so because it is necessary to decisions that must be made among conflicting but equally reasonable possibilities. Yves R. Simon, *A General Theory of Authority* (Notre Dame, Ind.: University of Notre Dame Press, 1962), 57–60.

5. If God were said to exercise "authority" over that other part of creation whose actions and ends are determined, the meaning would become a contradiction. He does not oblige the frog to jump; he has created him so.

6. Anyone inclined to exclude command and sanction altogether would need to explain Christ's confrontation with the money changers (Matthew 21:13).

7. See generally Etienne Gilson, *The Philosophy of St. Thomas Aquinas*, second ed., trans. Edward Bullough, ed. G. A. Elrington, O.P. (Cambridge: W. Heffer & Sons, 1929), 324–33. Gilson makes it specific that "human law cannot lay claim to any principle of its own." Ibid., at 329.

8. See, e.g., Aristotle, *The Nicomachean Ethics*, Bk I. Sec. 7, trans. J. A. K. Thompson (London: Penguin Classics, 1955).

9. See, e.g., Joseph Fuchs, "Good Acts and Good Persons," *The Tablet*, November 6, 1993, 1444–45; James Keenan, S.J., *Goodness and Rightness in Thomas Aquinas's Summa Theologica* (Washington, D.C.: Georgetown University Press, 1992). This usage, and my own, are not uncontroversial, see below.

10. See, e.g., John Finnis, *Natural Law and Natural Rights* (New York: Oxford University Press, 1980); John Finnis, *Aquinas: Moral, Political, and Legal Theory* (New York: Oxford University Press, 1998).

11. John Finnis is an example. Ibid.

12. See generally Fuchs, "Good Acts"; Keenan, *Goodness and Rightness.*

13. See this chapter, 88.

14. Immanuel Kant, *Foundations of the Metaphysics of Morals*, trans. Lewis White Beck (Indianapolis: Bobbs-Merrill, 1959), 20–21.

15. This event may occur far earlier than the traditional "age of reason" conceived as the time at which the child can with proper use of reason discover the content of Second Good. Recognition of the duty to seek that good can arrive long before. See my "Luck, Obedience and the Vocation of Childhood," in *Vocation of the Child*, ed. Patrick McKinley Brennan (forthcoming W.B. Eerdmans 2008).

16. See generally, Frank Jackson, "Weakness of Will," *Mind*, n.s., 93, no. 369 (1984).

17. See generally, Coons and Brennan, *By Nature Equal*. Alasdair MacIntyre puts it that "omniscience excludes the making of decisions." MacIntyre, *After Virtue: A*

Study in Moral Virtue, second ed. (Notre Dame, Ind.: Notre Dame University Press, 1984), 96.

18. W. F. R. Hardie, *Aristotle's Ethical Theory*, second ed. (Oxford: Clarendon Press, 1968), 258–93.

19. Milton adds from God's testimony, "he had of me all he could have." John Milton, *Paradise Lost*, Part III, in *The Portable Milton* (New York: Viking Press, 1949), 291.

20. See Etienne Gilson, *The Spirit of Medieval Philosophy*: Gifford Lectures 1931–1932, trans. A. H. C. Downes (New York: Charles Scribner's Sons, 1940).

21. See Coons and Brennan, *By Nature Equal*, 207–9.

22. Aquinas was not among those who took this proposition to heart. Ibid., 168.

23. Ibid., 85–88, 142–43.

24. The term "persona," as I use it, denotes every capacity of the person to engage in moral activity—except the capacity that is the self. The self is the unique and the invulnerable capacity to commit for or against the quest for truth and right conduct; the persona is its instrument. It consists of one's reason, health, wealth, reputation, habits, and relationships—of all one's being at a specific time that is contingent but potentially available to the self in the pursuit of its vocation. I defend the usage in "A Grammar of the Self," *First Things* 129 (2003): 37.

25. My conviction here is confirmed by James Keenan, who successfully narrows the distance between Aquinas and the anonymous Christian. However, Keenan candidly acknowledges the remaining gap. See generally Keenan, *Goodness and Rightness*.

26. Pope John Paul II, Encyclical *Veritatis Splendor* (1993).

27. See Coons and Brennan, *By Nature Equal*, 209–10.

28. Even the admirable James Keenan, S.J., seems on occasion to slip into this form of ambiguity:

> Goodness is the measure of persons, their habits of conduct, and their acts as proceeding from one who strives openly out of love to realize right living. . . . If the source is oneself motivated by goodness, the agent *and act* are good (emphasis mine). (Keenan, *Goodness and Rightness*, 174–75.)

Keenan puts the question rhetorically to representatives of this "contemporary" view with the following imagined reply: "They would respond unanimously: 'Yes, a wrong action can be called good when a person acts out of love but errs.'" James Keenan, "Can a Wrong Action Be Good? The Development of Theological Opinion on Erroneous Conscience," *Eglise et Theologie*, 24 (1993), 205, 206, 217, 218.

His real meaning seems plainer in many other passages such as this: "When we do something wrong, we should call our actions wrong; but when we act out in love . . . we are good." Ibid., 218. The cure is to distinguish the person from the act, as Keenan generally does.

29. A reader asks: "How is the integrity of Second Good maintained if its achievement is not necessary?" The short answer: Self-perfection depends on doing one's best toward Second Good; no one can do better. But the question is good. For a long answer see Coons and Brennan *By Nature Equal*, 66–90.

30. See Elaine Pagels, *The Gnostic Gospels* (New York: Vintage, 1981).

31. I have defended this usage at length elsewhere, because I am sensible that the label "gnostic," understood in its historic sense, might offend; I hope it is clear that I use it as a convenient generic for those theories that would disadvantage intellectual bunglers in their access to self-perfection. Coons, "A Grammar of the Self," 37.

32. Coons and Brennan, *By Nature Equal*, 14, 88–89, 235–36.

33. Simon, A *General Theory of Authority*, 47–50.

34. In the *Oxford English Dictionary* Sir Henry Maine is allowed to characterize John Austin's theory as "mentally uniting all forms of government in a group by conceiving them as stripped of every attribute except coercive force." *Oxford English Dictionary*, second ed., s.v. "Austinian."

35. See my "Law and the Sovereigns of Childhood," *The Kappan* 58, no. 1 (1976).

36. An excellent contemporary assessment of the commitment to predestination fairly expresses the gnostics' varying rationalia. Leszek Kolakowski, *God Owes Us Nothing: A Brief Remark on Pascal's Religion and on the Spirit of Jansenism* (Chicago: University of Chicago Press, 1995).

37. Finnis, *Aquinas*, 41.

38. See generally, Coons and Brennan, *By Nature Equal*.

39. Glenn Tinder, *The Fabric of Hope: An Essay* (Atlanta: Scholars Press, 1999), 38.

40. "Evangelicals and Catholics Together: The Gift of Salvation," *First Things* 79 (1998).

6

A Rock on Which One Can Build: Friendship, Solidarity, and the Notion of Authority

Thomas C. Kohler

INTRODUCTION

Like many Americans, I suspect, I have some strongly ambivalent reactions to the term "authority." On the one hand, I connect it with qualities like order, reason, truth, competence, or mastery of a field. For example, when I am ill or dealing with an issue I know little about, I want to consult with an authority—an expert who truly understands the nature of the problem that confronts me and knows how to approach its resolution. Likewise, as a lawyer, I have an acute awareness of the crucial importance of a good social order and a properly constituted structure of civil authority to our well-being. Sadly, experience repeatedly has demonstrated how their lack can place every aspect of human life at risk. History celebrates the great lawgivers with good reason. No society reaches an advanced state without having developed a sound system of legal authority.

Nevertheless, the word authority also calls some strongly negative associations to mind. I find that I tend to link the term with penalties and sanctions. In this sense, authority evokes vague feelings of being pressured or coerced, and calls up images of faceless bureaucrats who will respond with unpleasant steps should I fail to comply with a rule or standard promulgated by someone other than myself. Somehow, threat seems to lurk in the shadows that the word casts. From this perspective, authority stands as a challenge, if not an affront, to my insistent self-sovereignty. Such heteronomy offends my personal autonomy. Authority stands over and against me, and it only becomes domesticated through my consent—often only grudgingly offered—to its legitimacy. Like wary homeowners who acquire large and rather aggressive dogs to protect their property, as Americans we recognize the need for but never quite fully trust authority and those who claim to speak in its name. My nearly reflexive reactions to the term reveal that, like you perhaps, I have "issues" with authority and the threats it appears to pose to my dignity and my freedom to choose.

In my case, at least, I am afraid that some of my reactions go back to my law school days, where the term typically came tricked-out in some sort of Hobbesian, Rousseauian, or Weberian dress. It doesn't take much to grasp John Austin's command theory of authority, but it hardly seems very satisfying. Force, whether express or implied, does not constitute a stable basis for cooperation and the progressive development that is its fruit. By our very nature as reasonable beings, we spontaneously demand reasons for what we do. Doing something merely "because I say to" is not a sufficient justification, as any parent can tell you, even for a child. Something critically important has gone missing in an account of authority that links it primarily with force.

As I have thought about the topic, I have become intrigued by the relationship between friendship and authority and their tie to the notion of solidarity, which the catechism defines as "friendship" or "social charity." My thesis is that authority only properly can be understood through the lens of friendship, and that, in its fullest sense, solidarity constitutes a key aspect of authority. In a substantial sense, authentic authority represents the fruit of friendship, the achievement of real solidarity. The former cannot exist in the absence of the latter.

This claim may sound a bit jarring to contemporary ears. The integral relationship between authority and friendship actually represents an ancient insight, but one that, for the most part, somehow has gone missing in a time when authority implies force, agreement forged through subtle manipulation, or a reflection of consent based on private calculations of individual advantage. My starting place in these reflections will not be from the abstract world of theory, but from an assessment of my own concrete experiences and judgments. I invite readers to evaluate my comments in similar fashion, through reviewing them in light of their own experiences as mediated through their conscious operations of experiencing, judging, and valuing.

This discussion will unfold in four parts. In the first part, I will discuss the notion of friendship. In the second, I will turn to discuss the idea of authority and distinguish the colloquial meanings of the term and of the word "authorities." In the third section, I will outline the contours of the "rock" upon which one can begin to construct an authentic idea of authority. I will conclude with a brief summary of the notions of friendship and authority.

THE NOTION OF FRIENDSHIP

When I think about friendship and its significance, I naturally turn first to those I consider my friends and question why I regard them so. I find that those with whom I am closest are those from whom I have learned most, even if I do not necessarily consider myself their equal. Because I am drawn by their qualities of character and their way of being, I turn to them to test my as-yet-tentative judgments and to discuss life's issues, both the passing and the profound.

As these comments indicate, I am drawing a distinction from the outset between friends and acquaintances.[1] I have many acquaintances and good relations with a large number of people. Nevertheless, I find that I have very few friends. By friends, I mean the people with whom I am at one. These comprise that handful of people who know me as well, and at times, even better than I know myself. They somehow complete me. Our friendship exists around shared values and the sorts of questions and issues that we commonly regard as those most worth pursuing. The views of my friends matter to me, and I strongly tend to regard them and their judgments as normative or authoritative. This group constitutes the secret jury against whom I measure my actions and before whom I practice my inner deliberations when they are not present. I depend on them and their example in making my judgments. Their censure of me would be a stronger penalty than anything a legal system could impose.

Friendship of any sort involves some reciprocal exchange of belief and trust. In fact, a precondition to learning nearly anything is that we first, to some degree, trust the person who proposes to teach us. As the Germans put it, "Ich schenke ihm Glauben": "I give him credence, I grant him belief," in the sense of giving someone a gift. Friendship of any sort involves the granting of trust, an openness to the judgments of fact and meanings through which the friend has constituted himself. The more significant the friendship, the deeper the meanings that the friends share, and the more extensive and unquestioning the trust that the friends extend to one another. Friends assume no roles with one another behind which to conceal their true thoughts and feelings. In large part, friendship is a conversational activity.

Friendship sets the stage for willing cooperation. It moves us when nothing else would, and it opens us to ideas, propositions, arguments, and possibilities to which we otherwise might be closed. Friendship gives us the most powerful motive to act and to make self-sacrifices, even to the extent of laying down one's life for one's friends. No wonder that the ancients insisted that a specifically civic form of friendship was the *sine qua non* for any form of political society.

Before going any further, I should note that I am aware of the terrifically amorphous quality of notions like friendship and love. "We live with love," Jean-Luc Marion writes,

> as if we knew what it was about. But as soon as we try to define it, or at least approach it with concepts, it draws away from us. We conclude from this that love ought not and cannot be conceived accurately, that it withdraws from all intelligibility, and that every effort to thematize it belongs to sophistry or an unseemly abstraction.[2]

This attitude, he warns, leads us to conclude that "we can give love only an interpretation, or rather a noninterpretation, that is purely subjective, indeed sentimental."[3] As a result, "arbitrary individual choice becomes the sole law of love, which remains sunk in an intolerable but inevitable anarchy: we love arbitrarily, or rather, we believe that this arbitrariness still deserves the name love."[4]

Marion's description not only artfully captures the way people typically think about love and friendship, but also explains why it can be so difficult for us to take these topics with much seriousness. I think this might be especially true for those of us raised in an atmosphere dominated by the presuppositions of analytic philosophy. Preoccupied with our senses, we have a strong tendency to pass over the data of our consciousness, which causes us to overlook or misapprehend the very activities through which we know and that distinctly characterize us as humans.

Love can be surprising and it is undoubtedly powerful, as any well-adjusted adult can attest. Marion describes it as giving "the sole flavor and meaning to our life," while Aristotle sees it not only as the basis for political life, but proper self-love as the precondition for engaging in acts expressing practical and theoretical wisdom. Despite its power and the undeniable fact that we easily can be led to love the wrong things, love is not a completely random or wholly subjective emotion that exceeds our rational control. It is mysterious, but that does not mean that it is beyond any grasp of intelligibility.

In his haunting poem, "Dreams in Dialogue," the great Spanish poet, Antonio Machado, asserts that "[o]ne does not love by choice," but that is only partially correct.[5] Granted, in the first instance we are the "patient," the one acted upon. Someone or something, some perceived good, moves us. "Love leaps in through delighted eyes," as the old formula has it.[6] Love calls to us, some apparent good draws us, but we must choose whether and how to respond. We always remain free to decline the invitation, to turn away. It is left to us to judge whether we love rightly and whether what we might love is truly valuable. While everything is not completely up to us, we nevertheless do bear proportionate responsibility for what we love.

To suggest that love is integral to our conscious activities of reason may seem rather odd. After all, we tend to regard reason and emotion as standing in opposition to one another, or as characteristics that exist in separate spheres. Such views misapprehend the character of consciousness,[7] the range of human consciousness,[8] and the relation between our feelings and our knowings. As humans, we are not logic boards coldly operating away in the messy and often inconvenient clay containers in which we mysteriously have become lodged. Heidegger memorably characterized humans as mooded beings, and, in this instance, not without good reason.

Our feelings give us our bearings in the world. They relate and bind us to other people, spark our concern about wrongs that should be righted, and push us to work for better things that might be realized someday after we are gone. These feelings accompany our reasoning and give our activities of knowing, judging, and valuing their thrust and direction. Without feelings, these activities would be empty and directionless. We do not laboriously inquire into what we are indifferent to, but instead into what we are passionate about. Likewise, I not infrequently know perfectly well what I really ought to do. Unless spurred on by my conscience, however, or by a love that pulls me past my own self-centered inertia, I might stay planted in my chair, leaving what I know I should do undone, complaining all the while to myself that "I just don't feel like doing it," and cooking up rationalizations to justify my inaction. The trick in life is learning to judge our feelings properly by responding honestly to the questions about value that they constantly pose to us.

Feelings play an essential role in both our cognitive as well as our moral performance. The desire to know, the hunger for authentic meaning in life, is the most basic and characteristically human of all our drives. It is the silent vector that undergirds and conditions the rest of our longings. Because partial achievement leaves that desire unsatisfied, and troubles us with niggling questions about shortfalls in our performance, the craving for meaning serves as the generator of continually fresh questions. At the same time, it provides the standard for determining whether and to what degree our aspirations for responsible and meaningful living are being attained. We can try to drown those questions out, or mask the feelings that an unsettled conscience inflicts, but only at the cost of living a life that does not stand up to scrutiny and a psyche busy warring with itself.

As we will discuss a bit more in the third section, our questions come in two forms. Questions of fact invite us to understand what and how something is. Questions of value pose queries about such matters as how we ought to live and the sorts of arrangements we should bring into being. Answering either sort of question involves us in an act of self-transcendence. In answering questions of fact, we are invited to go past a world of our private imaginings and presuppositions to an understanding of what actually is. This is an act of what we can call cognitive self-transcendence. Responding to questions of value summons us past norms informed by self-regarding biases and guarded by rationalizations to arrangements that satisfy the test of disinterested intelligibility.

Feelings that respond to the good represent an opening to a more profound transformation than those involved in responding to what might possibly be true. For example, feelings of love for another can move me from good intention to good act. That movement is one from cognitional self-transcendence—knowing what the good is in a concrete situation—to moral self-transcendence, where in actually doing the good, in concretely bringing it about, we become different and better persons.

I will say more about the reasonability of love as I proceed. For the moment, however, we should not be surprised or misled by the seemingly amorphous quality of love and friendship. Friendship requires self-transcendence. Being a friend moves us beyond the narrow confines of our own limited state of being. In its more complete expressions, friendship involves both a passive response to the goodness immanent in another's way of being as well as the active effort on our part to comprehend it and achieve that goodness in ourselves. This is a dynamic process and we are changed as we proceed through it.

To link love and feeling with reason requires us to take at least some account of our knowing. At least since the time of Descartes, there has been a tremendous tendency to attempt to explain nearly everything in reductionist terms. For more than three hundred years, the approach recommended by the Cartesian universal method has been used to understand and explain nearly all phenomena, with stunning success. Take the whole, break it into its smallest constituent parts, study the differences among them, and then rebuild the whole. In this process, the fundamental laws that control nature will reveal themselves. As Francis Bacon put it, we "torture nature" to force it to divulge its secrets to us.

Given its previous accomplishments, it is little wonder that many people expect that a reductionist approach can be used to explain human life and behavior. Love and friendship, sexual orientation and tendencies toward altruism, shyness and a propensity to believe in a deity, some suggest, are all embedded in and controlled by our genetic makeup, the acids that compose our genes, etc. Reduce us to our smallest elements and we can discover what controls the way we tick.

As a result of work done by the Human Genome Project, however, how much our DNA alone can explain about the complexity of our bodies and our behaviors has come into question. We have too few genes, it appears, to justify the intricacy and variety of what we are. Likewise, there are too few genetic differences to account for all the observed differences among the species. Something more is going on. Things cannot be explained from the bottom up.

Some in the life sciences and other fields have proposed that in a fashion not wholly understood, "organizational" or "emergent" principles come into play at higher levels of complexity to produce properties not observed in the lower constituent elements. At the protein or cellular level, for example, properties emerge that cannot be extrapolated from the underlying chemical or molecular structures. Things happen at these levels that the atoms or chemicals that compose these structures cannot themselves do. At each level of complexity, a qualitative differentiation takes place and a new degree of freedom appears. The new whole is not only greater, but also different than the sum of its parts. As some describe it, nature operates through schemes of "broken symmetry."[9]

Because new properties appear at each level of complexity, attempts to reduce explanation to the mechanical operation of simple fundamental laws will not succeed. At each level, new relations among the observed data exist that require new insights and the formulation of new laws to explain. This results in a hierarchy of autonomous sciences. The basic entities of the higher science observe the laws of the lower. But the higher sublates the lower, enabling the lower to realize a latent potential it could not achieve on its own. The lower entities operate according to their own laws, but they participate in higher order and its laws.[10] For example, the laws of chemistry are not violated in the generation of hemoglobin by mammals. At the same time, the higher activity is not simply an application of the lower. "Psychology is not applied biology," Phillip Anderson observes, "nor is biology applied chemistry."[11]

Development is not a two-way street that allows one to understand the higher simply by reversing direction and taking account only of the lower operations. At each higher level, properties appear whose emergence was not completely predictable. Their manifestation occurs not by necessity, but according to a schedule of probabilities. As contingent events, they come into being when the conditions are right, and survive as long as those conditions are fulfilled. Even small events can shift the probabilities of the emergence of new systems or the decline of established ones. As humans, we are part of and subject to this emergent order, which is not completely under our control. Because of the degree of freedom that we embody, however, we play a role in determining what happens next and bear some share of the responsibility for it.

The physicist, Robert Laughlin, illustrates some of the points we have been discussing through an analogy to Impressionist art. "A field of flowers rendered by Renoir or Monet," he explains, "strikes us as interesting because it is a perfect whole, while the daubs of paint from which it is constructed are randomly shaped and imperfect. The imperfection of the individual brush strokes tells us that the essence of the painting is its organization."[12]

Grasping the intelligible relations in the patterns of organization constitutes the essence of human understanding. It describes precisely what we are doing when we are knowing. This fact has vast implications. It defines how we appropriate our knowledge of reality and what we mean by that extremely elusive and dangerous term—real. As I will outline in the third section, the invariant pattern by which we engage in this activity also provides us with a normative method through which the further development of understanding occurs. Likewise, it cuts the ground from under determinist and reductionist accounts. "Ironically," Laughlin observes,

> the very success of reductionism has helped pave the way for its eclipse. Over time, careful quantitative study of microscopic parts has revealed that at the primitive level at least, collective principles of organization are not just a quaint side show but everything—the true source of physical law, including perhaps the most fundamental laws we know. . . . [N]ature is now revealed to be an enormous tower of truths, each descending from its parent, and then transcending that parent, as the scale of measurement increases.[13]

"The reason our minds can anticipate and master what the physical world does," Laughlin continues, "is not because we are geniuses but because nature facilitates understanding by organizing itself and generating law."[14]

This last point bears some emphasis. The intelligible patterns that we grasp in our acts of understanding constitute the structure immanent in reality. They are intrinsic to it. Consequently, our acts of knowing and what we know are the same. An isomorphism exists between them. Real is not some body or object "out there" somewhere beyond us that we seek to understand by squinting at it intently, or by assiduously jabbing and poking at its constituent parts. Real is what we grasp when we make correct judgments about a set of patterned relations through which a thing or concrete situation is constituted and that make it to be the way that it is. We participate in reality, and achieve identity with it, to the degree that we make accurate judgments about it.

Now, as this suggests, any act of understanding tends to be unstable. Such acts always point past themselves. After some effort, we might get our heads around one set of patterned relations. As we do, however, questions immediately will arise about the character of the subsequent set of terms and relations that govern them. We never catch a break. Reality teases us forward. Like the boy or the girl that your mother warned you about, it inveigles us to go just a little further, to take that next step. We can always ignore its entreaties and hang up on its calls. But even if we do, reality will just keep pestering us. A convinced and persistent suitor, it just won't go away.

Our liberty to choose whether and how to respond to these promptings tells us something further about human character. A degree of freedom pertains to each level of existence. Plants, for example, systematically organize and employ chemical compounds to bring about regular processes that the underlying elements could not achieve on their own. Plants function under the governance of a set of intelligible relations that reveal themselves in the plant's growth and development. Sentient beings exploit plants, thereby subjecting them to sets of higher schemes that permit conscious operation and response. Unlike other animals, however, humans have to choose how they will live their lives. We do not operate under the control of instinct alone. Bernard Lonergan points out that animals respond to substantially new conditions by slowly developing a new species. In humans, however, "there occurs the transition from the intelligible to the intelligent."[15]

This shift means that we participate in the world in a way unique from the other animals. For us, discoveries in science and mathematics, novel ways of symbolizing understandings through art and music, and new economic and legal arrangements that institute and regularize new ways of living in the world all come about through new manners of attending to data. We must identify, deliberate, and choose among the possibilities as we go about making the world in which we live. Consequently, unlike the other animals, at the most fundamental level we live under the control of our questioning.

This is the point where love makes its entry. As we have seen, questioning draws us out of ourselves. Questions are the invitations that reality ceaselessly issues to know it and in so doing, to become one with it. Questions, however, occur to us. We do not generate them ourselves. Try as we might, we cannot make ourselves have a good idea. Instead, by paying attention, by being alert to the data or to an issue, we make it more likely that a question will crop up and, through our wrestling with it, lead us to a new insight, to a fuller understanding. Consequently, our feelings lead our knowings. What we love determines the sorts of things to which we will be attentive. It is the motive that (for better or worse) kicks our potencies into action.

Love represents our response to a perceived good, to something that we identify as worthwhile. Love specifies those for whom we will sacrifice and the goals toward which we will work. It reflects itself in our habits and identifies the persons on whom we will lavish our attention and the issues that will occupy our concerns. Love directs our doings, but even more importantly, it gives us the impetus to act. What we love ultimately determines the sorts of questions to which we will be open and what we will do in response to any knowledge that we gain. The desire to know characterizes human beings. To the extent that we love in a disinterested and unrestricted fashion, the more we act in concert with our most fundamental drives. Disordered loving, on the other hand, frustrates our spontaneous orientations. It leads to missed opportunities and nonsensical results. On the personal level, it can lead to ever more frenzied but blunted efforts to satisfy our most fundamental drives.

Knowing and loving stand in an integral relationship. Like knowing, the act of loving and that which we love are the same. An identity, an isomorphism, exists between them. This is what Aristotle means, I think, when he states that a friend is another yourself, or Christ's teaching that in marriage, "the two shall become as one." There is an identity between the friends, between the loving and the loved, which occurs through the common value judgments that they make. The meanings that friends share, which form them to be who they are and through which they live, are the same. The greater the commonality in the meanings shared, the more complete the community, the identity, that the friends enjoy, and accordingly, the deeper, the more significant, their friendship is. Their solidarity exists in and through the self-transcendence embodied in their decisions and determined by their valuing.

As this suggests, we are constituted through what we know, but far more significantly, by what we love. "Love and do as you will," St. Augustine breezily tells us. It sounds easy enough, but as we have seen, doing it authentically puts us in the struggle of—and for—our lives.[16] To the degree we learn to value correctly, to the extent that our feelings respond to and actively move us toward what is authentically valuable, we enjoy identity with the good. We participate in and, to the degree we do so, become one with it. Thus, as the quote from St. Augustine continues, "Let the root of love be within. From such a root nothing but good can come."[17]

Consequently, there is potential for development, or what I might call ascent, in all this. As we all know, love can transform us. Friends who are themselves good induce me—give me the motive—to become a better, more complete, person myself. While good friends move each other to become better, and more fully human, we never fully realize or completely understand the good, despite the fact that we have concrete, lived experiences of it. This problem with attempting to define love or friendship takes us back to Plato's problems with definitions and the sorts of difficulties he and his conversation partners encountered in *The Lysis* in trying to nail down what love and friendship are.

Definitions are abstract. The good, however, is always concrete, but its aspects—the instances of its appearance to us—truly are innumerable. As a result, there is a mysterious aspect to the good and to friendship. By mysterious, I do not mean that the good ultimately is unintelligible or somehow occult. Instead, to the degree we are open to it, we constantly are being drawn more deeply into it. For example, I long ago now fell in love with my wife, but I am still coming to know her and the good she embodies. She continues to move and humble me through who she is and the meanings that she incarnates, and I continue in my halting way to try to live up to them. I have been changed in that process. To the degree that others have aided each of us in realizing our authentic humanity, we all have had similar experiences. *Cor ad cor loquitur.*

AUTHORITY

Friends may speak to one another's heart. But authority seems to speak in an entirely different voice. Friendship represents a response to a motive good. The thing that impels us to respond to authority appears to lie in a certain sort of irresistibility. Authority compels our acceptance of it. It leaves us no reasonable alternative but to recognize and to cooperate with it.

"Authority," Bernard Lonergan tells us, "is legitimate power."[18] This sounds surprisingly Weberian, but Lonergan goes on to perform something of a transvaluation of values with the term and its meanings. "The source of power," he points out, "is cooperation" and cooperation takes place in two ways.[19]

Cooperation exists across time, and, as Lonergan observes, "Power today results from all the achievements of the past that have been accumulated, developed, integrated. Any present is powerful in the measure that past achievement lives on in it."[20] Those previous attainments serve as the foundation for future developments. Through our communities, we live simultaneously in the present and the past, availing ourselves of the capital bequeathed us through the efforts of our ancestors, and, if we act reasonably and responsibly, adding to the stock from which future generations will draw. Authentic authority accumulates power over time.

Cooperation also occurs in the present. As the notion of positive subsidiarity suggests, groups can achieve things the individual simply cannot do and larger associations can be effective where the smaller may fail. Cooperation in the present through associations of various types amplifies the effective ability to get things done. These associations sublate the insights and potential that individuals embody and the efforts they expend to enable them to achieve through the organization what would not have been possible for its members to realize on their own. Concrete pluralities cooperatively working together can produce new understandings and novel solutions to the problem of living that could not be predicted and could not be achieved by any given person on his or her own. This explains why cities so frequently have been the locus of discoveries in the arts as well as the natural and human sciences. Our naturally social nature reveals itself in the fact that most of our operating takes the form of cooperating with others.

"As the source of power is cooperation," Lonergan observes, "so the carrier of power is the community."[21] Authorities are the officers to whom the community delegates authority to exercise power in the community's name. Authority itself rests in the community.

Therein lies the rub. As humans, we only live in communities and these communities give us our orientations and our identities. We do not live in a world of mere biological immediacy, or one that is intrinsically conditioned by space and time. Instead, we encounter life largely through the understandings that others have bequeathed to us. Cultural, philosophical, and religious traditions, literature, art and architecture, the natural and human sciences, and most especially language mediate the ways in which we apprehend our existence and its meanings. These meanings constitute us and shape our affectivities. They thereby condition us to what and to whom we will be open. We can leave our communities, but in a real sense, they never leave us. Their imprint remains a perpetual part of who we are. The meanings of the communities in which we live soak into our pores in ways that makes the awareness and critical judgment of them difficult.

A community represents the achievement of shared judgments, meanings, sentiments, and values. The solidarity that a community embodies vanishes at the point that meanings lose their commonality and values are no longer shared. Beyond that point, as we say, people really live in different worlds, whose meanings and values remain largely opaque to outsiders.

The shared sentiments and feelings that help to ground community respond to values, which can be ranked in an ascending order.[22] Vital values stand on the first rung. These include the goods most basic to sustaining life, such as health, physical safety and well-being, bodily vitality, and mental acuity. The value we place on these goods disposes us to work to secure ourselves from the consequences that flow from their lack. Social values stand at the next level. These include the concrete social, economic, legal, and political institutional orders through which the demands for the vital values regularly and consistently can be met. Because the intelligent and responsible arrangement of these ordering schemes set the conditions for supplying the vital values to all the members of a community, social values constitute a higher order good than the vital values. The breakdown of the social order directly threatens individual well-being.

Cultural values constitute the third level of human goods. Cultural values mediate the meanings that explain and justify the social order of the community to its members. These values supply the shared motives and sentiments that support social cohesion and ongoing cooperation. Cultural values recount the community's story, and help us to locate our place within it and within the greater world. When the cultural order shifts or disintegrates, the social order and schemes that it regularizes lose their meaning and coherence. A new and stable social order only emerges after the community accepts a new set of cultural meanings. The culture plays a normative role. In a flourishing society, the culture identifies what is authentically worthwhile and provides a framework for critiquing what is not. To the degree that it fulfills its tasks, the culture sustains and promotes development of individuals and the society alike.

Community exists for the individual. It grounds and conditions the possibilities for the achievement of one's true individuality. Consequently, personal values lie at the fourth level of the human good. When rightly oriented, they find their full expression in the individual's ability to engage in the most distinctly human of activities: experiencing, understanding, judging, and valuing in a reasonable and responsible way. In other words, personal values reflect themselves in the ability to love in an ordered fashion, value properly, and engage in acts of intellectual and moral self-transcendence in a sure-handed and regular way. Those who embody authentic personal values are autonomous. They act as the originators of values in themselves and in their communities.

At the highest level stand terminal values, to which personal values are closely linked. These represent the values that orient all of our other undertakings and the meanings for the sake of which we do everything else. They are the values that give us the impetus for all of our other acts. They represent what we most love. The authentic apprehension of value at any level represents the proportionate achievement of solidarity with the good that becomes increasingly unrestricted as one progresses to ever-higher levels of value. Solidarity grounded in the terminal values involves an ever-greater participation in and identity with an unlimited good. This is community at its most significant and unrestricted level.

As the reader will have noticed, each higher level of valuing sublates the operations and goods on the lower. At each level, a new degree of human freedom appears and the probabilities for individual and group development are enhanced. At the same time, to the extent that the community coheres around values that stand the test of authentic intelligibility, to the extent that they reflect an understanding and agreement around what is truly valuable, the community rests on the sort of identity that grounds friendship. At the same time, because such values form the basis for ongoing cooperation and development, they have the power, the irresistibility, that the mind seeking genuine meaning demands.

Authentic community is not a permanent achievement. Life is always in flux and we steadily are confronted with new situations that require us to deliberate and choose in light of what is truly valuable. Personal inauthenticities and biases, both individual and social, constantly threaten to throw our judgment off. Shared meanings set the conditions for willing cooperation on which authority rests. But we will not buy just any story. We demand that our actions and our values make sense and that they actually be meaningful. Over the long run, we will not cooperate with anything less. Nevertheless, it is very easy to go wrong. Our shortcomings and biases easily mislead us. Just as community can represent the achievement of authentic good, so we can have a deformed sort of solidarity in misery and suffering. Can we, and if so, how do we go about distinguishing the truly valuable from the only apparently good? How do we identify truly flourishing communities from those caught up in a cycle of decline?

TRANSCENDENTAL METHOD

The task is not an easy one. Nevertheless, we are not without hope. The human mind constitutes itself through a basic pattern of operations that are employed in every cognitional enterprise, in every effort to resolve issues of fact, in every circumstance in which we make judgments of value. These operations occur consciously and it is through them that we are conscious. Importantly, this pattern does not merely assign the structure through which we know. It is intrinsic to what is to be known through it. In recognition of these facts, Lonergan refers to this pattern of operations as a "transcendental method"; he goes on to define a method as "a normative pattern of recurrent and related operations yielding cumulative and progressive results"[23] (italicized in original).

Let me mention a few points before I proceed. Firstly, what I briefly will describe is not a set of rules, but instead a normative set of operations from which one may derive rules. Secondly, the operations of our consciousness are self-assembling. They progressively unfold one to the other and are transitive—that is to say, that they have objects. Finally, as our consciousness unfolds from level to level, we realize our humanity more fully and completely.

Intelligent questioning about why something is, how it came to be, what it means, what we ought to do, and why that course is desirable constitutes the heart of a method. It requires being truly attentive to data, trends, potential problems, and the work and observations of others. Such a state of attentiveness is not easily achieved or maintained. Not only does it require enormous energy, but our biases also perpetually threaten to sabotage the process by deflecting our attention from raising questions about long-held suppositions, cherished but ultimately untenable beliefs, or, most stubborn of all, norms of behavior based on self-regard. By ruling certain questions out of court because we simply do not want to deal with them, we can halt the process before it begins. Frustration, incomplete or false explanations, uneasy consciences, and badly ordered societies are the fruit of failing to attend to relevant data and appropriate if unsettling questions.

From questioning follows the effort to understand, to develop explanations or proposed courses of action that jibe with all the relevant facts and can take into account all the data. This stage of method entails the exercise of true intelligence and creativity, the entertainment of new possibilities and efforts at assembling information in novel ways. It also marks another point for collaboration, for taking into account what those working in other fields might know, and for raising questions to them about what the data may suggest.

In this second stage of method, one formulates hypotheses, attempts explanations, or plots out what ought to be done. We attempt to describe what we think we know and ask ourselves whether our account squares with all the relevant data. We try out our proposals on others to see whether they can poke holes in what we have managed to formulate. This is a stage of searching, probing, and testing. When we have a response for all the questions others have posed to us, and an answer to all the misgivings we have about our own proposal, when we have tortured ourselves and others but no further relevant questions emerge, we reach the stage of judging. Is this explanation right? Do I have it? Could it truly be so? Can I really justify why the proposed course of action is better than the other things I might do?

Making judgments unavoidably entails making commitments. In judging, we take a stand. We make claims about how something really is or works or what in human affairs objectively ought to be. We thereby bind ourselves to a certain understanding of the world. Judgments, in other words, deal with meanings. As we have seen, judgments take two forms: judgments of fact and judgments of value. In the first, we seek to settle the question "Is it so?" In the second, we attempt to answer the more profound questions "Is it desirable? Should something be?" Answering either sort of question involves an act of self-transcendence. Our answers make claims about how something actually is, or a state of affairs that should be, apart from my private imaginings, wishes, or arbitrary assertions, and that others may themselves verify. The question of fact, however, involves only cognitive transcendence. The question of value deals not just with knowings, but also with actions and doings, and involves moral self-transcendence. In deciding questions of value, we are determining the meanings in which we live and shaping the communities in which we act. Our authenticity depends on the degree of our self-transcendence, i.e., the degree to which our answers are not the product of self-regarding whim and rationalizations, but something others objectively can validate.

This little outline of our conscious operations is rather compact. Nevertheless, it represents the rock on which one can build not only a sketch of the meaning of authority, but a framework for understanding the meaning of meaning itself. It affords the foundation for working out a new, comprehensive, and integrative philosophy that permits us, among other things, to unite the human and natural sciences, to develop an ethics based on something more than mere consensus.

Some other points about this scheme deserve mention. The first is that it is irreversible, since revisions to it would involve us in conscious operations that follow the scheme. Objections to the scheme amount to objections to the revisions. The second is that the scheme avoids the subject-object split that has haunted so much of philosophy since the time of Descartes. It also avoids the problems of perceptualism and the concern about the "privileging of the present" that rightly has been the subject of postmodernist critics. Lastly, it avoids conceptualism and the notion that there are concepts that exist prior to understanding and reason.

One might object that understanding as Lonergan presents it puts a tremendous amount of weight on very weak reeds. That is true enough, but it is a function of our free will. As St. Paul puts it, "we must work out our salvation in fear and trembling."[24]

FRIENDSHIP AND AUTHORITY IN SUMMARY

The good news in all of this is that we have help. We do not engage in these intentional operations totally on our own. Everything is not completely up to us. It may offend our modern sensibilities, bottomed as they are on notions of individual sovereignty, but as humans, we are far less an actor than a being who constantly is acted upon. For example, we are not fully responsible for our feelings. In a real sense, they inflict themselves on us. Nevertheless, we are responsible for the way we react to them. We must evaluate and choose amongst our feelings, decide how to react to them, and determine which ones truly are pleasurable, and hence constitute the feelings that will give us the motives for acting. In this process, we are making value choices. Value then is a transcendental notion, and as such, it regulates the meanings in which we live.

The transcendent quality of value also represents the entry point for grace, the invitation to go beyond ourselves and to love what is truly valuable, to participate in what is truly good, to enjoy a limited identity with the source of all goodness. We are drawn to seek that which is truly valuable, and admittedly, it is terrifically easy to make mistakes about it. My mistakes, or those made through time by any group, society, or culture, do not extinguish it, even though these errors may make its realization far less probable. Meanings that are not truly valuable eventually collapse from the weight of their own unintelligibility.

In summary then, authentic authority requires authentic friendship, embodied in shared judgments about what is objectively and verifiably valuable. Authority is meaningful. Authority that is not may have temporary force, but that force will be unstable because it lacks the motive power that sustains the willing cooperation on which authority ultimately rests.

NOTES

1. Aristotle distinguished among three kinds of friendship: relations based on advantage, on pleasure, and on excellence. Only the last truly deserves the name. The other states reflect certain characteristics of authentic friendship, but they are not species of a common genus. Relations based on something other than excellence gain the name friendship only by analogy. Nevertheless, they hold the potential to ripen into authentic friendship. Rightly ordered self-love is the foundation for true friendship, and as we will see, for the appropriation of one's full humanity. Gadamer points out that this way of understanding friendship retained its validity until the eighteenth century. Hans-Georg Gadamer, "Friendship and Self-Knowledge: Reflections on the Role of Friendship in Greek Ethics," in *Hermeneutics, Religion, and Ethics*, trans. Joel Weinsheimer (New Haven, Conn.: Yale University Press, 1999).

2. Jean-Luc Marion, "The Intentionality of Love," in *Prolegomena to Charity*, trans. Stephen E. Lewis (New York: Fordham University Press, 2002), 71.

3. Ibid.

4. Ibid.

5. Antonio Machado, "Dreams in Dialogue" ("Los sueños dialogados") (Poem XLV), in *Antonio Machado: Selected Poems*, trans. Alan S. Trueblood (Cambridge, Mass.: Harvard University Press, 1982), 209.

6. Sometimes the word eros is substituted for love in that statement, but it does not change the point. Gadamer notes that a Doric harmony exists between eros and logos, an insight this paper should help to support.

7. Consciousness is a famously slippery term. By consciousness, I do not mean any form of perception, i.e., a subject's explicit attentiveness to someone or something. Instead, I mean the range of human awareness. Part of its structure, perception is a conscious operation, but not its entirety.

Merely perceiving something, giving it my explicit attention, does not make me conscious. I can be aware of something without attending to it. Directing my attention to something makes me conscious in a different way. For example, it is one thing to be in a funk, but it is another to realize it and to examine the sources of the feelings of uncertainty and depression. There is a prior conscious reality that is pure experience—a state of "feelings as felt"—that is very much part of who we are, but that is a mode of consciousness that exists prior to our appropriation of any degree of self-knowledge. Thus, "[b]eing oneself is prior to knowing oneself.

St. Ignatius said that love shows itself more in deeds than in words; but being in love is neither deeds nor words; it is the prior conscious reality that words, and more securely, deeds reveal." Bernard Lonergan, "Existenz and Aggiornamento," in *Collection: Papers by Bernard Lonergan*, eds. Frederick E. Crowe and Robert M. Doran (Toronto: University of Toronto Press, 1988), 229.

We do not know ourselves immediately, but as mediated through the process of inquiring into our felt experiences, seeking to understand and evaluate the feelings evoked by those experiences, and then judging our understandings of those feelings and their meanings. Self-knowledge involves a certain "heightening" of our consciousness. Nevertheless, consciousness is prior to and different than the process through which our self-knowledge is appropriated. As a result, "[c]onsciousness . . . as an internal self-presence or awareness has to itself not only a dimension of explicit, foreground awareness, but a tacit or background dimension—namely, the most radical presence of ourselves to ourselves—that can never be made explicit exhaustively." Fred Lawrence, "The Fragility of Consciousness: Lonergan and the Postmodern Concern for the Other," 54 *Theological Studies* 55 (1993), 59. Thus, our consciousness is not an object that we contemplate through some form of inner perception, as Descartes imagined; not an inward perception of feeling, as Rousseau and the Romantics taught; nor, as Kant suggested, something that cannot be objectively known, but only postulated, because we can have no direct sense perception of it.

8. If consciousness is the range of awareness, of what can we be aware? The answer is, of anything that we can question. Our ability to question shows that the range of human consciousness is unrestricted. We can and do raise questions about everything. The unrestricted desire for meaning that drives our questioning reveals an awareness that constantly pushes beyond what we already know to an unknown that is to be known. Questioning represents a normative human activity, one that is dyed into our bones. We are born questioners and cannot help but ask what things are, why things are and what they mean, what should be, what we should do, or why one course of action is better than another. We know our consciousness through the very acts by which we inquire into, devise understandings about, and then judge whether the relationships we have proposed square with what we can verify in the experiences themselves. We exist in and through these operations.

Accordingly, "questioning not only is about being but is itself being, being in its *Gelichtetheit* [luminosity], being in its openness to being, being that is realizing itself through inquiry to knowing that, through knowing, it may come to loving." Lonergan, "Metaphysics as Horizon" in *Collection*, 192. Our intentionally conscious activities of experiencing, understanding, judging, and deciding decenter us. We transcend ourselves through our engagement in them. By being attentive to experience, "we attend to the other; by understanding we gradually construct our world; by judgment we discern its independence from ourselves; by deliberate and responsible freedom we move beyond the merely self-regarding norms and make ourselves moral beings." The questions that draw us, the desire to know that constitutes our most basic drive, the disinterestedness of authentic morality "is fully compatible with the passionateness of being. For that passionateness has a dimension of its own: it underpins and accompanies and reaches beyond the subject as experientially, intelligently, rationally, morally conscious." Bernard Lonergan, "Mission and the Spirit," in *A Third Collection: Papers by Bernard J. F. Lonergan, S.J.*, ed. Frederick E. Crowe, S.J. (New York: Paulist Press, 1985), 29.

Our consciousness is sheerly given. There is nothing "behind" it and nothing outside of it. The "crucial upshot of a correct analysis of consciousness as experience leads us to the realization that there is nothing in our consciousnesses that has not been, in a precise sense, given to us, including consciousness itself." Lawrence, "Fragility of Consciousness," 72.

9. P. W. Anderson, "More Is Different: Broken Symmetry and the Nature of the Hierarchical Structure of Science," *Science* 177 (1972), 393.

10. "Nor does the introduction of the higher autonomous science interfere with the autonomy of the lower," Bernard Lonergan explains, "for the higher enters into the field of the lower only in so far as it makes systematic on the lower level what otherwise would be merely coincidental." Bernard J. F. Lonergan, *Insight: A Study of Human Understanding* (San Francisco: Harper & Row, 1978), 256.

11. Anderson, "More Is Different," 393. As Bernard Lonergan notes, "The laws of physics hold for subatomic elements; the laws of physics and chemistry hold for chemical elements and compounds; the laws of physics, chemistry, and biology hold for plants; the laws of physics, chemistry, biology, and sensitive psychology hold for animals; the laws of physics, chemistry, biology, sensitive psychology, and rational psychology hold for men. As one moves from one genus to the next, there is added a new set of laws which defines its own basic terms by its own empirically established correlations." Lonergan, *Insight*, 255.

12. Robert B. Laughlin, *A Different Universe: Reinventing Physics from the Bottom Down* (New York: Basic Books, 2005), 7.

13. Ibid., 208.

14. Ibid., 209.

15. Lonergan, *Insight*, 267.

16. Cf. Jeremiah, 45: 4–5: "But your life I will leave you; as a prize of war"—life is the prize of this struggle. The point of living is to engage in it, to wage the campaign.

17. Augustine, *Sermon on 1 John*, 7, 8.

18. Lonergan, "Dialectic of Authority," in *A Third Collection*, 5.

19. Ibid.

20. Ibid.

21. Ibid.

22. For a fuller account, see Bernard J. F. Lonergan, *Method in Theology*, second ed. (Toronto: University of Toronto Press, 2003), 27–36; also see Thomas C. Kohler, "The Integrity of Unrestricted Desire: Community, Values, and the Problem of Personhood," in *Autonomy and Order: A Communitarian Anthology*, ed. Edward W. Lehman (Lanham, Md.: Rowman & Littlefield, 2000), 61–67.

23. Lonergan, *Method*, 5.

24. Philippians 2:12.

7

Society, Subsidiarity, and Authority in Catholic Social Thought

Russell Hittinger

SOCIETAL PERSONS

Margaret Thatcher famously said that "there is no such thing as society," there are only "individual men and women, and there are families."[1] Lady Thatcher was surely right that groups like families and polities, clubs, teams, and colleges do not possess the unity of an individual substance. The two creation myths of Genesis, for example, clearly distinguish between the one-flesh unity of Adam and Eve (Gen 2:21–25) from the sequence of natural kinds. In this, scripture seems to confirm common sense and untutored observation of the facts on the ground. Marriage does not have a nature in the same sense as a plant, a bird, a mammal, or even a human being. When two or more people are constituted in a society, a second or third natural kind is not produced.

In answer to the question "What kind of a thing is society?" the right answer seems to be that society is a "person." We can recall Aquinas's definition of a person as that which is "distinct by reason of dignity"[2]:

> For as famous men were represented in comedies and tragedies, the name "person" was given to signify those who held high dignity. . . . And because subsistence in a rational nature is of high dignity, therefore every individual of the rational nature is called a "person." Now the dignity of the divine nature excels every other dignity; and thus the name "person" pre-eminently belongs to God.[3]

Thomas refers to the Latin word *persona*, a mask used by actors to impersonate a well-known character—someone distinct in dignity. Ancient theologians and philosophers transferred the idea of impersonation to a rational, individual substance—to the very thing personated, to persons both human and divine.

In the older tradition common to jurists, philosophers, and theologians there were at least three kinds of persons. First, there are natural persons. Here, the word "natural" can be used to denote whatever or whoever possesses a unity of rational substance: human persons, angelic persons, or divine persons sharing the unity of a single substance. In each case, what is distinct in dignity has the unity of an individual. Second, there are what the law calls *fictional persons*. As Thomas Hobbes noted, "[t]here are few things that are incapable of being represented by fiction."[4] Inanimate things like bridges, hospitals, and houses can receive endowments, and thus bear interests and rights at law. Like Caligula's horse, made a senator by imperial decree, such entities are distinct in dignity not on account of their own nature, virtue, or power, but rather by a *fictio legis*, the construction of law. Third, there are what should be called *real* persons, which have neither the unity of a substance, nor a unity merely imposed on things insofar as they can be imputed or made to stand for things really having dignity.

Such persons—real but not substantial—are called societies. A society possesses what Thomas called a unity of order:

> It must be known that the whole which the political group or the family constitutes has only a unity of order [*habet solam ordinis unitatem*], for it is not something absolutely one [*aliquid simpliciter unum*]. A part of this whole, therefore, can have an operation that is not the operation of the whole, as a soldier in an army has activity that does not belong to the whole army. However, this whole does have an operation that is not proper to its parts but to the whole.[5]

Things enjoying a unity of order each possess what is individually proper to themselves—certain operations and acts not reducible to the commonality, but which flow, rather, from a natural or spontaneous unity of their nature—in a human person, sensing, thinking, judging, willing, and so forth.[6] These natural properties are not dissolved or canceled by membership in a group. At the same time, a society enjoys a real unity transcending mere aggregation of the members. Wherever there are plural rational agents, aiming at common ends, through united action, and where the unity is one of the intrinsic goods aimed at, we have a society—something distinct in dignity. To be sure, it is real—the crew team, the college, the city, the marriage. But it is neither a substance nor a mere imputation. A society will hold itself out to the rest of the world as something distinct in dignity, possessing certain rights and responsibilities.

In his seminal essay on "Moral Personality and Legal Personality," the British legal historian F. W. Maitland writes:

> When a body of twenty, or two thousand, or two hundred thousand men bind themselves together to act in a particular way for some common purpose, they create a body, which by no fiction of law, but by the very nature of things, differs from the individuals of whom it is constituted.[7] . . . If the law allows men to form permanently organized groups, those groups will be for common opinion right-and-duty bearing units; and if the law-giver will not openly treat them as such, he will misrepresent, or, as the French say, he will "denature" the facts . . . For the morality of common sense the group is person, is right-and-duty bearing unit.[8]

For Maitland, when individuals, with a note of permanence, engage in united action for a common purpose, there comes into existence a unity that transcends the aggregation of its parts. That is to say, there comes into existence a group-person (a society) that requires the rest of us to recognize not only the individuals, but, as Maitland puts it, "$n + 1$ persons."[9] Between the poles of natural persons and fictional persons, there is yet another kind of person: a society, which is the bearer of rights and duties just because of the kind of thing that it is. It would "denature" the facts, as Maitland says, to pretend otherwise.[10]

Hence, in the *Digest* the jurist Modestinus defines marriage as "the union of a man and a woman, a consortium for the whole of life involving the communication of divine and human rights."[11] It is the society itself, the *union*, that is the bearer of the rights communicated. This is what John Paul II meant by the "subjectivity of society"—something more than simple inter-subjectivity; rather, an inter-subjectivity that constitutes a "subject" in its own right.

> [T]he social nature of man is not completely fulfilled in the State, but is realized in various intermediary groups, beginning with the family and including economic, social, political and cultural groups which stem from human nature itself and have their own autonomy. . . . This is what I have called the "subjectivity" of society which, together with the subjectivity of the individual, was canceled out by "Real Socialism."[12]

In addition to individual persons, there is society; neither can be reduced, one to the other. If individual persons are reduced to the group, what follows is substantialism: the group has the unity of substance rather than a unity of order. If, on the other hand, the group is reduced to the individuals, the group ceases to be a subject; it only enjoys a unity of composition or aggregation. Dignities are attributed to it, but only as a kind of fiction. For example, we can speak of the retailers of Chicago, and go on to attribute to these retailers a certain legal status (rights, privileges, and responsibilities) without supposing that any two of them know one another, much less that there exists a society of retailers.

Societies therefore are distinguished from mere partnerships. Admittedly, this distinction is easier to draw abstractly than it is from social facts. For one thing, partnerships can become societies, and societies can evolve into mere partnerships. For another, both societies and partnerships can be brought into existence through the instrument of a contract. To make the distinction more difficult, apropos of Lady Thatcher's remark, we often speak of societies as partnerships even when we mean something more than that. In a commercial society, our rough-and-ready discourse about polities, churches, and marriages is tinged with the language of contracts and partnership.

Yves Simon writes: "In a mere partnership each action is traceable to some partner, e.g., all the work is traceable to the handicraftsman and all the financing to the money-lender, [but] none is traceable to the partnership itself." The fact that several persons know the same object and wish to bring it about is enough to explain the kind of inter-subjectivity characteristic of a partnership. A society, on the other hand, "implies, in addition to immanent acts relative to the same object, my knowing that the others know and desire the same object and want it to be effected by the action of our community." "Mere partnership" Simon observes, ". . . does not do anything to put an end to the solitude of the partners."[13] One who leases a car from Daimler-Chrysler, for example, does not intend to bring a society into being. No corporate personality is aimed at. The reciprocity has no aspect of permanence; it has no united action; indeed, it requires no society whatsoever—except incidentally, perhaps, in the breach of contract, in which case the partners repair to the courts of the political society. In the contract of partners, we can predicate certain reciprocities; but there is no society that is the proper bearer of those predicates. For the same reason, we may doubt that a temporary consortium of individuals to produce a child constitutes a group-person—a unity distinct in dignity.

In the case of a real group-person, common action is an intrinsic aspect of the common end or purpose. Think, for example, of a family, a faculty, a crew team, or an orchestra. In each case, the reason for action includes the good of common action. Achievement of a mutually agreeable result is not enough. To be sure, an orchestra aims to produce the music, just as a crew team aims to win the race; for their part, spouses aim to raise children and to send them into a wider world of societies. Yet for each of these groups, their respective corporate unity is one of *reasons for action*—unity is one of the goods being aimed at.[14] In the case of a society, unity is an intransitive good—ordinarily, it survives the failure of the crew team to win the race, a marriage to produce children, or a polity to negotiate a treaty with another state. By the same token, partnerships usually do not survive failure of the partners to secure the mutually agreeable ends for which the arrangement was constructed.

Moreover, partnerships ordinarily do not require the existence or internal allocation of authority. Authority is accidental. Its absence is noted only when the partnership breaks down, when the agreements fail to achieve the mutually anticipated results. A society, however, aims at the good of united action. Whatever other failures it may incur by way of external, transitive ends, a society will not survive a chronic failure of united action. Societies need authority—at the very least for the purpose of coordinating actions among a number of individuals who enjoy what Thomas called a "unity of order," or what Maitland meant by an "n +1" unity.

MODELS OF CIVIL SOCIETY

The diverse set of nongovernmental associations called "civil society" includes economic corporations, private trusts, schools and faculties, charitable organizations and foundations (both religious and secular), the press, clubs, churches, sodalities, and labor unions. In a free society, these groups will possess juridical personality—not as individual substances or as Caligula's horse—but nonetheless as real persons according to the criteria we sketched in the previous section.

Among Western nations today, we find a broad consensus that the flourishing of these "right-and-duty" bearing societies marks an important difference between free and despotic societies—or, worse still, a totalitarian society in which the state is regarded not only as the preeminent group-person, but perhaps even a substantial person. Without a flourishing civil society, the external constitutional structures and devices of democracy—even the charters and covenants of human rights—cannot succeed in maintaining a free society. Experience teaches that whenever we attempt to promote or to implant democracy outside of the Western world, we discover that constitutions prove to be an empty shell of ordered liberty without what Ernest Gellner has called "the miracle of Civil Society."[15]

That there be a civil society distinct from the formal organs of the state, and that civil society be recognized as public law, are uncontroversial propositions. Yet, since the seventeenth century, we have inherited quite different understandings of the nature of civil society and the ontology of group-persons upon which it would seem to depend. These are quite different reasons for valuing civil society and group-persons. Maitland's position emphasizes the intrinsic value of group-persons, at least those that pursue morally good ends by honest means. Civil society is also valued for its efficiencies in providing goods and services, or for its utility in checking the power of the state. It is often difficult to cleanly distinguish one from the other in the course of political and policy debates. We shouldn't be surprised, for they have emerged within a common history of Western polities, in response to the post-Westphalian system of sovereign nation states.

When we think of modern man we think of the Enlightenment, the sovereignty of reason, and of ideologies of liberty; we think especially of his technologies. But his greatest and most sustained work was the state. Scholars debate exactly what makes a polity a modern "state," but some criteria will appear on every list: territorial homogeneity, monopolies over lethal force, education, police, taxation, and, of course, *sovereignty as indivisible, perpetual, and inalienable power*.[16] History testifies that the peoples of Europe and her former colonies were prepared to make almost any sacrifice to transform their polities into *states*.

Beginning in the seventeenth century, one of the most urgent questions was how to reconcile the state, with its monopoly over public authority and power, with the myriad of other groups claiming authority, rights, and liberties according to custom, natural law, and ecclesiastical law. How does state sovereignty (which recognizes the state as the preeminent, if not the exclusive group-person) comport with what Maitland called the "right-and-duty bearing" unities that we are calling civil society?

Thomas Hobbes (1588–1679) provided an early, and very clear, model for understanding the relationship between groups and the sovereign state. It has been called the "concession" theory.[17] In *Leviathan*, Hobbes contends that a "person, is he, whose words or actions are considered, either as his own, or as representing the words or actions of another man, or of any other thing to whom they are attributed, whether truly or by fiction."[18] In the natural as well as in the legal world, there are three kinds of "person": (a) natural, individual persons who speak and act for themselves; (b) artificial persons who represent the speech and actions of others; and (c) purely fictional persons, such as bridges, churches, or hospitals. Seeing clearly enough that the state could not count as a natural, individual person, Hobbes concluded that the state is an artificial person, which is to say that the state has a corporate nature by virtue of a multitude being represented. This representative is called the "sovereign."

This division of persons and personations brings us to the crucial issue. Into what category do we place nongovernmental entities of this sort? Can they be persons? Can there be more than one legitimate artificial person? The nature of civil society stands or falls on the answer to these questions. Hobbes writes: "For power unlimited is absolute sovereignty. And the sovereign, in every commonwealth, is the absolute representative of all the subjects; and therefore no other, can be representative of any part of them, but so far forth, as he shall give leave."[19] For Hobbes, once the sovereign comes into existence, there can be only one legitimate artificial or representing person.[20]

From such premises, Hobbes then draws a reasonable but troubling conclusion. Artificial persons other than the state are entitled to exist only insofar as the sovereign "shall give leave."[21] That is, they rightfully exist by the permission or *concession* of the sovereign.[22] Thus, "private bodies regular, but unlawful, are those that unite themselves into one person representative, without any public authority."[23] Hobbes does not deny that these corporate persons *can* exist on their own initiative and actions; at issue is whether they have a *right* to exist apart from the sovereign's concession. Interestingly, he did not regard spontaneous modes of market behavior as threatening to the state. Where there is a "mere concourse of people, without union to any particular design, by obligation of one to another, but proceeding only from a similitude of wills and inclinations"—in one way, a pure market—there is no artificial person, no representation, and therefore no group authority to compete with the state.[24] The private, therefore, does not mark the absence of public sociality of various kinds (covering everything from daily courtesies to markets, to the myriad of exchanges amenable to contracts and partnerships), but rather the absence of authority. The absence or suppression of authority is usually the clue that we are not considering a real society, or that the society is not recognized by the state.

Crucial to the concession model is the idea that groups are not merely regulated by the state's public law, but rather are given a reason to exist, or not to exist. The modern French state began precisely on this note. Consider article 3 of the French *Declaration of the Rights of Man and Citizen* (1789): "The source of all sovereignty resides essentially in the nation; no group, no individual may exercise authority not emanating expressly therefrom."[25] Two years later, the state passed a law against corporations:

> Since the abolition of all kinds of corporations of citizens of the same occupation and profession is one of the fundamental bases of the French Constitution, re-establishment thereof under any pretext or pretence or form whatsoever is forbidden (§1). Citizens of the same occupation or profession . . . may not, when they are together, name either president, secretaries, or trustees, keep accounts, pass decrees or resolutions, or draft regulations concerning their alleged common interests (§2).[26]

Other laws were enacted against religious orders, including teaching and hospital nuns.[27]

Now, we must ask why the sovereign should ever grant a concession. For our purposes today we might think of *devolution*, which often has a very strong resemblance to the older concession model. Imagine a homogeneous power formally belonging to the state. But the state decides to parcel out aspects of this power from the top-down, or from the center to the periphery. While the state does not deny its own plenitude of power or sovereignty, it does recognize the contingent fact that it cannot effectively or efficiently reach all of the objects within its formal power. Accordingly, the state will outsource power, by way of a quasi-delegation, to other groups for the purpose of efficiently creating and distributing certain goods and services: education, charitable relief of the poor, the orderly transfer of property, or investment; mercenaries or civilian contractors might become right-and-duty bearing entities insofar as they are instruments of state policy.

The concession model helps us to see a paradox of the modern state. On the one hand, the achievement of sovereignty requires the state to assert its monopoly over what Hobbes called "artificial" or representative personhood. Especially in the early phases of statemaking, and typically during revolutions, the sovereign will severely assert its monopoly to the detriment of civil society. When a state does not leave this phase, such as in Communist regimes, the state becomes totalitarian; that is, it refuses to grant concessions, and therefore all business is conducted within the organs of a single power. But the complexity and scale of modern states practically guarantee that the sovereign must make concessions. It must, in this sense, learn to "devolve."

The golden age of concession theory was the eighteenth and nineteenth centuries, because it was during this time that states were created according to the modern idea of sovereignty. Yet this model is quite durable, never entirely disappearing, even in our time. Take, for example, the debates in Europe and the United States over the issue of marriage. What kind of juridical person is a marriage? What are the state's interests and powers with regard to marriage? In 1992, the Hawaiian Supreme Court defined marriage as "a partnership to which both parties bring their financial resources as well as their individual energies and efforts."[28] On this view, marriage is but one example of juridical personality based on financial partnership. Presumably, the state gives recognition to the partnership because of its policy interests in the orderly possession and distribution of property.

This point was reiterated in the controversial 2003 decision of the Massachusetts Supreme Court, which prohibited the legislature from giving legal title of marriage only to one man and one woman.

> We begin by considering the nature of civil marriage itself. Simply put, the government creates civil marriage. *Civil marriage is created and regulated through exercise of the police power.* Civil marriage anchors an ordered society by encouraging stable relationships over transient ones. It is central to the way the Commonwealth identifies individuals, provides for the orderly distribution of property, ensures that children and adults are cared for and sup-

ported whenever possible from private rather than public funds, and tracks important epidemiological and demographic data.[29]

This contains several telling traits of concession theory. In the first place, we read that the state does not merely regulate marriage, but creates it through the exercise of the police power. What aspects of good order move the state to allow married people to be a right-and-duty bearing unity? The Court mentions economic reasons (property), sociological reasons (stable relationships), health reasons (care for the old or indigent), and scientific reasons (collection of epidemiological data). The state breathes into the dust of sexual relationships and private aspirations to intimacy, and creates a "person" at law. This person, then, becomes the site or occasion for bringing about more efficiently certain results that are in the interest of the state.[30] All that remained for the Massachusetts Court to do was to judge that one gender or two genders are immaterial to the state's interest in having other agents procure the publicly desirable results. The actual reason that most private persons have to cause a matrimonial society—the precisely heterosexual nature of the union—is irrelevant to its status as a group-person; and it is irrelevant, first and foremost, because the public reasons upon which the conferral or concession of status depends can be achieved in a way indifferent to the subjective valuing of particular modes of union. The Massachusetts decision is a pure example of concession theory. Interestingly, the Court leaves untouched the question whether this juridical person is a society or a partnership. The public efficiencies falling within the purview of the positive law could be attached to either a partnership or a society.

While the concession model is by no means dead, its star has been in eclipse during the second part of the twentieth century. At least in the West, the reason for the decline of the concession theory is not difficult to explain. After the trauma of two world wars, we have witnessed an erosion of confidence in the doctrine of state sovereignty. The Protestant theologian Karl Barth aptly called the postwar history (in the West) the era of "disillusioned sovereignty."[31] The concession theory depends upon a lively sense of sovereignty; it is precisely this idea of state power that triggers the need for concessions. Take away or weaken the claims of sovereignty and the concession theory has less to do, less to explain, and less to justify.

Especially after World War II, there has been interest in reviving another strand of liberalism on the issue of civil society—one that emerged in the eighteenth and nineteenth centuries in reaction to state absolutism. In France, we think of Montesquieu and Tocqueville—in England, and in the new American republic, James Madison. As Emile Durkheim observed: "[I]f that collective force, the State, is to be the liberator of the individual, it has itself need of some counterbalance; it must be restrained by other collective forces, that is, by . . . secondary groups . . . it is out of this conflict of social forces that individual liberties are born."[32]

We may call it the power-checking-power model, because it estimates the value of civil society chiefly in terms of a check upon untrammeled state power. Montesquieu wrote: "Political liberty is found only in moderate governments. . . . It is present only when power is not abused, but it has eternally been observed that any man who has power is led to abuse it; he continues until he finds limits. . . . So that one cannot abuse power, power must check power by the arrangement of things."[33] Hence, the famous idea of civil society as "intermediate powers." What interested Montesquieu was not the specifically social landscape of corporate persons (an ontology that perhaps he took for granted) so much as the distribution of "powers." Civil society is useful as an arrangement that checks abuse of power and thereby inclines a political society to moderation.[34]

Tocqueville revisited this subject in *Democracy in America*. What, he asked, can check the power of the state when it is driven by the spirit of democracy? In the old regime, the state was practically constrained, despite its claims to absolutism, by the aristocratic class and by the lower orders of society. They could exert their own interests over and against monarchical power. In a democracy, however, the state *is* the people. What can induce the people to limit themselves? Tocqueville surmised that the key is civil society.

> The morality and intelligence of a democratic people would risk no fewer dangers than its business and its industry if the government came to take the place of associations everywhere. Sentiments and ideas renew themselves, the heart is enlarged, and the human mind is developed only by the reciprocal action of men upon one another. I have shown that this action is almost nonexistent in a democratic country. It is therefore necessary to create it artificially there. And this is what associations alone can do. . . . The idea of secondary powers, placed between sovereign and subjects, naturally presented itself to the imagination of aristocratic peoples because those powers contained within them individuals or families whom birth, enlightenment, and wealth held up as without peer and who seemed destined to command.[35]

Tocqueville perhaps was more attentive to the specifically social aspects of civil society than was Montesquieu. Even so, Tocqueville estimates civil society principally in the light of powers. In a democratic age, what seems "natural" are the twin colossi of the individual and the state; the social estate of so-called secondary powers seems artificial. But artificial things can be useful.

This line of thought concedes to the state its monopoly over public things. Importantly, it differs from the concession model with regard to the end to be achieved. Whereas the concession model seeks to protect and maintain state sovereignty, the power-checking-power model endeavors to shrink its scope. Let the state be sovereign in the classically "modern" sense of the term; but let this sovereignty be diminished. One way to achieve this goal is to create a vast sphere of the *private*—a sphere of judgments, choices, and actions by individuals and associations.

As we saw, the concession model regards devolution as the outsourcing of state power. Subtly, but importantly, the power-checking-power model treats devolution as *privatization*. But it does have a public function. It checks untrammeled state power.[36] This view of civil society need not, and usually does not, depend on a strong ontology of the nature, character, and virtues of group-persons. The late Ernest Gellner has made this point very convincingly. He argues that civil society "checks" power in two ways. On the one hand, it liberates economic relationships from political ones by constituting a sphere of private interests and resources. On the other hand, civil society liberates economic relationships from social ones by constituting a sphere of liberty to create or revoke bonds of association.[37]

The beneficiary of this kind of civil society is what Gellner calls the "modular man." "The [Western conception of civil society] has not committed itself either to a set of prescribed roles and relations, or to a set of practices. . . . The associations of modular man can be effective without being rigid."[38] For Gellner, civil society is nothing other than a market in which individuals negotiate and choose not merely commercial transactions, but lifestyles.

Patterning civil society on the interests of the "modular man" will prove very attractive in the age of "disillusioned sovereignty." Over the past half century, we have seen that when the sovereignty of the state ceases to have the same purchase on the minds and loyalty of men, it does not necessarily imply a recovery of older social authorities; it does not automatically give credit to a deep ontology of corporate personality—one that makes clear the difference between what we have called a society and a partnership. Just the opposite. As Gellner explains, suspicion of the efficacy of state sovereignty tends to give credit to a malleable sphere of social entities and roles chosen by the individual. Fear of the fixed character of the state's nature as a corporate person is mirrored in fear of fixed boundaries of other corporate persons as well: churches, families, economic corporations, and indeed any kind of group that exercises authority over its members.[39]

To be sure, Gellner is prepared to admit that small, tightly knit groups, as well as the state, have the properties of a society. Both, for example, are meant to endure beyond the kind of temporal spans fixed by contract, and neither are purely voluntary. More importantly, families and polities include authority over their members. Civil society, on the other hand, is marked by the opposite traits of revocable bonds that can come into and out of existence without authority—except where authority is externally necessary to broker disputes.

> But the real situation is at the very least triangular . . . there are the segmentary communities, cousin-ridden and ritual-ridden, free perhaps of central tyranny, but not really free in the sense that would satisfy us; there is centralization which grinds into the dust all subsidiary social institutions or subcommunities, whether ritually stifling or not; and finally, there is the third alternative we seek to define and attain. It excludes both stifling communalism and centralized authoritarianism. It is *this* kind of Civil Society which concerns us.[40]

In sum, the power-checking-power model does not aim at a multiplicity of societies, which necessarily brings in turn a multiplication of authorities. Rather, it aims to check the power of state sovereignty by shrinking its scope. And this is to be accomplished by expanding the sphere of the private, and, as Gellner suggests, where the private is distinguished by indifference to the difference between partnership and society, and therefore to the role of authority in associations other than the state. The concession model worries about a diminution of state authority. For it, devolution represents a contingent outsourcing of authority governed by public estimation of "the scale of effects" of a proposed action.[41] As a social scientist has put it, subsidiarity "can increase the problem-solving capacity of policy-making" by respecting what can be called "output legitimacy."[42] Accordingly, we measure the legitimacy of policy objectives in terms of persons and powers best positioned to act efficiently. The value of civil society is contingent upon, or at least consistent with, purely "technocratic criteria of policy success."[43] The power-checking-power model will understand devolution similarly, as the demonopolizing of state power. It is compatible with the idea that, all other things being equal, it is better to decentralize power in view of its tendency to be abused, its lack of transparency from the top-down, or perhaps its "democratic deficit" in bringing ordinary people into the processes of decisionmaking (so-called input legitimacy). Other social scientists use terms like "social capital" or "untraded interdependencies" to describe the social networks not reducible to individuals or to the formal organs of the state.[44]

CATHOLIC SOCIAL THOUGHT

The question whether there exist social persons distinct in dignity, reducible neither to the individual nor the state, stands at the outset of

Catholic social doctrine. Earlier, I said that our models of civil society have developed chiefly in response to the post-Westphalian situation of sovereign states. In Europe and in her former colonies, the Catholic Church lost its political privilege in the new nation-states. Beginning in France during the Revolution, the Church, along with her religious orders, schools, seminaries, and sodalities were stripped of juridical personality—except such as remained by concession of the states. In France, the hard version of the concession model was expressed in the *Civil Constitution of the Clergy*, drafted in 1790. The Church effectively became a department of the civil government. A softer version was enacted more than a century later, in the formal law of separation in 1905, when church properties were transferred to the so-called *associations cultuelles*, overseen by laity and regulated by state law.

Catholic social doctrine, accordingly, emerged in defense of two propositions: first, that the state does not enjoy a monopoly over group-personhood; second, that societies other than the state not only possess real dignity as right-and-duty bearing unities, but that they enjoy modes of authority proper to their own society. Like the liberal, power-checking-power position, Catholic thought wished to limit untrammeled state power. Eventually, the Catholic view came to include liberal insights regarding the external devices of limiting sovereignty, particularly in the fashion of constitutional divisions of power as well as other artificial constraints necessary for the rule of law. From the beginning, however, the Catholic view was interested in social pluralism and the multiplication of authorities. In this way, it differed markedly from the liberal program of expanding the sphere of privacy, at least as we have discussed this notion in connection with Gellner. The private/public distinction, for Catholicism, is not measured by the presence or absence of authority, for in both spheres there exist real societies, and therefore authority.

In his famous encyclical *Rerum novarum* (1891), Pope Leo XIII defended the right of workers to form associations. The following passage reaches the nerve of the issue:

> Private societies, then, although they exist within the body politic, and are severally part of the commonwealth, cannot nevertheless be absolutely, and as such, prohibited by public authority. For, to enter into a "society" of this kind is the natural right of man; and the State has for its office to protect natural rights, not to destroy them; and, if it forbid its citizens to form associations, it contradicts the very principle of its own existence, for both they and it exist in virtue of the like principle, namely, the natural tendency of man to dwell in society. There are occasions, doubtless, when it is fitting that the law should intervene to prevent certain associations, as when men join together for purposes which are evidently bad, unlawful, or dangerous to the State. In such cases, public authority may justly forbid the formation of such associations, and may

> dissolve them if they already exist. But every precaution should be taken not to violate the rights of individuals and not to impose unreasonable regulations under pretense of public benefit. . . . The State should watch over these societies of citizens banded together in accordance with their rights, but it should not thrust itself into their peculiar concerns and their organization, for things move and live by the spirit inspiring them, and may be killed by the rough grasp of a hand from without.[45]

According to Leo, such societies spring from the same source as the state, the "tendency of man to dwell in society."[46] When the state recognizes the social principle animating a group, it recognizes a principle of its own existence. Society does not devolve from the state or come into existence because of the state's need to outsource powers for socially useful ends.

In *Rerum novarum*, Leo introduces another issue. He writes: "In order that an association may be carried on with unity of purpose and harmony of action, its administration and government should be firm and wise. All such societies, being free to exist, have the further right to adopt such rules and organization as may best conduce to the attainment of their respective objects."[47] Wherever a society is marked by common ends and unity (or harmony) of action, there must be authority. Leo XIII's point is that the state will do an injustice if it allows societies to exist, but denies their capacity for self-government. Where there is no right to group authority, common action will depend entirely on spontaneous unanimity. This is hardly possible in a family, much less in an economic corporation, a university faculty, a church, or even a sports team. Hence, a state that recognizes the existence of civil society, but not the diverse modes of authority appropriate to those societies, reduces civil society to mere partnerships.

To understand the relationship between society and authority, we can consider Yves Simon's useful distinction between *substitutional* and *essential* functions of authority. Regarding the use of authority to substitute for the judgment and decision of another, Simon observes:

> Just as an individual may need to be directed in the pursuit of his individual good, so a community may be unable to attain its own common good without guidance. Thus, if certain duties relative to the welfare of a city [municipality] and normally discharged by it are taken over by the state on account of the city's inability to discharge them satisfactorily, the authority so exercised by the state is of the paternal type: it is not concerned (at least directly) with the common good of the state but with the *proper* good of the city; it is *substitutional,* since it does things that the governed should be able to do for themselves; and it aims at its own disappearance or becomes abusive.[48]

Thus, in the exercise of paternal authority, the parent is in charge of immature persons, not only in regard to their ordering to the common good of the familial society, but, more significantly, in regard to the child's own good. In this sense, the authority is substitutional, or we might say, remedial. By analogy, the state might have good reason to substitute itself for the authority ordinarily residing in a smaller group (civic or private) for the purpose of remediating a defect. It does so not immediately for the good of the polity, but for the good of the society needing such assistance. As Simon concludes, this specific function of authority aims to make itself obsolete. The difference between authority and authoritarianism consists precisely in this aim. Authoritarianism may well order a person or persons to their own good, either individually or communally, but at the cost of removing or permanently deferring the good of ordering themselves.

Simon contends that the essential function of authority does not imply efficiency in bringing about a certain range of ends; rather, it implies the existence of a society attempting to bring about certain ends through united action. "Even in the smallest and most closely united community," he points out, "unity of action cannot be taken for granted; it has to be caused, and, if it is to be steady, it has to be assured by a steady cause."[49] Further, "unity of action depends on unity of judgment, and unity of judgment can be procured either by way of unanimity or by way of authority; no third possibility is conceivable."[50]

> A society enjoying a supremely high degree of enlightenment would, all other things being equal, enjoy much more choice than ignorant societies and have to choose among many more possibilities. It would not need authority to choose between two courses of action one of which is bound to lead to disaster, since, by hypothesis, knowledge would rule out illusory means. But it would need authority, *more than ever*, to procure united action, for, thanks to better lights, the plurality of genuine means would have increased considerably. The function of authority with which we are concerned, i.e., that of procuring united action when the means to the common good are several, does not disappear but grows, as deficiencies are made up; it originates not in the defects of men and societies but in the nature of society. It is an essential function.[51]

Even in a society beset with no natural or moral imperfections, authority is necessary to solve issues of coordination.[52] If, indeed, there is a real society (transcending partnership), authority has an essential function not reducible to remediation of deficiencies. Simon insists that the absence of material or moral deficiencies make the function more rather than less important.[53] As Thomas says in *De regno*:

> To be sure, the light of reason is placed by nature in every man, to guide him in his acts towards his end. Wherefore, if man were intended to live alone, as many animals do, he would require no other guide to his end. Each man

> would be a king unto himself, under God, the highest King, inasmuch as he would direct himself in his acts by the light of reason given him from on high. Yet it is natural for man, more than for any other animal, to be a social and political animal, to live in a group. . . . [I.8] If, then, it is natural for man to live in the society of many, it is necessary that there exist among men some means by which the group may be governed.[54]

Simon allows that unanimity can be a cause of united action. A society will ordinarily depend *at some level* on unanimity—on united action, mutually attuned in such a manner that no deliverance of authority (commands, laws, or ad hoc managerial decrees) is immediately needed. For Simon, this is the principle of autonomy. "Wherever a task can be satisfactorily achieved by the initiative of the individual or that of small social units, the fulfillment of that task must be left to the initiative of the individual or to that of small social units. From the association of the principle of autonomy with the principle of authority results an order which is hierarchical. In such an order, the autonomy of the inferior social unit supplements and balances the authority of the higher social unit."[55] It seems that Thomas had something like this in mind when he distinguishes between regnal and civic prudence. "Rulers imposing a law," he writes, "are in civic matters as architects regarding things to be built," whereas civic prudence is concerned "with individual operable things." As legislative prudence "gives the precept," so also "civic prudence puts it in effect and conserves the norms stated in the law."[56]

This effectuating and conserving of a norm (precept, law), which Thomas here calls civic prudence, is in one sense the lowest level of any social order. We can imagine an individual who has appropriated the command of his superior, and who is able to attune that norm to contingent, operable matters. There is no need of a further command except that which flows from the individual judgment. Thus, even in a hierarchical system of command, we will reach a level at which a command can no longer substitute for individual judgment. A husband and wife, for example, participate in the norms pertaining to marriage—natural, canonical, and civil. Where there is a legitimate diversity of means to achieve the ends of matrimony, the spouses act in concert without immediate need of further commands (either from on high, or from one to the other). Small groups are capable of this kind of unanimity—perhaps we can call it interpersonal prudence. The unanimity is not accomplished in the absence of law or authority; it is not antinomian, but rather supranomian. In any social order, this represents the lowest level at which common action is accomplished without the immediate intervention of extrinsic authority. Think of two or more craftsmen installing a window just by virtue of mutual attunement of judgment and action to the operable matter at hand.

They have no need to call upon the architect or the foreman in order to put into effect and conserve the norms. The essential function of authority does not erase spontaneous unanimity of action. Were authority to attempt to reduce unanimity to authority, society would not be directed but paralyzed. Simon's point is that whenever a society must achieve united action, and where unanimity cannot be presupposed, authority is necessary.

On that score, we can distinguish devolution from the older notion of subsidiarity.[57] The term was coined by the nineteenth-century Italian Jesuit Luigi Taparelli. For Taparelli and the tradition of Catholic social doctrine, subsidiarity is not a freestanding concept. As a principle regulating and coordinating a plurality of group-persons, subsidiarity presupposes a plurality of such persons, each having distinct common ends, kinds of united action, and modes of authority. It is not, therefore, a question of whether there shall be group-persons, or whether they are efficient or immediately useful to the state. Rather, the question is how these groups stand to one another and to the state. In its negative formulation, subsidiarity demands that when assistance (*subsidium*) is given, it be done in such a way that the sociality proper to the group (family, school, corporation, etc.) is not subverted. Taparelli used the term *ipotattico*, taken from the Greek *hypotaxis*—the rules governing the order of clauses within a sentence. Rendered in Latin as *sub sedeo*, subsidiarity evokes the concept of auxiliary troops in the Roman legion that "sat below," ready and duty-bound to render service. Hence, it describes the right (*dritto ipotattico*) of social groups, each enjoying its own proper mode of action. While sometimes identified with the word *subsidium* (help, assistance), the point of subsidiarity is a normative structure of plural social forms, not necessarily a trickling down of power or aid.[58] Taparelli used the expression *associazione impotattica* to emphasize the interdependence of societies, each maintaining its own unity (*conservare la propria unità*) without prejudice to the whole.[59]

Subsidiarity, however, cannot be construed as judgments, decisions, or actions at the "lowest level." The notion of a "lowest" level perverts the concept of subsidiarity. The better term is *proper* level. The term "proper" is taken from the Latin word *proprium*, denoting what belongs to, or what is possessed by, a thing or person. From *proprium* we derive the word "property." On the modern view of the state, there are only two persons having *propria*: the artificial person of the state, and natural, individual persons. The "lowest" level can only mean the individual, or, perhaps, partnerships that are but aggregations of individuals. Subsidiarity, on the other hand, presupposes that there are plural authorities and agents having their "proper" (not necessarily lowest) duties and rights with regard to the common good—immediately, the common good of the particular society, but mediately the common good of the body politic. Pius XII noted that "every social activity is for its nature subsidiarity; it must serve as a support to the members of the social body and never destroy or absorb them."[60] To be sure, subsidiarity is often described and deployed in a defensive sense—as to what the state may *not* do or try to accomplish—but the principle is not so much a theory about state institutions or of checks and balances, as it is an account of the pluralism and sociality of society. Once we distinguish subsidiarity from the similar but misleading notions of devolution, it is easier to grasp why it was introduced as an aspect of social justice. For Pius XI, social justice is that kind of order that ensues when each person is capacitated to "exercise his social *munus*," to contribute to the common good according to his proper office and role.[61] This may or may not require the giving of aid, the correction of a deficiency, or the removal of a barrier to the performance of social duties, but what it always entails is respect for a pluriform social order.

In his encyclical *Centesimus annus* (1991), Pope John Paul II weaves together the different strands of these ideas:

> [The] primary responsibility in [social justice] belongs not to the State but to individuals and to the various groups and associations which make up society. . . . In addition to the tasks of harmonizing and guiding development, in exceptional circumstances the State can also exercise a *substitute function*. . . . Such supplementary interventions, which are justified by urgent reasons touching the common good, must be as brief as possible, so as to avoid removing permanently from society and business systems functions which are properly theirs [*propria munera*]. . . . Here again the principle of subsidiarity must be respected: a community of a higher order should not interfere in the internal life of a community of a lower order, depriving the latter of its functions [*propriis officiis*].[62]

This passage helps to illuminate how authority and subsidiarity, in Catholic thought, stem from the same principle. Both presuppose the existence of a society—as Maitland said, an "n +1" unity, where the unity is an intransitive good. Recall our earlier point that a society ordinarily survives defeat or failure of one or more of its purposes; it does not, however, survive the dissolution of united action. Since united action cannot depend entirely on unanimity, authority has an essential function within a society. The principle of subsidiarity also presupposes the existence of societies. It cannot be expressed adequately as the imperative that decisions be made at the *lowest possible level*. The lowest level is either a cost-benefit calculation, which can be considered while prescinding from the society altogether, or it simply designates a spontaneous unanimity of action—neither of which notions reach functions *proper to* a given society.

Subsidiarity is nothing other than the principle that, when aid is given, it not remove or destroy the authority or functions (*munera*) proper to the society being assisted. As Pope John Paul noted, in "exceptional circumstances" the state may exercise a "substitute function," but not in such a manner as to deprive the society of its proper modes of union.[63] Like Simon's rubric of substitutional authority, such interventions must aim to make themselves obsolete. If we were treating a mere partnership, or a market-like order of aggregation, we might think otherwise; that is to say, we would apply the requisite power or authority so long as it instrumentally produces the right results. Subsidiarity, on the other hand, requires that the sociality of society be preserved. No argument to good results external to the society will suffice, unless, indeed, one has moral reason to dissolve a society, regime, or party.

Some Catholic commentators have pointed out that subsidiarity need not imply deficiency. Calvez and Perrin, for example, contend that "the exercise of a subsidiary function consists primarily and above all in interventions made by society in its own right, interventions which are necessary even when there is no failure by individuals to perform their functions."[64] They go on to say that "subsidiarity looks only one way. The state brings aid (*subsidium*) to other societies, but they do not bring aid to the state—at least not in the same sense."[65] This position is unobjectionable so long as we are speaking of the unique role of the state in coordinating the united action of plural societies. In this case, the authority and obligations of the coordinating power do not imply deficiency in the other societies. So conceived, the *subsidium* is authority, considered according to what Simon called its essential function. But this "aid" must be sharply distinguished from the idea of the state imparting, outsourcing, or conceding the social forms and functions of other groups. In *Mater et Magistra*, John XXIII refers to the state's work as "directing, stimulating, co-ordinating, supplying and integrating" a plurality of societies.[66] "Of its very nature," he concludes, "the true aim of all social activity should be to help members of the social body, but never to destroy or absorb them."[67] These groups must "be really autonomous [*suis legibus re ipsa regantur*], and loyally collaborate in pursuit of their own specific interests and those of the common good. For these groups must themselves necessarily present the form and substance of a true community."[68]

CONCLUSION

I mentioned at the outset that, in modern times, these three models (concession, power-checking-power, and subsidiarity) emerged together. All three share a conviction that there is something deficient in the system of state sovereignty. The concession theory holds that formal sovereignty is contingently, but nonetheless, chronically incompetent to reach effectively all the things pertaining to the public good or interest. The state, therefore, must learn to outsource, devolve, and concede the status of other social dynamisms and powers.

The power-checking-power theory holds that state sovereignty itself is dangerous. But constitutional division of powers is not enough. The state also needs to be checked by intermediate powers. Sovereignty is not denied, but restricted by the expansion of the private sphere. A proponent of this model can agree that devolution is efficient, but with the value-added reason that it is also useful in checking power.

The Catholic theory sets out neither to make state sovereignty more effective or less effective. Rather, it defends the intrinsic dignity of group-persons in their own right. The sin of the modern state is the injustice of its claiming a monopoly over group-personhood—reserving what is "distinct in dignity" for itself and for individual persons. The Catholic position holds that the political sovereign is limited by the very existence of real group-persons. A normal society, then, is not so much an expansion of the private as a multiplication of authorities embedded in group-persons. On this view, subsidiarity is not devolution—rather, it is a principle governing the harmony and coordination of group-persons.

NOTES

1. *Women's Own Magazine*, October 31, 1987.
2. St. Thomas Aquinas, *Summa Theologica*, trans. Fathers of the English Dominican Province, I, 29.3 ad2
3. Ibid.
4. Thomas Hobbes, *Leviathan*, XVI.81.
5. Thomas Aquinas, *Ethicorum Aristotelis Ad Nicomachum*, ed. Raymond M. Spiazzi, O.P. (Genova, Italy: Marietti, 1964), I.5.
6. Not every thing having unitas ordinis is a society deserving the predicate "person." The world, Thomas says, "is called one by the unity of order, whereby some things are ordered to others." *Summa Theologica*, I, 47.3.
7. F. W. Maitland, "Moral Personality and Legal Personality," in *State, Trust and Corporation*, ed. David Runciman and Magnus Ryan (Cambridge: Cambridge University Press, 2003), 63 (quoting Albert Venn Dicey, 17 *Harvard Law Review* 511, 513 (1904)).
8. Ibid., 68.
9. Ibid., 69.
10. On the *genosenschaftliche* character of polity, as a harmony of group-persons, see Otto von Gierke, *Natural Law and the Theory of Society, 1500–1800, with a lecture on the ideas of natural law and humanity by Ernst Troeltsch*, trans. Ernest Barker (1934; reprint, Boston: Beacon Press, 1957). A translation of five subsections in vol. 4 of Gierke's *Das deutsche Genossenschaftsrecht*.
11. Modestinus, *Digest*, 23.2.1.

12. Pope John Paul II, Encyclical *Centesimus annus* (1991), §13.

13. Yves Simon, *Philosophy of Democratic Government* (Chicago: University of Chicago Press, 1951), 65.

14. Should parents outsource their acts of parenting, or an orchestra the acts of attuning and playing music one with the other, or a crew team the acts of training and rowing, we may well judge that the group has lost, or abandoned, one of the perfections inherent to its corporate identity.

15. Ernest Gellner, *Conditions of Liberty: Civil Society and Its Rivals* (New York: The Penguin Press, 1994), 32.

16. To mention only a few covered in Christopher Pierson, *The Modern State* (London: Routledge, 1996), 6–34.

17. The term "concession" derives not explicitly from Hobbes's own writings, but rather from the magisterial work of Otto Friedrich von Gierke (1841–1921), who attempted to recover the juristic concept of corporate personality from what he called the "concession" theory. For Gierke, it was Hobbes who gave the most challenging version of it. Otto von Gierke, *Natural Law and the Theory of Society*.

18. Hobbes, *Leviathan*, XVI.80.

19. Ibid., XXII.115.

20. "Corporations must be capable of exercising jurisdiction over their members because any group that acts in its own right must be able to compel its members to recognize the authority of its actions, and to condition their own actions accordingly. Hobbes recognized this, which is why he was able to compare the commonwealth to a corporation, and why he was so insistent that corporations should be regulated by the sovereign." David Runciman, *Pluralism and the Personality of the State* (Cambridge: Cambridge University Press, 1997), 121.

21. Hobbes, *Leviathan*, XXII.115.

22. At least one aspect of "concession" was well known in Roman and ecclesiastical law. Associations claiming a share of public authority in the civil or ecclesiastical spheres require permission to so exist. Thomas Aquinas, for example, readily admitted that public associations cannot rightfully exist without the consent of authority. "The objection that, according to law, no one can be forced to join an association against his will, applies only to a private society, established by two or three members. But a man can be compelled to form part of a public association, which cannot exist without the consent of authority. Thus, a prince may force the inhabitants of a certain city to accept an individual as their fellow-citizen; and an ecclesiastical society can be compelled to accept a man as a canon, or a brother." St. Thomas Aquinas, *Contra impugnantes* (1257), I, cap. 3.

23. Hobbes, *Leviathan*, XXII.121.

24. Ibid.

25. John Hall Stewart, *A Documentary Survey of the French Revolution* (New York: Macmillan, 1951), Document 17, at 114.

26. Ibid., Document 28, at 165.

27. Indeed, more than a century later, the Third Republic enacted such legislation: "No religious congregation may be formed without an authorization given by law which that determine the conditions of its exercise. . . . The dissolution of

a congregation or the closing of any establishment may be declared by a cabinet decree." *French Law of Associations*, title III, §13 (July 1, 1901).

28. *Baehr v. Lewin*, 852 P. 2d 44, 58 (1993) (citing *Gussin v. Gussin*, 73 Hawaii 470, 483, 836 P. 2nd 484, 491 (1992)).

29. *Goodridge v. Dept. of Public Health*, 440 Mass. 309, 321–22 (2003).

30. Compare to Justice Joseph Story: "[Marriage] may exist between two individuals of different sexes, although no third person existed in the world, as happened in the case of the common ancestors of mankind. It is the parent and not the child of society." Joseph Story, *Commentaries on the Conflict of Laws* (Boston: Hilliard, Gray and Company, 1834), 100.

31. Karl Barth, *Church Dogmatics*, vol. 3, part 4 (Edinburgh, Scotland: T&T Clark, 1976), 410.

32. Emile Durkheim, *Professional Ethics and Civic Morals* (New York: Free Press, 1958), 63.

33. Montesquieu, *Spirit of the Laws*, ed. and trans. Anne M. Cohler, Basia C. Miller, and Harold S. Stone (Cambridge: Cambridge University Press, 1989), 155.

34. Montesquieu looked to England for such a model; for in England, it was not merely Parliament, but also the businessmen who moderated the abstract principle of monarchical absolutism. "It is against the spirit of commerce," he wrote, "for the nobility to engage in it in a monarchy. . . . The usage that permitted commerce to the nobility in England is one of the things that most contributed to weakening monarchical government there." Ibid., 350.

35. Alexis de Tocqueville, *Democracy in America*, trans. Henry Reeve, Esq. With an Original Preface and Notes by John C. Spencer (New York: Adlard and Saunders, 1838. Repr. Clark, N.J.: The Lawbook Exchange, 2003), II.2.5, and II.4.2.

36. While constitutions provide only external and static distributions of power, civil society is a dynamic force, representing the sum of all those private actions that are initiated, negotiated, and pursued without asking for a "concession."

37. Gellner, *Conditions of Liberty*, 211–12.

38. Ibid., 100.

39. Left to its own logic, this position allows corporate personality in the mode of temporary partnerships. The associational choices of individuals must be respected. The state exists not to protect its own sovereignty so much as to protect individual liberty against social authority. So, for example, the state's interest in marriage is not to be defended on the basis of the institution's usefulness in collecting scientific or demographic data, but its usefulness in facilitating individual choice. Consider, for example, an opinion written by Justice Brennan in a case that contested the state of California's defining the nature and value of marriage:

> [T]he plurality ignores the kind of society in which our Constitution exists. We are not an assimilative, homogeneous society, but a facilitative, pluralistic one, in which we must be willing to abide someone else's unfamiliar or even repellent practice because the same tolerant impulse protects our own idiosyncrasies. Even if we can agree, therefore, that "family" and "parenthood" are part of the good life; it is absurd to assume that we can agree on the content of those terms and destructive to pretend that we do. In a community such as ours, "liberty" must include the freedom not to conform. The plurality today squashes this freedom by requiring specific approval from history before protecting anything in the name of liberty. (*Michael H. v. Gerald D.* 491 U.S. 110, 141 (1989) (J. Brennan dissenting))

40. Gellner, *Conditions of Liberty*, 12.

41. Here, quoting from the new, and politically troubled, *Treaty Establishing a Constitution for Europe* (2004) on the principle of subsidiarity. *European Convention*, Treaty, I.11 (3).

42. For the notions of input and output legitimacy, see Fritz W. Scharpf, *Governing in Europe: Effective and Democratic?* (Oxford: Oxford University Press, 1999).

43. Paul D. Marquardt, "Subsidiarity and Sovereignty in the European Union," 18 *Fordham International Law Journal* 616, 637 (1994).

44. See R. Leonardi and C. Paraskevopoulos, *Social Capital and Learning Institutional Networks: Making Sense of Subsidiarity in European Regional Policy* (paper presented at the thrity-sixth conference of Regional Science Association (RSA), Zurich, August 26–30, 1996).

45. Pope Leo XIII, Encyclical *Rerum novarum* (1891), §§51–52, 55.

46. Note this paragraph from the *Catechism of the Catholic Church*, written more than a century after Leo's encyclical: "A society is a group of persons bound together organically by a principle of unity that goes beyond each one of them. As an assembly that is at once visible and spiritual, a society endures through time: it gathers up the past and prepares for the future. By means of society, each man is established as an 'heir' and receives certain 'talents' that enrich his identity and whose fruits he must develop. He rightly owes loyalty to the communities of which he is part and respect to those in authority who have charge of the common good." *Catechism of the Catholic Church*, rev. ed. with amendments following the publication of the *Edito Typica* (Vatican City: Libreria Editrice Vaticana, 1999), §1880.

47. Pope Leo XIII, Encyclical *Rerum novarum* (1891), §56.

48. Simon, *Philosophy of Democratic Government*, 11 (emphasis added).

49. Ibid., 19.

50. Ibid.

51. Ibid., 33.

52. Consider John Finnis, who seems to rely on Simon: "Authority (and thus the responsibility of governing) in a community is to be exercised by those who can in fact effectively settle co-ordination problems for that community. This principle is not the last word on the requirements of practical reasonableness in locating authority; but it is the first and most fundamental." *Natural Law and Natural Rights* (Oxford: Clarendon Press, 1980), 246.

53. Yves Simon, *A General Theory of Authority* (Notre Dame, Ind.: University of Notre Dame Press, 1962), 21–22.

54. St. Thomas Aquinas, *De regno*, I.2,4,8. Simon relies heavily on Thomas's response to the Augustinian position, that mastership of one person over others was the effect of sin. Thomas contends that, even in a state of innocence, mastership is natural.

> But a man is the master of a free subject, by directing him either towards his proper welfare, or to the common good. Such a kind of mastership would have existed in the state of innocence between man and man, for two reasons. First, because man is naturally a social being, and so in the state of innocence he would have led a social life. Now a social life cannot exist among a number of people unless under the presidency of one to look after the common good; for many, as such, seek many things, whereas one attends only to one. Wherefore the Philosopher says, in the beginning of the Politics, that

wherever many things are directed to one, we shall always find one at the head directing them. Secondly, if one man surpassed another in knowledge and virtue, this would not have been fitting unless these gifts conduced to the benefit of others, according to 1 Pt. 4:10, "As every man hath received grace, ministering the same one to another." Wherefore Augustine says "Just men command not by the love of domineering, but by the service of counsel" and "The natural order of things requires this; and thus did God make man" (*De Civitate Dei* xix, 14, 15) (Aquinas, *Summa theologica* I, 96.4).

55. Yves Simon, *Nature and Functions of Authority* (Milwaukee, Wis.: Marquette University Press, 1940), 47.

56. Aquinas, *Ethicorum Aristotelis Ad Nicomachum*, lectio 9.

57. For communitarian and libertarian accounts of subsidiarity, see Viktor Vanberg, "Subsidiarity, responsive government and individual liberty," in *Subsidiarität: Idee und Wirklichkeit Zur Reichweite eines Prinzips in Deutschland und Europa*, eds. Knut Wolfgang Nörr and Thomas Oppernmann (Tübingen, Germany: J. C. B. Mohr, 1997), 253–69 (author's own translation).

58. The history and philosophy of subsidiarity are covered with unusual clarity by Thomas C. Behr, "Luigi Taparelli D'Azeglio, S.J. (1793–1862) and the Development of Scholastic Natural-Law Thought as a Science of Society and Politics," *Journal of Markets & Morality*, vol. 6 (Spring, 2003), 99–115.

59. Luigi Taparelli D'Azeglio, *Saggio Teoretico Di Dritto Naturale Appogiato Sul Fatto*, eighth ed. (Rome: Societa Grafica Romana, 1949), 685, 694 (author's own translation).

60. Pope Pius XII, *La elevatezza e la nobilità* (1946), AAS/38, 144f.

61. Pope Pius XI, Encyclical *Divini redemptoris* (1937), §51.

62. Pope John Paul II, Encyclical *Centesimus annus* (1991), §48.

63. "In every government the best thing is that provision be made for the things governed, according to their mode: for in this consists the justice of the regime. Consequently even as it would be contrary to the right notion of human rule, if the governor of a state were to forbid men to act according to their various duties,—except perhaps for the time being, on account of some particular urgency,—so would it be contrary to the notion of God's government, if He did not allow creatures to act in accordance with their respective natures." Ibid.

64. Jean-Yves Calvez, S.J. and Jacques Perrin, S.J., *The Church and Social Justice: The Social Teachings of the Popes from Leo XIII to Pius XII* (1878–1958) (Chicago: Henry Regnery, 1961), 122–23.

65. Ibid., 332.

66. John XXIII, Encyclical *Mater et Magistra* (1961) §53.

67. Ibid.

68. Ibid., §65.

III

AUTHORITY IN LAW?

8

How a Constitution May Undermine Constitutionalism

J. Budziszewski

Lex facit Regem. In these three words, Henry de Bracton expressed the essence of constitutionalism. The king is supreme *within* the system of laws but not *over* it; it is law that makes the king, not the king the law. The aphorism, of course, is not just about kings; it endorses "the rule of law" in opposition to "the rule of men." More precisely, constitutionalism is the principle that the real authority of government, as distinct from its sheer ability to compel, depends not on the personality of the rulers, but on antecedent principles of right. What we commonly call the law—governmental enactments—is not the ultimate ground of right, but an elaboration and specification of these antecedent principles in the light of the circumstances at hand.[1] Because the elaboration and specification of these principles is necessary to the common good, when the enactments that result from them meet certain conditions they "bind the conscience" of the citizens. In other words, they become real obligations. The authority of the government is simply its ability to bind conscience, *subject to these conditions*. Power, then, is justified by authority, not authority by power.

One would think that a written constitution would provide constitutionalism with its highest and most perfect expression. Of course not just any such document would do. It would have to be simply phrased, properly ratified, publicly promulgated, and compatible with the antecedent principles of right that we have been talking about. This would enable it to serve as a "higher law"—not in the sense that it replaced these antecedent principles, but in the sense that it regulated all subsequent attempts to elaborate and specify them. Should some rulers declare lawful what the constitution forbade, then other rulers, or perhaps citizens, could appeal to the constitution in opposing them.

This was certainly how the American founders expected their constitution to work. As always with big ideas, what actually happened is more complicated. No doubt, having a written constitution does promote constitutionalism in some respects. However, in other respects it actually undermines the concept. Surprisingly, at the time critics anticipated some of the ways in which this can happen, especially Brutus, a pseudonymous Anti-Federalist who was probably the New York judge Robert Yates. Brutus did not propose doing without a written constitution. What he proposed was drafting the document differently, with a greater awareness of the ways in which such an instrument can backfire.

THE SHAPE OF THE FOREST

As I hope to show, Brutus was an exceptionally acute theorist. However, he was not as talented an expositor and rhetorician as the Federalist writers with whom contemporary Americans are more familiar. James Madison always sets the trees in the context of the forest. Brutus describes the trees, but he leaves his readers to work out the shape of the forest for themselves. It is not that he doesn't see the forest; if he didn't, his pictures of its various localities would not connect up as well as they do. The problem is that he lavishes his powers of portrayal on the localities rather than on the forest as a whole. I hope it will not be presumptuous, then, if I sketch the big picture that all of Brutus's smaller pictures presuppose but which he does not actually paint for us.

Brutus's big picture coincides with Madison's big picture in certain respects, but diverges from it in others. He plainly agrees with Madison that government is both necessary and dangerous. Though indispensable for keeping order, it is also prone to tyranny, because officeholders labor ceaselessly to make themselves more important. Always they seek to expand their spheres of action and enlarge the definitions of their official responsibilities. Human government is always government under the conditions of the Fall.

The disagreement between Brutus and Madison concerns not the identity of this malady, then, but its remedy. Madison had written:

> In framing a government which is to be administered by men over men, the great difficulty lies in this: you must first enable the government to control the governed; and in the next place oblige it to control itself. A dependence on the people is, no doubt, the primary control on the government; but experience has taught mankind the necessity of auxiliary precautions.[2]

What makes these words interesting is that although the language of "dependence on the people" being the "primary control on the government" conjures up images of direct popular rule, Madison never says that "the people" *as such* are the primary control on the government. No, he says that the government is to "control itself." What he has in mind is checks and balances. The various parts of the government certainly do depend on the people in various circuitous ways, but the crucial thing is not simply that they do depend on the people, but that they depend on them in such *different fashions,* making it impossible for the government to have a unitary will to oppress them. To put it another way, what makes the government trustworthy is not its similarity to "the people," but the sharpness of the contrast among its own parts. Although each part may reflect some element in the character of the people, there is no part of the government that reflects the character of the people as a whole.

The Madisonian Senate, for example, depends on the considered judgment of the people as filtered through state legislatures interested in protecting their own authority. The House of Representatives, by contrast, depends on the shifting opinions of the people, or to be more exact, on what is left of these shifting opinions after competing factions have canceled each other out. The presidency depends on the compromise of the various regions of the people, as filtered through the Electoral College, and, when the college cannot pick a winner, through the House of Representatives. The judiciary depends on the specialized knowledge of those members of the people whose qualities persuade the president to nominate them and the Senate to confirm them. And so on. Direct popular government, had it been instituted, would have been like a mirror that perfectly reflected the people's image. Republican government, as Madison conceived it, is more like a prism that breaks up the light of that image into a multitude of different hues, coupled with a filter that blocks certain hues from passing through.

Brutus is somewhat more sympathetic to popular government than Madison is, and much less sanguine about the possibility of getting the government to "control itself." He does not oppose the idea of checks and balances *per se.* He does oppose the Federalist theory of how checks and balances will work. In the traditional theory of checks held by most Anti-Federalists, including Brutus, the parties who are checking each other are social classes, and the place where they are checking each other is a single branch of government—the legislature. In the Federalist theory, by contrast, the main parties checking each other are the branches of government themselves—legislature against executive against judiciary. Note well that for the Federalist innovation of branch-to-branch checking to work, the Federalists must be right about three things: (1) They must be right that just as members of social classes view themselves as vested in the protection and aggrandizement of these classes, so holders of government offices view themselves as vested in the protection and aggrandizement of these offices; (2) they must also be right that officeholders of different branches view their vested interests in these offices as diametrically opposed, so that the more power and prestige that officeholders in one branch enjoy, the less power and prestige the officeholders in the other branches enjoy; and (3) they must be right about the inherent advantages that each branch of government brings to the competition, because otherwise the strongest checks will not be awarded to the weakest branches, as they ought to be.

Some Anti-Federalists challenged even the first of these three points of confidence. They refused to admit that self-interest is actuated just as strongly by office as by social class. Thus Patrick Henry complains in the Virginia ratifying convention, "Tell me not of checks on paper, but tell me of checks founded on self-love."[3] Brutus's approach is quite different. He readily admits the psychological realism of the first point, but he challenges the realism of the other two.

It may seem that I am straying from the original question of how having a written constitution may undermine constitutionalism. Not so. Brutus recognizes that a written constitution is not merely a statement of political ideals, but a legal instrument. It is all well and good to say that the three branches shall be coequal, but courts normally interpret legal instruments. A differently drafted legal instrument might have distributed the power of interpretation among all three branches. It might have identified particular respects in which the legislature, the executive, and the judiciary are each interpreters of the constitution. What the Constitution actually does, argues Brutus, is just the opposite. Rather than distributing the power of interpretation, it concentrates it in the courts. To make matters worse, he holds, the language by which this is done encourages judges to exercise this concentrated power of interpretation in extravagant ways that bear but a distant relation to what the Constitution actually says.

The Federalists' response to such concerns is that we need not fear the judiciary because the other two branches would immediately check usurping courts. Brutus has a double response, for the Constitution dramatically misjudges not only where checks are most needed, but also where they will actually be used. In the first place it assumes that the judiciary will be the weakest of the three branches, when in fact it will be the strongest. In the second place, it assumes that the other two branches will be jealous of its power, when in fact they will collude with it. The consequence of these two misjudgments is that under the Constitution, the legislature, executive, and judiciary will be coequal in name only, and "the real effect of this system of government, will . . . be brought home to the feelings of the people, through the medium of the judicial power."[4] So it is that the very instrument ordained to insure the sober rule of law comes instead to advance the arrogant rule of men—that is, of judges. This is the lie of the forest. Now let us examine the trees.

JUDICIAL INDEPENDENCE AND FINALITY

Under the Constitution, Brutus argues, the national courts will be unlike the courts of any other republic in history, endowed with both radical independence and interpretive finality.[5]

He does not oppose a moderate judicial independence; in fact, he supports it. Constitutional provisions that prohibit Congress from holding the jobs and salaries of judges for ransom are all to the good. The problem, in his view, is that the Constitution also makes it impossible to remove judges from office for making legal errors. The only grounds mentioned in the Constitution for the impeachment of any official are bribery, treason, and other high crimes and misdemeanors.

Central to his argument is the difference between England and America. Some degree of judicial independence is essential in both settings. However, the reasons that make judicial independence essential to England have less weight on this side of the Atlantic. The important question about judicial independence is always "Independence from whom?" In England, when we speak of the independence of the courts we mean their independence from the king. In America, we mean their independence from the legislature.

To be sure, both kings and legislatures desire to increase the powers and prerogatives of their offices. Independence from the latter may therefore seem just as important as independence from the former. According to Brutus, however, such reasoning is specious. Members of Congress will hold their offices only for fixed terms. By contrast, not only does the king hold his office for life, but he also transmits it to his posterity. This gives him a far stronger motive to draw power to the Crown. For this reason, independence of English courts from the Crown must be very strong indeed, but independence of American courts from the legislature need not be nearly so strong.

Paradoxically, even though the reasons for judicial independence are less weighty under American than English conditions, the Constitution makes the independence of American judges far greater. In the first place, it is obvious that American judges will have the power of judicial review. English judges have no such power; they may declare the meaning of laws passed by Parliament, but they may not set these laws aside on grounds that they are inconsistent with the English constitution. In the second place, although English judges are accountable for errors in the interpretation of the law to the House of Lords, American judges will not be accountable for errors in the interpretation of law to any tribunal. Consequently, the interpretations they render will be utterly final. The consequence of these differences is that whereas English judges are controlled by Parliament, in America judges will be supreme. Although the Federalists may have thought that they had learned from the English experience, in fact they had gravely misunderstood it.

INTERPRETIVE MONOPOLY AND EXTRAVAGANCE

In Letter No. 11, Brutus scrutinizes the constitutional language by which the judicial power is characterized. Article III, section 2 declares without qualification that it extends to all cases arising *both* under the Constitution *and* under the laws of the United States.[6] It is unreasonable to suppose that this language is redundant; therefore, these two provisions—"arising under the Constitution" and "arising under . . . the laws of the United States"—must have distinct meanings.[7] In that case, what does it mean to extend the judicial power to all cases arising under the Constitution? Evidently, that courts will be able to declare what the Constitution *means*. Because the constitutional language is stark and unqualified, we must further assume that this power will be a judicial monopoly, unshared by Congress or the president.

Section 2 also states that the judicial power extends not only to all cases in law, but also to all cases in equity. Quoting Blackstone, Brutus defines equity as "the correction of that, wherein the law, by reason of its universality, is deficient."[8] What he has in mind is the fact that every law is a universal rule; it says, "In all cases that fit into category P, do Q." Unfortunately, because of the infinite variability of circumstances, there will always be some cases in the category P where doing Q would achieve a result opposite to that intended by the legislature. In such cases, a court renders judgment equitably—not according to the words or letter of the law, but according to what the court takes to be the spirit of its reasoning.

If we now put the fact that the judicial power extends to cases "arising under the Constitution" together with the fact that it extends to cases arising both "in law and equity," we conclude that the judiciary will be empowered to interpret not only ordinary laws, but also the Constitution itself, not only according to its letter, but also according to the spirit of its reasoning. If we put this conclusion together with the fact that the decisions of the court will be final, we further conclude that no one will be able to second-guess the speculations of the courts as to what the spirit of the Constitution may be.

This immensely expands the power of the courts. If anything, the structure of the rest of the Constitution encourages the courts to indulge their speculations about the spirit of the document with extravagance rather than restraint. In the first place, the government's powers "are conceived in general and indefinite terms, which are either equivocal, ambiguous, or which require long definitions to unfold the extent of their meaning."[9] In the second place, by suggesting that more power is conveyed than expressed, the Necessary and Proper Clause requires courts to attend not only to the words of the Constitution "in their common acceptation," but also to its "spirit, intent, and design."[10]

Strong as they are, Brutus's arguments seem even stronger today than they did at the time they were written. Historically, references to the spirit of the law in discussions of equity can mean either of two things: the particular intention of the law under examination, or the general intention of fairness that all law is presumed to have. This is why law dictionaries sometimes define "equity" simply as a set of principles of fairness used in interpreting the law. If we view the particular intention of the Constitution, we find that it was not conceived as an instrument for enforcing fairness in general; rather, it picks and chooses among the kinds and aspects of fairness that it guarantees. Today, however, judges treat it as though it really did guarantee all-around fairness, even when this leads to absurd consequences like reading the principle "one man, one vote" into a document that expressly gives the same number of senators to each state.

CHECKS AND BALANCES: COLLUSION OR COMPETITION?

Brutus's assumptions about the nature of checks and balances directly contradict those of James Madison. To be sure, the Brutusian and Madisonian assumptions do not contradict each other at every point; in particular, both thinkers recognize the deep thirst of officeholders for power and dignity. "It will not be denied," says Madison in *Federalist* No. 48, "that power is of an encroaching nature." Similarly, says Brutus in Letter No. 11, "Every body of men invested with office are tenacious of power; they feel interested, and hence it has become a kind of maxim, to hand down their offices, with all its rights and privileges, unimpaired to their successors; the same principle will influence them to extend their power, and increase their rights." The natural tendency of judges, therefore, is to try to make themselves all-around social umpires, with no limits to the cases and controversies that they can adjudicate.

However, while Madison views the branches as fighting over who gets the biggest slice of a pie of fixed dimensions, Brutus views them as cooperating to get a bigger pie so that each of them may have a bigger slice. To put this another way, Madison thinks in terms of what we now call a zero-sum game. Each gain in the power of one branch diminishes the power of all the others, making their members natural enemies. By contrast, Brutus thinks in terms of what we now call a positive-sum game. *Certain* ways of increasing the power of one branch can actually increase the power of the other branches too, making their members natural allies. If Brutus is right, then Madison has made a catastrophically serious error, for the name of the game is not competition, but collusion. Instead of "obliging the government to control itself," interbranch relations will encourage the government to become ever more powerful.

The pivotal observation in Brutus's argument is that federal courts can hear cases and controversies that would otherwise be reserved for state courts by allowing Congress to make laws on subjects that would otherwise be reserved for state legislatures. Thus, besides the obvious motive to increase their powers directly, judges have a further, though less obvious, motive to increase them indirectly, simply by expanding the power of legislators. One hand washes the other. "Every extension of the power of the general legislature, as well as of the judicial powers, will increase the powers of the courts," Brutus says, "and the dignity and importance of the judges, will be in proportion to the extent and magnitude of the powers they exercise."[11]

In Letter No. 12, Brutus goes on to explain that the collusion of the judiciary with the legislature in increasing the size of the pie is perfectly compatible with an ever-larger *share* of the pie being given to the courts. He is not convinced that courts will be able to tell Congress *directly* what to do:

> Perhaps the judicial power will not be able, by direct and positive decrees, ever to direct the legislature, because it is not easy to conceive how a question can be brought before them in a course of legal discussion, in which they can give a decision, declaring, that the legislature have certain powers which they have not exercised, and which, in consequence of the determination of the judges, they will be bound to exercise.[12]

But he is confident that courts will be able to achieve the *effect* of telling Congress what to do, just because the members of Congress will internalize the principles devised by courts to guide their own decisions:

> These principles, whatever they may be, when they become fixed, by a course of decisions, will be adopted by the legislature, and will be the rule by which they will explain their own powers.
>
> What the principles are, which the courts will adopt, it is impossible for us to say; but it is not difficult to see that they may, and probably will, be very liberal ones.[13]

The judiciary becomes therefore the practical, if fitful, sovereign, limited mainly by the fact that it can rule on issues only as, and to the extent that, they arise in particular cases. It might be objected that Congress will *not* internalize the judiciary's explanation of its powers—that this is one of the points at which we should expect Madisonian competition, not Brutusian collusion. However, two centuries of hindsight allow us not only to confirm Brutus's argument, but also to fortify it. First, constitutional separation of the legislature from the executive makes party discipline in our regime much weaker than in parliamentary regimes. This weakness of party discipline, coupled with the vast increase in the range of the government's activities, makes it impossible for the legislature to fully regulate its own agenda. Positive control over the agenda passes largely to the executive, which finds it easier to seize the initiative; negative control passes to the judiciary, which can overturn laws it does not like. Another fact bolstering Brutus's case is that whereas federal legislators periodically face the electorate, federal judges don't. This makes Congress much more risk-averse than courts are. Rather than resenting the judiciary for taking hot-button issues out of its hands, the legislature may be relieved and grateful that someone else has made the decision for them. Finally, although the public perceives the president and members of Congress as politicians, it tends to view the courts, unrealistically, as nonpolitical guardians of the Constitution. This makes it still more difficult for any politicians who might wish to resist the puissance of the courts to stir up the political will to do so.

The upshot of all this is that an ever-larger share of the power pie goes to the judiciary—but for a variety of reasons (not least the fact that the pie itself is getting bigger), the other branches acquiesce in the change.

LEGAL FICTIONS

We have seen that Brutus thinks the courts will expand their powers indirectly, through expansion of the powers of the legislature. It remains to discuss how he thinks that the courts will expand their powers *directly*, through employment of legal fictions. This technique is so effective, he suggests, that courts in England have been able to use it even in actual defiance of Acts of Parliament. How much more effective might it be in America, where no legal barriers stand in the way of its exercise?

His illustrations of the technique are borrowed from William Blackstone.[14] Originally, the Court of Exchequer was intended for suits by debtors of the king who pleaded that the actions of third parties had made them less able to pay their debts; the Court of the King's Bench, in turn, was restricted to suits by parties who had suffered trespasses, or other injuries, by violence. In passage of time, however, the Court of Exchequer lost interest in whether the party bringing suit really was a debtor of the king, and the Court of the King's Bench lost interest in whether the party really had suffered an injury by violence. Let the plaintiff only say the words—or file the writ—and his suit would be heard by the court.[15] Brutus expects American courts to follow an analogous strategy to overcome their own jurisdictional limits.

In fact, the Constitution only mentions a single exception to the jurisdiction of federal courts in civil cases: They are prohibited from hearing lawsuits between citizens of the same state, unless the parties claim land under grants of different states. Needless to say, if the federal courts could somehow pack this category of case into their jurisdiction too, their civil jurisdiction would be universal. As Brutus explains in Letter No. 12, this would be trivially easy to do. Courts might simply make a routine practice of declaring the parties to be citizens of the same state. If this seems absurd, says Brutus, remember that article 4, section 2 guarantees to the citizens of each state all of the "privileges and immunities" of citizens in the several states. If we are entitled to all of the privileges and immunities of citizens in every state, then can we not be regarded as citizens of every state? By this reasoning, the claim of a Virginian to be a citizen of New York would appear perfectly truthful. Even if its falsehood were conceded, if the courts were to allow such a legal fiction who could contradict them?

The bizarre lengths to which this sort of thing could be taken is suggested by the dissenting opinion of Justice Douglas in the 1972 case *Sierra Club v. Morton*, in which an association of environmental activists sought to halt the construction of a resort in a national park.

> The critical question of "standing" would be simplified and also put neatly in focus if we fashioned a federal rule that allowed environmental issues to be litigated before federal agencies or federal courts in the name of the inanimate object about to be despoiled, defaced, or invaded. Contemporary public concern for protecting nature's ecological equilibrium should lead to the conferral of standing upon environmental objects to sue for their own preservation.[16]

The prospect of vegetables and minerals bringing suit in federal court makes arguments about animal rights seem almost quaint.

THE TRIUMPH OF VIRTUAL JURISPRUDENCE

Although the members of the *Morton* Court declined to swallow the particular legal fiction suggested by Justice Douglas, it would be a grave mistake to suggest that they are averse to fictitious claims. For example, a fictitious *history* has been employed to conclude that the First Amendment requires neutrality between religion and irreligion[17]; a fictitious *psychology* has been employed to maintain that the only possible motive for opposing special preferences for homosexuals is animus[18]; a fictitious *embryology* has been employed to insinuate that a child in the womb does not enjoy actual life but only "potential life"[19]; a fictitious *classification* has been employed to characterize antireproductive behavior as reproductive behavior[20]; a fictitious *semantics* has been employed to interpret the phrase "exercise of religion" as having no reference to religious acts[21]; and a fictitious *grammar* has been employed to treat categorical prohibitions as implying qualified permissions.[22] The use of fictitious suppositions is so pervasive a feature of constitutional construction that we should no longer speak of actual jurisprudence, but of virtual jurisprudence.

The pivotal moment in the development of virtual jurisprudence was probably *Griswold v. Connecticut*,[23] the 1965 case that established the doctrine of a general right to privacy. Not all of *Griswold*'s methods are still used; the importance of the case lies rather in its demonstration of just how much a determined court could get away with. Writing for the plurality, Justice Douglas set loose not just one legal fiction but an army of them. The argument is most ingenious. Certain clauses of the First, Third, Fourth, and Fifth Amendments provide, respectively, that citizens may peaceably assemble, that soldiers may not be quartered in private houses during peacetime without the consent of the owners, that unreasonable searches and seizures may not be conducted, and that no one may be compelled to give testimony against himself. Appealing to the Ninth Amendment idea of unenumerated rights, Douglas argued (1) that each of the four provisions protests some aspect of privacy; (2) that by doing so they imply a right to privacy *as such*; and (3) that because this right is general, it encompasses the particular behavior which the statute under challenge had prohibited.[24] All three claims are specious; this is virtual jurisprudence at its finest.

As to the first claim, the liberty of peaceable assembly guaranteed by the First Amendment is not a private act but a highly public one, connected with petition for redress of grievances. Moreover, the immunity from self-incrimination in the Fifth Amendment prevents government from eliciting confessions through torture; privacy is not the issue in this clause either. As to the second claim, although the protection against the quartering of soldiers in houses and the protection against unreasonable searches and seizures do have some connection with privacy, neither protection is absolute; the former allows an exception for wartime, the latter an exception for reasonable cause. Moreover, they protect citizens only against certain kinds of intrusions on their homes, bodies, records, and property, not against all intrusions. Plainly, it is unreasonable to suggest that they imply a protection of privacy *as such*. As to the third claim, even if these provisions did imply a generalized right to privacy, the alleged conclusion would not follow. Privacy concerns what other people may do with my property and what others may know about my affairs. Justice Douglas is not talking about what others may do or know; he is talking about what I may do. What he calls privacy might better be described as self-sovereignty.

THE COURT BECOMES KING

The idea of self-sovereignty is given its purest expression in the 1992 case *Planned Parenthood v. Casey*.[25] By this time the Court no longer finds it necessary to appeal to the Ninth Amendment or allude to "penumbras, formed by emanations."[26] It simply composes a confession of faith:

> At the heart of liberty is the right to define one's own concept of existence, of meaning, of the universe, and of the mystery of human life. Beliefs about these matters could not define the attributes of personhood were they formed under compulsion of the State.[27]

To understand this creedal statement one must recall what occasioned it. What the Court meant by defining one's own concept of human life was not so much deciding what to think, but deciding what to do: *Because* I have liberty to define my own concept of life, I may kill. In strict logic, it would seem to follow that I may kill anyone. In fact, it would seem to follow that I may do anything whatsoever. For the time being, the Court restricts its universal permission to the taking of life not yet born. This serves as a salutary reminder of what may be called the first principle of judicial usurpation: Formulae of universal permission never really mean universal permission; they are always instruments for the transfer of the power to prohibit from one set of hands to another. That king who says "Everything is permitted" will always add, "But I decide for everyone what 'everything' includes."[28]

The Court seems to recognize the extraordinary nature of what it is doing, for in the very same decision that it assumes such unprecedented power, it goes to unusual lengths to say that doing so is nothing out of the ordinary. Its argument neatly illustrates the *second* principle of judicial usurpation: In an age when candid monarchy has gone out of fashion, kings cannot be expected to call attention to themselves by announcing *l'état c'est nous*. Inevitably, it is in the name of the rule of law that the rule of men is proclaimed. "Our analysis would not be complete," says the Court, "without explaining why overruling Roe's central holding would not only reach an unjustifiable result under principles of stare decisis, but seriously weaken the Court's capacity to exercise the judicial power and to function as the Supreme Court of a Nation *dedicated to the rule of law*"[29] (emphasis added).

The introductory paragraphs of this essay defined constitutionalism as the principle that the real authority of government depends not on the personality of the rulers, but on antecedent principles of right. Governmental enactments are not the ultimate ground of right, but elaborations and specifications of these antecedent principles in the light of the circumstances at hand. Because necessary to the common good, under certain conditions these elaborations and specifications "bind the conscience" of the citizens; that is, they generate a real obligation to obey.

The Court's argument is a sort of parody of these ideas. It does not deny them; on the contrary, it nominally affirms them. The twist is that by declaring itself uniquely qualified to comment on these antecedent principles, it puts itself, in effect, in their place. By so doing, it arrogates to itself the power to bind the conscience of the citizens. In fact, it claims authority to tell them not only what to do, but also when to shut up—for it regards itself as the umpire of national moral controversies.

The Court puts these claims in loftier language, of course, but their meaning is clear nonetheless. Here is where it proclaims the uniqueness of its qualifications to elaborate and specify the antecedent principles of right from which the authority of government arises:

> The root of American governmental power is revealed most clearly in the instance of the power conferred by the Constitution upon the Judiciary of the United States, and specifically upon this Court. As Americans of each succeeding generation are rightly told, the Court cannot buy support for its decisions by spending money, and, except to a minor degree, it cannot independently coerce obedience to its decrees. The Court's power lies, rather, in its legitimacy, a product of substance and perception that shows itself in the people's acceptance of the Judiciary as fit to determine what the Nation's law means, and to declare what it demands.[30]

Here, in turn, is where it declares itself the umpire of national moral controversy, so that, for example, when it tells the proponents of the sanctity of life that the debate is over, they should be quiet and go home:

> Where, in the performance of its judicial duties, the Court decides a case in such a way as to resolve the sort of intensely divisive controversy reflected in *Roe* and those rare, comparable cases, its decision has a dimension that the resolution of the normal case does not carry. It is the dimension present whenever the Court's interpretation of the Constitution calls the contending sides of a national controversy to end their national division by accepting a common mandate rooted in the Constitution.[31]

The Court goes so far as to claim that the measure of the people's fitness to be governed by the rule of law is nothing more than whether the people are willing to agree with what it says:

> Like the character of an individual, the legitimacy of the Court must be earned over time. So, indeed, must be the character of a Nation of people who aspire to live according to the rule of law. Their belief in themselves as such a people is not readily separable from their understanding of the Court invested with the authority to decide their constitutional cases and speak before all others for their constitutional ideals.[32]

Confusing this willingness of the citizens to believe as they are told to believe with its "legitimacy" as an organ of government, the Court concludes with dark warnings that should its "legitimacy" in this sense be undermined, then so would the country be undermined in its "very ability to see itself through its constitutional ideals." Plainly, the members of the Court can no longer distinguish themselves from the nation, their lawlessness from the law, or their arbitrary will from those principles of right that are antecedent to their own authority.

L'Etat, c'est nous—such is the unvoiced motto of the monarchs of our day. It was Brutus who saw how such an order of things might come to pass, but it was Bracton who told us how to answer. Against such kings we must say, as he did: *Lex facit Regem*. They may believe that they make the law, but it is not so. Law makes the king.

NOTES

1. Specification of these principles means more than simply declaring what would have been right even in the absence of enacted law. The enacted law in our country specifies that in the interests of safety, automobiles on two-way roads must drive on the right, not the left. Even apart from law, citizens would have been obligated to drive safely. However, they would not have been obligated to drive on a particular side.
2. James Madison, *The Federalist* 51 (1788).
3. Patrick Henry, "Speeches of Patrick Henry in the Virginia State Ratifying Convention," in *The Anti-Federalist*, ed. Herbert J. Strong (Chicago: University of Chicago Press, 1985), 319:5.16.14.
4. Brutus [Anti-Federalist who was probably the New York judge Robert Yates], *New York Law Journal* 1787–1788, Letter No. 11.
5. Brutus's argument is first sketched in Letter No. 11, and elaborated in Letter No. 15. It may fruitfully be contrasted with the argument of Alexander Hamilton in *The Federalist*, No. 78.
6. U.S. Const. art. III, § 2, cl. 1.
7. Id.

8. Brutus, Letter No. 11 (quoting Sir William Blackstone, introduction, sec. 2, *Commentaries on the Laws of England* (1765), quoting Grotius, *On the Law of War and Peace*, bk 2, chap.16, sec. 26, which in turn relies on Aristotle, probably either *Nicomachean Ethics*, bk. 5, chap. 10, or *Rhetoric*, bk. 1, chap. 13).

9. Brutus, Letter No. 11.

10. Ibid.

11. Ibid.

12. Brutus, Letter No. 12.

13. Ibid.

14. The first is discussed in Brutus's Letter No. 11 and the second is discussed in Letter 12.

15. J. Budziszewski, "The Future of the End of Democracy," *First Things* 91 (March 1999), 15–21.

16. *Sierra Club v. Morton*, 405 U.S. 727 (1972).

17. "The wholesome 'neutrality' of which this Court's cases speak thus stems from a recognition of the teachings of history that powerful sects or groups might bring about a fusion of governmental and religious functions or a concert or dependency of one upon the other to the end that official support of the State or Federal Government would be placed behind the tenets of one or of all orthodoxies. This the Establishment Clause prohibits. And a further reason for neutrality is found in the Free Exercise Clause, which recognized the value of religious training, teaching and observance and, more particularly, the right of every person to freely choose his own course with reference thereto, free of any compulsion from the state. This the Free Exercise Clause guarantees." *Abington School District v. Schempp*, 374 U.S. 203 (1963), at 221. Notice that the Constitution is inconsistently said to require neutrality between religion and irreligion because it recognizes the value of religion.

18. "[T]he amendment seems inexplicable by anything but animus toward the class that it affects"; later in the same case, "laws of the kind now before us raise the inevitable inference that the disadvantage is born of animosity toward the class of persons affected." *Romer v. Evans*, 517 U.S. 620 (1996), at 631, 633.

19. "With respect to the State's important and legitimate interest in potential life, the 'compelling' point is at viability. This is so because the fetus then presumably has the capability of meaningful life outside the mother's womb." *Roe v. Wade*, 410 U.S. 113 (1973), at 163.

20. "[F]or two decades of economic and social developments, people have organized intimate relationships and made choices that define their views of themselves and their places in society, in reliance on the availability of abortion in the event that contraception should fail. The ability of women to participate equally in the economic and social life of the Nation has been facilitated by their ability to control their reproductive lives." *Planned Parenthood v. Casey*, 505 U.S. 833 (1992), at 856.

21. "Our cases do not at the farthest reach support the proposition that a stance of conscientious opposition relieves an objector from *any* colliding duty fixed by a democratic government." *Gillette v. United States*, 401 U.S. 437 (1971), 461 (emphasis added). Notice that the statement of the Court goes far beyond the mere assertion of a tacit condition that religious conduct be within the bounds of good order.

22. "The essence of all that has been said and written on the subject is that only those interests of the highest order and those not otherwise served can overbalance legitimate claims to the free exercise of religion." *Wisconsin v. Yoder*, 406 U.S. 205 (1972), at 215. According to this alleged interpretation of the First Amendment, even "legitimate" claims to the free exercise of religion can be overbalanced by "interests," not defined in the Constitution, that judges consider sufficiently important. Yet the First Amendment states that "Congress shall make *no* law . . . prohibiting the free exercise of religion" (emphasis added). Again notice that the statement of the Court goes far beyond the mere assertion of a tacit condition the religious conduct be within the bounds of good order.

23. *Griswold v. Connecticut*, 381 U.S. 479 (1965).

24. Id., at 484–86.

25. *Planned Parenthood*, 505 U.S. 833 (1992).

26. *Griswold*, 381 U.S., at 484.

27. *Planned Parenthood*, 505 U.S., at 851.

28. J. Budziszewski, "The Roots of Law," *Religion & Liberty* 11, no. 5 (2001).

29. *Planned Parenthood*, 505 U.S., at 851.

30. Id.

31. Id., at 867.

32. Id., at 868.

9

Locating Authority in Law

Patrick McKinley Brennan

NAME IT WHAT YOU PLEASE

What is the locus of authority in what we do in the name of law? This is my concern, which, it should be apparent, is both circumscribed and expansive. From the angle of circumscription, the question postulates: (1) authority (2) as an isolable element (3) in a practice in which (4) we are engaged (5) "in the name of law." The angle that highlights the "we" forebodes the expansion. After all, in order to locate authority's place in what we do in the name of law, we must say who "we" are. What could be easier—or less possible? "'Know thyself' we hear suggested for our own good. Yet we hardly know ourselves."[1]

Our resistance to self-knowledge has no doubt many causes, but among the legally orthodox, the asymptotic elimination of the human subject is virtually axiomatic. The orthodox vouchsafe law's objectivity exactly by denying or minifying the subject's appearance in our legal undertakings. As one critic of the orthodoxy relates:

> Sometimes it seems as if there is only one story in American legal thought and only one problem. The story is the story of formalism and the problem is the problem of the subject. The story of formalism is that it never deals with the problem of the subject. The problem of the subject is that it's never been part of the story.[2]

The heterodoxy I wish to develop and defend here takes the subject as starting point—the font of law and authority.

This competing theory observes that both the possibility and exigence of law—and the authority that alone makes law possible—arise from our subjectivity. Force and violence reach us from without, and they do so arbitrarily and with no regard for who we are; we become lawful, however, from the inside out, if we choose to do so at all. This is because—or, so I shall argue—we subjects are normatively oriented, but not determined, to the real and the good. We humans are not mere objects, nor does the normative order arrest us from without in episodes of "now for something totally different." Before we advert to or thematize the fact, the fact is that we are ordered out of ourselves, first, to affirm what is (the real) and, second, to affirm and then realize the valuable that might yet be (the good). Because this normativity is indefeasibly ours, all additional or subsequent normative claims—including those made "in the name of the law"—must meet its anterior and concomitant demands. Which is why we can say, with Joseph Vining: "The question what the law 'is' is not so very different from the question who we 'are.'"[3]

The jurisprudential mandarins who keep orthodoxy afloat are at pains to keep this a secret. Ronald Dworkin's signal defection from humanity to Hercules is only the limit case; most mainstream legal theorists are content to prosecute the more modest quest for the rule of law that is as much as possible not a rule of men. We are all legal realists now, of course; "no adult needs to be told that we live under a rule of men in the sense that laws are made, interpreted, and administered by real men and women."[4] However, at least from the moment the eager first realists spotted the camel in the vicinity of the tent of law, those concerned for law's rule have been trying to reconstruct law by constructing theories of how proto-realists can be made lawful.[5] Robert Bork's originalism, Justice Scalia's textualism, Bruce Ackerman's dualism, Owen Fiss's disciplining rules, Ronald Dworkin's integrity[6]—from the right and from the left they come bearing theoretical gifts designed to ensure law's rule in this world brought to us by Charles Darwin and Justice Holmes. This is the world in which the idea that there is a norm that precedes what we do in the name of the law—a norm to which we are obligated freely to conform our living and the "positive law" by which we structure and govern it—has to compete with the idea that the only "laws" are statistical regularities.

Some students of law oppose the embarrassing surfeit of theoretical riches by denying that the game is worth the candle; the aspiration to a rule of law, they say, is simply misplaced, a holdover from prelapsarian naiveté. Paul Kahn, for instance, in a very profound study of what we do in the name of the law, concludes that "the rule of law may be our deepest political myth" and recommends—citing the authority of Abraham Lincoln—that in place of law, we appeal first to charity.[7] Others counter the grand theories with more modest, more prosaic, more "pragmatic" aims and means. Judge Posner proposes legal pragmatism simpliciter, and Cass Sunstein, to pick another example, advocates "incompletely theorized agreements."[8]

This is all very interesting, to be sure—but the trouble, as I see it, is that the "grand theory vs. muddling through" false dilemma has largely blocked the human subject from view, and, along with him or her, the very possibility of authority and, therefore, of law. The result of this theory-driven occlusion of the potentially lawful subject is that what is put forward as law cannot but look "largely irrelevant to the self,"[9] no better than "an unintelligible restraint."[10] What we adults do "need to be told"—or rather, what we need to discover for ourselves—is what in us generates authority and thus makes law possible, thereby preempting or displacing the authoritarian and the arbitrary. The availability of the authoritarian and arbitrary we can take for granted, but law's possibility needs to be made out afresh, and this requires—or so I am arguing—that we get to know ourselves.

What we do in the name of law has its externalia such as courthouses and capitols, codes and codicils, robes and ritual action, and these import "authority" of a sort. Furthermore, for reasons to which we shall come, we cannot do without externalia in law and the "authority" associated with them. But whereas no one mistakes robes and courthouses for the law itself, some do mistake texts for the law itself, thereby collapsing the possibility of genuine authority into one of its usual conditions. Texts, like other artifacts of our creation, are not self-moving, self-justifying marionettes of law; texts do not rise of themselves to wield authority over us. A book of black marks, the cover of which is embossed "Revised Statutes of the State of Utopia" or "Restatement (Seventh) of Everything," is an unlikely contributor to law; but if on the cover were etched "California" instead of "Utopia" or "Contracts" instead of "Everything," we might—or we might not—have a different case, as anyone familiar with "unconstitutional" statutes and the "persuasive authority" of a Restatement knows. In figuring out what might make the difference in the latter case, what I am after is what in us is the root of law—in a phrase, the inner experience of law.[11]

On the account I shall develop, "the inner experience of law" includes the cognitional and volitional experience of the legislator promulgating texts, of the judge interpreting these texts, and of the sheriff determining how to give coercive effect to judicial decisions bearing on the community; it also includes the experience of individual subjects understanding those rules and then receiving or rejecting them as guides to conduct. Underneath and uniting all these (and other) inner experiences of law, however, there is the focal case of the inner experience of law; it precedes and is the condition of the possibility of all those others. I shall refer to it as the experience of inner law. It is what I earlier referred to as our normative orientation out of our interiority to the real and the valuable, the human subject's (free) subordination to a primal norm issued within his own rational consciousness. "Inner law" is my name for what Bernard Lonergan, S.J. (1904–1984), refers to as the criterion that precedes "the criteria of truth invented by the philosophers"[12]: it is "the dynamic criterion of the further question immanent in intelligence itself." Lonergan continues:

> Name it what you please, alertness of mind, intellectual curiosity, the spirit of inquiry, active intelligence, the drive to know. Under any name, it remains the same and is, I trust, very familiar to you. This primordial drive, then, is the pure question. It is prior to any insights, any concepts, any words, for insights, concepts, words, have to do with answers; and before we look for answers, we want them; such wanting is the pure question.[13]

Our texts, our decisions, and our actions are, I shall argue, contributions to law exactly inasmuch as they are governed by inner law.

Lonergan was right to insist that, in general, what you name this primal criterion is secondary to acknowledging its hegemony. The project at hand here, however, will not tolerate such linguistic license. The task of locating authority in what we do in the name of law forces, or at least invites, us to face the fact that operative within us is an eros for the real and the good that just is the basic law to which all our undertakings must bow, lest they lack authority and end up, therefore, lawless. Those bent on a univocal definition of law will resist the usage that refers to what is within us as law and to "positive law" as various, analogically related, forms of law. The burden to show that law just is "positive law," however, would be on the one denying the correctness of the analogical usage that is the rule, not the exception. The limitation of law to the command of the sovereign, as by John Austin and others, is the exception, not the rule, and it flies in the face of common usage and understanding.

The project of tracing our communal lawfulness to inner law, by way of authority, will upset the sensibilities of souls bent on finding law that is so objective as to be able (almost) to claim its own instances. But, getting to know ourselves, we just might discover that inner law provides the foundation, a rock from and on which we can build.[14] Our compliance with it can create authority, and authority can speak law to us as individuals and as community. Inner law is not a rock after the manner of a "rail that runs surety through our judgments,"[15] but it does promise to lead us, if we would choose to follow, to the real and the good. The authority that it makes possible is not forceful, but it is correlative to our dignity as free beings capable of choosing intelligence over violence. A rock that is the human spirit working itself out may not be what H. L. A. Hart's absolute absolutist had wanted, but it just may be what we need in order to assure authority, instead of authoritarianism, in what we do in the name of law.[16]

THE TEMPTING OF SCALIA

To recognize "inner law" for what it is entails the subordination of all else to it, and we should recognize right away that this rectification thwarts a familiar and forceful aspiration, the one Thomas Paine thought was satisfied in what the colonists were creating: "In America, the law is king."[17] David Dudley Field was of the same mind: "The law is our only sovereign. We have enthroned it."[18] The aspiration to which Paine and Field gave famous American expression is to displace the modern personal sovereign—conjured variously and menacingly by Thomas Hobbes, Jean Bodin, Jean-Jacques Rousseau, and John Austin, among others—with a sovereign that just is the law. On the typically modern conception, the (personal) sovereign was to be above the law, possessed of absolute and unconstrained power. On the view Paine and his progeny propound, by contrast, positive law is as high as it gets. The substitution of sovereign law for the unconstrained personal sovereign is modernity's hope to do better than Hobbes.[19] Hans Kelsen had something of the sort in mind, and, for its part, even the *Compendium of the Social Doctrine of the Church* (published in English in Rome in 1994) refers to "the principle of the 'rule of law,' in which the law is sovereign."[20] Closer to home, Justice Antonin Scalia, having made a profound genuflection to democracy, has been tireless in his privileging of positive law: "It is the law that governs us."[21]

Among the grand theorists named above, the justice and his jurisprudence deserve our special attention, and this for two reasons. First, unlike most of the other grand theorists named above, he is sometimes in position to implement his theory in the name of the Constitution of the United States, without risk of being overruled by a higher court.[22] Second, the justice is, I wish to suggest, putting forward what those observant of inner law must regard as a specially treacherous form of pseudo law, a system of rules backed by a species of authoritarianism, not authority. Justice Scalia's well-known "just apply the rules of law" injunction, reinforced as it is by the common political bromides about the glories of democracy and the evils of "legislating from the bench," perhaps sounds banal or even commonsensical. Behind its presuppositions and modes of proceeding, however, are entailments that, I would suggest, cut the legs of law out from under it by removing all possible sources of authority.

Justice Scalia's announced twin aims have been to make what we do in the name of law as much as possible a system of *rules* contained in, or constructed from, a closed universe of texts. Textualism is the technical name for the second aim, and its boast, according to Justice Scalia, is that, by treating as the law itself the "objectified intent" lodged in the text the lawgiver promulgated, it delivers "a government of laws and not of men."[23]

> We look for a sort of "objectified" intent—the intent that a reasonable person would gather from the text of the law, placed alongside the remainder of the corpus juris. . . . [T]he reason we adopt this objectified version is, I think, that it is simply incompatible with democratic government, or indeed, even with fair government, to have the meaning of a law determined by what the lawgiver meant, rather than by what the lawgiver promulgated. . . . Men may enact what they will; but it is only the laws that they enact which bind us.[24]

Recognizing that not everything that we might seek to cover with law is reducible to rules, Scalia continues: "Only by announcing rules do we hedge ourselves in. . . . All I urge is that . . . [totality of the circumstances tests and balancing modes of analysis] be avoided where possible; that the Rule of Law, the law of rules, be extended as far as the nature of the question allows."[25]

This concession, such as it is, leaves the system, or the aspiration thereto, intact: texts are the law, and authority (and the lack thereof) is hardly tarried over. What the lawgiver, a person (either individual or corporate), "meant" has been suppressed to make way for a text, what the lawgiver "promulgated." This limitation of law to text and the judicial role to giving coercive effect to text is a strategy that Justice Scalia took the occasion of a lecture at the Gregorian University in Rome to defend in particularly poignant terms:

> [M]y only authority as a judge to prevent the state from doing what may be bad things is the authority that the majority has given to the courts. . . . To say, "Ah, but it is contrary to the natural law," is simply to say that you set yourself above the democratic state and presume to decide what is good and what is bad in place of the majority of the people. I do not accept that as a proper function. . . . Yes, it is dogmatic democracy. . . . I have been appointed to apply the Constitution and positive law. God applies the natural law.[26]

Here, "authority" amounts to a democratically conferred license; the judge's "authority" is to function, as much as possible, as something of a conduit for democratically generated texts and the rules they contain. The "distinguishing features" of Justice Scalia's jurisprudence are, in sum, that "(1) it is a system; (2) it is a system selected for plainly pragmatic reasons. It represents an intentional effort to diminish the role of discretion and personality in the judicial enterprise."[27]

To listen to Scalia describe the features of the system, of textualism and "dogmatic democracy," one might suppose that he is doing little more than reporting what is largely beyond dispute. Just beneath the surface of the description, however, just beyond the modest "[a]ll I urge . . ." is a normative campaign drastically to shorten (what H. Jefferson Powell refers to as) "the list of legitimate modalities"[28] by which to approach the work of a federal judge and, with it, law in general. The grand theory urged must contend, like it or not, with the unacknowledged fact that the Constitution simply does not fix the modalities of its own construction and implementation, nor, for that matter, does it define "the Judicial Power" that it undertakes to vest. These points are too plain to merit argument here. Whatever its merits or demerits, textualism is one man's (or a group's) argument for a constitutional order of a certain kind. At the very least, then, Scalia's position should be acknowledged for what it is: "a proposal for radical reform."[29]

That other judges on the Court are doing worse things than Scalia is no reason not to put Justice Scalia to the test. Though I shall say a word about the upside of Scalia's proposal at the end, first I wish to highlight the general, adverse consequences of constructing and inhabiting such a system as Scalia has in mind. According to Scalia, the people have spoken; from now on, the law rules *ex proprio vigore*—at least, that is, to the extent judges succeed in that all-important legal work of hemming themselves in by creating rules and construing them formalistically. "Authority" amounts for Scalia simply to a democratically generated warrant, backed by the coercive power of the state, to behave in certain ways (but not others).

What has become of authority in the robust sense we usually think of it? That is, authority not as mere licensed power, but as that power that is worthy of respect and even intelligent obedience? The suggestion I made at the outset is that, like it or not, the axiomatic, asymptotic elimination of the human person by the interposition of a system of texts entails the elimination of any possible source of authority in law. Has Justice Scalia not sacrificed the authority of law on the altar of text and democracy?

A possible preemptive reply to this suggestion is that the democratically enacted text, given effect by a constitutionally licensed judge, is itself just as much authority as one can hope for. Such a reply becomes the more plausible the more one scratches the surface of Scalia's textualism and observes that the textualist judge, his claimed passivity notwithstanding, invents and justifies his own role (through his campaign for radical reform), thus becoming a sort of *sub rosa* authority, at least to the extent that his plea for a "textualist" judiciary succeeds in winning judicial adherents. To the extent, moreover, that the textualist succeeds in using law to create conditions in which justice has more of a chance of being done (than by, say, the judicial "activists" Scalia fingers), there is objective merit in what he is doing.

This line of reply eventually founders, however, on the fact that, whatever the admirable consequences of his efforts, the textualist judge is engaged in a systematic campaign to eliminate the problem of authority in law by eliminating the source of authority. This he does by severing the link between the meaning of texts human subjects create in the name of law and the meaning those texts will have in the mind and hands of the judge giving them effect (and of the citizen receiving them and deciding what action to take). Notwithstanding his vigorous protestations that his role is virtually supine, the textualist does not so much conform to the meaning of the legal text as construct it. Not looking for the real meaning of the text ("what the lawgiver meant"), he supplies a meaning for "what the lawgiver promulgated."[30] The decisive point is that the successful textualist has decamped from a world in which texts come to him with a meaning to be mined to a world of his own creation, a world in which he supplies the legislator's texts with a meaning of his own construction. One might call this an act or appearance of authority—except that it is, in fact, authoritarian, for the simple reason that it amounts in the end to *ipse dixit*. Yes, the textualist canvasses dictionaries and other sources, but can they provide anything other than schedules of probable—rather than real—meanings?[31] *Auctoritas, quo vadis*?

The textualist judge turns out to be an "activist" of a novel and remarkable sort, but meanwhile the appearances (of his deference and passivity) are kept up. Persons are not allowed to appear—this in order to make text, as much as possible, the only appearance in law. The result is texts awaiting the assignment of meaning, authority in abeyance. Joseph Vining catches the underbelly of textualism and "dogmatic democracy," its ineluctable lack of authority:

> There is always an enormous difficulty, an enormous struggle in law particularly, to recall and keep in mind that language is evidence of meaning, not meaning itself. The struggle comes from the thirst to know, for closure, that can always be slaked for the moment by illusion, but at a cost and often a terrible cost. The difficulty, the struggle, is the difficulty of listening, and it is a person one listens to—only a person, whom one approaches in good faith, which includes faith that there is a person to be heard. Axiomatic elimination of the person, at least from conscious presence in the reasoning mind, is a way of cutting short the struggle, stopping the work of listening. It is precisely the elimination of the person that permits one to think of rules not as linguistic evidence but as having a real existence of their own. . . . So there is always the temptation in law to approach a statute as if its words had meanings in themselves and by themselves—the authoritarianism sometimes shown by those devoted to maintaining the supremacy of democratic politics and legislative authority. . . . But over the long run lawyers do not succumb. They pull themselves away from the common temptation. Something that

has authority pulls you into the spirit of it. Without spirit there can be no authority. Without authority there is no law.[32]

The trouble with a system such as Scalia's, so Vining suggests, is that it does what it can to hide—and thus to leave unregulated—the potential human sources of authority, thereby becoming authoritarian in the name of "dogmatic democracy." One might be tempted to reply that the lawgiver's texts really do carry authority lodged within themselves, and that my fear for authority's absence is unfounded. But if black marks on white pages carry authority in themselves, then perhaps too the etchings on rocks caused by centuries of random rubbings and collisions? And the configurations of the clouds blowing by, of sticks and twigs washed up on the sea's shore?

I submit that authority in law requires the presence and appearance of persons, human subjects living out their orientation to the real and the valuable. Though inevitably present in the legal world Justice Scalia confronts, these human sources of authority are eclipsed and law's claim to bind is loosened to the extent that they are denied. In developing this thesis, I shall put particular emphasis on the work of Joseph Vining, whom Steven Smith describes as "one of the most provocative but elusive legal thinkers of our time."[33] Whether the approach to authority can now be other than oblique remains to be seen.

DENZINGERTHEOLOGIE IN LAW?

"Over the long run lawyers do not succumb," Vining assures us. But Scalia succumbs, and invites—and sometimes forces—the rest of us to come along. Gordon Wood has opined that "[t]he real source of the judicial problem that troubles Justice Scalia lies in our demystification of the law, which is an aspect of the general demystification of all authority that has taken place in the twentieth century." Wood suggests that perhaps we should "remystify some of what lawyers and judges do"[34]—a suggestion Scalia would counter with the unexceptionable observation that the bell announcing legal realism cannot be unrung.[35] There is another alternative, however, one that only requires that we get to know ourselves—not according to the reductive descriptions offered by the realists, but as we really are. Rather than "remystify" law, we might follow Joseph Vining and observe that what we do in law, notwithstanding what we sometimes say about it, is everywhere full of the traces of genuine authority, the legal manifestation of human spirit working itself out—or, in my idiom, subjects obedient to inner law. To observe and heed these appearances of authority is always a struggle, one that Scalia rejects with his frank and final preference for a system of legal rules.

Why, we might ask, does Justice Scalia succumb? Why is Antonin Scalia, of all people, engaged in an "intentional effort" to construct as closed a system of law as possible? "Dogmatic democracy" and textualism do not make the only response to legal realism, and some of the other possible responses, which mount a more frontal assault than Vining's invitation to attend to what we in fact do that breathes authority in law, appear quite in line with the Catholic tradition with which Scalia generally aligns himself.[36] Scalia's fervent Catholicism and deep immersion in the Catholic intellectual tradition are *concessa* on all sides. Justice Scalia, without engaging in a pseudo-remystification project, indulging a single woolly idea, or even struggling to follow Vining's charting of authority's pulse in the breadth and depth of our legal practice, could take his stand with St. Thomas Aquinas and say, contra textualism and "dogmatic democracy," that an unjust law is no law at all. Antonin Scalia, of all people, knows better than that "God applies the natural law." He also knows that one can travel a long way with "legal positivism" without denying, as textualism welded to "dogmatic democracy" does, that positive law cannot violate the natural law without thereby losing *pro tanto* its capacity to bind as a legal norm.[37]

George Kannar's insightful study of Justice Scalia's jurisprudence sheds light on this question, and, by doing so, contributes to an answer to our guiding question about the locus of authority in what we do in the name of law. Kannar's critical insight is that Scalia the Catholic was acculturated into a religious-theological world in which, when it comes to articulating what we believe in, or to stating the norms by which we are to live, "we" do nothing or as little as possible—or, at least, we cause ourselves to appear to do as little as possible. According to Kannar, more formative of Scalia's legal mind than the "'higher elements' of the Catholic legal tradition" is the approach to text and history that prevailed in those self-effacing religious-theological circles of Scalia's youth. Kannar avers that "in understanding that experience, a page of the Baltimore Catechism may be worth a volume of Aquinas."[38] Even more helpful than a page of the Baltimore Catechism, perhaps, would be a page from the *Enchridion Symbolorum Definitionum et Declarationum De Rebus Fidei Et Morum*, the text that in many ways provides the background not only to the Baltimore Catechism, but also to much else that grew up in Catholic practice during the period before the 1950s and 1960s.

Although Catholics who knew the Church before the Second Vatican Council (1962–1965) were plenty familiar with the idea that in the Church's magisterium there is "authority," paradoxically the magisterium and many of the Church's influential theologians minimized the need for or function of the voice of authority in the life of Catholics. (Which no doubt has something to do with why so many Catholics of that period, and those who view them uncharitably, see the Church as an authoritarian institution.) If it is too crude to say that the appearance created was one of the teaching Church engaged in a kind of ventriloquism, we can say, with Bernard Lonergan, that the theologian, or perhaps even the magisterium itself, was frequently engaged in *Denzingertheologie*:

> What Karl Rahner refers to as Denzingertheologie, the late Pierre Charles of Louvain named Christian positivism. It conceived the function of the theologian to be that of a propagandist for church doctrines. He did his duty when he repeated, explained, defended just what had been said in church documents. He had no contribution of his own to make and so there could be no question of his possessing any autonomy in making it.[39]

This way of doing theology takes the epithet by which it is known from the book of quotations of papal and conciliar pronouncements originally edited by Heinrich Denzinger in 1854.[40] As the book went through dozens of editions over a century and a half, Denzinger was succeeded by other editors, including the estimable Karl Rahner, S.J. (1904–1984), but his name remained and named a method of theology enabled by the handy book of quotations. The practitioner of *Denzingertheologie* proceeded by adducing proof-texts that were treated as timeless nuggets to be arranged and rearranged as fresh situations might invite. The truths given voice were said to be "semper et ubique eadem," always and everywhere the same; the Church, in reaching new formulations of these dogmatic truths, was neither adding nor subtracting, merely giving new expression. This is a complex phenomenon that is not readily summarized, but Kannar captures its thrust:

> [The Catholic worldview sought] to reduce thought to "formulae" rather than to inspire a deeper reflection on ultimate historical or moral values, or on any abstract higher law. "The mode of theology was constant—a simultaneous linking and severing in the Scholastic distinguo. To know the terms was to know the thing, to solve the problem. So we learned, and used, a vast terminology," all in the service of a life-absorbing, habit-forming "urge to codify reality and capture it in rules." . . . Linguistic essentialism seems second-nature. To reject "policy" as a starting point is thus a rather easy thing to do.[41]

This was the world of a decadent scholasticism, in which, as Bernard Lonergan describes, "[t]he chair is still the chair of Moses, but it is occupied by scribes and Pharisees. Traditional doctrine is still taught, but it is no longer convincing. The religious order still reads out the rules, but one may doubt that the home fires are still burning."[42] In such a world, some people's ideal theologian comes to resemble "a parrot with nothing to do but repeat what has already been said."[43]

Such was the way of much of the Catholic world in the period immediately before the Second Vatican Council did its work. It is often said that the council "made changes" in the Church, and as regards discipline and practice this is plainly true. But more important is the council's work on change itself: "The meaning of Vatican II," Lonergan says, "was the acknowledgment of history."[44] The point Lonergan here makes epigrammatically, and expounds and elaborates extensively elsewhere, is that at Vatican II the Church recognized her place in an ongoing process called history.[45] No longer pretending to live outside of time and above change, the Church reinstated reality—which includes the "deposit of faith" as well as the warp and woof of the change in which it is transmitted and received—as the object of concern and inquiry. Moving from what Lonergan called the "classicist" to the "historicist" operative stance, the Church recognized that her call to live in and by the truth entails the subordination of texts, even inspired texts, to fresh insights into those texts and the reality they concern.[46] In its Dogmatic Constitution on Divine Revelation (*Dei verbum*), the council explained that "[t]here is a growth in insight into the realities and words that are being passed on."[47] Texts were thus freed to be the contingent and conditioned—if hugely important, and, in the case of scripture, inspired—helps to understanding reality that they are.

What exactly the Church acknowledged in this connection at Vatican II is much debated,[48] but present purposes do not require the taking of a stand on a disputed question. This much is beyond dispute: any acknowledgment of change—and there was some—makes inescapable the question of what assures or guarantees, if anything does, that such change will be in the right direction. In short, without timeless texts as a putative last word, the role of authority in both assuring authentic development and preventing false development is out in the open. Thus exposed, the question has been the occasion of a most vigorous debate over the last half century. With respect to growth in insight into divine revelation, however, *Dei verbum* already affirmed that those "in the episcopate," to whom as a group in union with the Bishop of Rome the "deposit of faith" is entrusted, possess "the sure charism of truth" ("charisma veritatis certum").[49] The question of authority can be debated, but there is no question but that the magisterium will not err in its interpretation of the deposit of faith.

Thus the magisterium of the Church, on herself and divine revelation. When it comes to matters of state and statecraft, however, there can of course be no hope of landing anyone or a group possessed of "the sure charism of truth"—indeed, we justly fear and flee those who are cocksure of themselves as concerns the extent of our and the neighbors' civil liberties. The Church's divine assurance of not slipping into error assures that the discussion will concern how—not whether—her teaching is certainly true as concerns divine revelation and what is contained in it. Architects of state, by contrast, lacking all assurance of access to the truth about human living, are remitted to what means of argument meet the test of our desire for the real and the valuable. To return to a proximate example, even textualism in constitutional interpretation is not self-certifying, a point even Justice Scalia would be quick to concede (preferring to end his regress with "dogmatic democracy").[50] We are possessed of a constitution and a tradition of its interpretation, but even for the legal force of these a case must be made out and minds persuaded.

It would make sport of a most serious matter to say that, in the face of our reliable fallibility, Scalia punts. This is no game. Which is why we should say instead that, faced with no guarantees that we shall succeed in our efforts to know the truth and live by it in law, Scalia preempts the whole enterprise of seeking the truth in hope of living by it. "Dogmatic democracy" is Scalia's sufficient justification for this interdict, to which he sometimes adds the proposition that statecraft has nothing to contribute to. Leaving it to God to implement the natural law, Scalia is content with democratically generated rules—a system of texts—as our bottom line.

In sum, the Church put away positivism by reminding us that what matters is living according to the truth, not according to formulations; Justice Scalia, by contrast, has staked his claim, and our collective living, on the legal analogue of *Denzingertheologie*. Can we blame him? "[T]here is always the temptation in law to approach a statute as if its words had meanings in themselves and by themselves—the authoritarianism sometimes shown by those devoted to maintaining the supremacy of democratic politics and legislative authority."

RESISTING THE TEMPTATION—HOLDING OUT FOR AUTHORITY

"When literate cultures are in crisis," David Tracy observes, "the crisis is most evident in the question of what they do with their exemplary written texts."[51] Scalia is an important phase in—not the whole of—legal history; "over the long run lawyers do not succumb." But if they do not succumb—because they discern that nothing less than living in a way equal to our human dignity is at issue—still we have to ask exactly how it is that we can use texts in law without becoming authoritarian about them. If Scalia's solution to the problem of human living has the faults that we have been outlining, still we should not underestimate the problem to which an authoritarian textualism seems to Scalia to be the solution. As Mary Ann Glendon has commented cryptically but clearly enough, "Our legal culture also explains why many friends of democratic and rule-of-law values have been driven to expound what most civil lawyers would regard as excessively rigid forms of textualism."[52] Texts have the apparent advantage that they are there to be paid attention to—whereas everyone acknowledges that authority, even if it is real, is nothing anyone can touch.

Although there is some serious (if generally shallow) discussion of it in the Anglo-American jurisprudential literature, authority remains an outlier in scholarly legal discourse. In fact, law's initiation rites disparage the conditions of authority from the threshold, only half by accident. I refer to the "orientation" in which first-year law students are told—frequently by instructors (not professors) parroting some out-of-date, photocopied text provided by someone "in charge of orientation"—that our way of doing law, which will be the object of their attention for the next three years of their lives, affirms and depends upon "a hierarchy of authorities." But such stilted discourse rings hollow, and within days or at most weeks, disorientation takes hold. No longer delayed by questions of "authority" and implausible "hierarchies" of the same, students are busy dividing the legal engine between "law" and the lawless—that is, between "black-letter law" and "policy." Echoing too many professors and a profusion of "study guides," law's students have begun to imagine that law is what it is and speaks for itself; and policy, no one need be told, has always its advocates to advocate for it. This is only one man's report from the classroom, but he has heard the basis of it a thousand times: "Professor, are you making a policy argument or is this the black-letter law you're talking about?" As for Justice Scalia, it's just as simple as that—or, at least, one can always *say* that it's that simple.

But practicing lawyers, or at least the better ones, know better—know that texts are not as handy as the textualist would have you believe and that "policy" isn't an adequate description of the "what else" that goes into making law. Lawyers do not just find texts, black marks packed with rules ready to be dislodged and "applied," or dislodged and then massaged with policy until ripe to be given effect. Lawyers turn to texts all right, but as part of a process very different from the one outlined during "orientation." As Vining observes, "the texts to which they turn are selected and are old, necessarily from the past, requiring translation over time and between languages and places, year to year, decade to decade."[53] Denzinger left the texts in the Greek or Latin in which he found them, but he did do the work of selection for generations of Catholic theologians, many of whom forgot that there had been selecting[54]—this despite the introductory note "Selectio documentorum," and the additional introductory note on the authority of the included selections, "Valor documentorum." Lawyers lack a Denzinger. As practicing lawyers know, they, and judges too, must do their own selecting.

Denzinger limited his selections to papal and conciliar pronouncements, for reasons that find ready (though by no means uniform) resonance in the Catholic tradition. But what are the practicing lawyer's or judge's principles of exclusion and inclusion? It would seem to be at least in part a matter of "selection" that the Constitution of the United States rather than, say, the Articles of Confederation or the Code of Justinian, or a recipe on a shelf in Gary Lawson's kitchen[55] is to be consulted for what is to be law for us here and now—but on what principle? The constitutions and statutes of forgotten empires line the walls of the great museums and libraries, but are they to be selected? What of "foreign law"? What of the assertions by members of the current Supreme Court that foreign sources of law should—or should not—be consulted? "Overruling" is a fact of legal life the legitimacy of which no one denies; but if *Plessy v. Ferguson* is still "on the books"—or at least "in" the U.S. Reports, it is no longer evidence of what is law for us. And so forth.

Resisting this destabilizing claim, an objector will object that "surely" what the legislature, "our legislature," gives us is "the law." "Certainly," it will be said, "what the U.S. Congress casts into the world, that has gone unvetoed and survived judicial-review, is law for us in America. Which is why," the etymologically edified objector will continue, "we call it a legislature, not a consideration-bearer. Surely, at least within the confines of these United States, what the Congress launches is law, it being granted on all sides that in a cloistered monastery lodged on the coast of a remote island on the opposite side of the world, what the U.S. Congress issues by way of the Government Printing Office is no more 'the law' than is the wisdom of a Doonesbury cartoon that appears on the same day."

What this well-intentioned line of objection overlooks is how and why even here and now the achievement of Congress's voting for, promulgating, and publishing some black marks, which then go unvetoed by the president and survive "judicial review," does not achieve law for us. As Vining says, "Statutes and regulations are only candidates for attention, not just in competition for enforcement resources, but in the very analysis of situations. This is to be observed historically from without. It is also experienced by lawyers, from within."[56] Vining softens the blow of this insight by exemplifying the point from another continent:

> the piece of writing that emerges from Parliament is not the law. It is evidence of the law, which is used in the course of arriving at a statement of law. Legislation is the arbitrary that we allow—but also limit. To make the point in its strongest form, it could be said legislation is lawless behavior, except that by a paradoxical trick we make legislative statutes materials we use in determining what the law is.[57]

To take a more proximate example from contemporary administrative law as it is practiced on this continent, section 706 in the Administrative Procedure Act (1946) states that a "reviewing court shall . . . hold unlawful and set aside" agency action that fails any one of a number of statutorily defined criteria. But when, in 2002, it was presented with an argument that it must set aside an agency action that it had found unlawful, the U.S. Court of Appeals for D.C. Circuit said, per Judge Silberman, that it "is simply not the law" that it must set aside the unlawful agency action; and for this proposition of discretion to decide whether to set aside the unlawful agency action the Judge Silberman cited earlier precedent of the same court decided in 1993 (while ignoring the contrary precedent decided in 1994).[58] To say what the law is requires taking all this—what is said, what is done—and more, into consideration.

To put the point more broadly, the possibility of the executive veto, which invites the possibility of the supermajority, the possibility of judicial invalidation on review or on collateral attack—these are but incidents of legislative text's not being law *ex proprio vigore*. With exceptions that prove the rule, we do not give effect as law what we cannot or will not say is worthy of being acted upon intelligently. No lawyer arguing to a court about the correct disposition of agency action found unlawful can ignore section 706; at the same time, it would fly in the face of intelligent practice to ignore that the text has not been dispositive of what has been done in all cases in which it was relevant. Lawyers and others engaged in the process of ascertaining the law look both to what has been, and to what is being, done:

> Words of law are not givens of the world. . . . The very words themselves are not given. They are found. Even focal texts, that become concrete particulars of the lawyer's world from time to time, carry no meaning a lawyer can reach up and break off like a bit of crystal. Constructing a statement of law to be acted upon, a lawyer constantly seeks a real meaning, drawn from all the evidence. The evidence is not only other words. It includes action, what is done.[59]

And this fact about what we do, that trumps what we sometimes say, brings us nearer the heart of the matter. We might say that the principle of exclusion and inclusion is given in part by something operative inside the lawyer engaged in what we call "the legal process." In Vining's way of putting it, "[t]he past and its texts enter the experience of legal authority through legal method and its presuppositions, which are subtler than statements commonly made about them would suggest."[60]

Lost on—or denied by—the maestro who looks for law exactly in text is the fact that before there can be law, there is a person making a decision. Democratically enacted rules of general applicability—whatever their wisdom and whatever their appeal to Friedrich Hayek—do not of their own vigor rise to the level of law for any community. No particular text or assemblage of texts stands as the law; and though it makes sense as a kind of shorthand to refer (as we do) to law's textual sources as the law itself, it makes nonsense of law to go on then to imagine that it exists apart from decisions leading to conduct. "There is always, in law, a decision maker, and what are called rules in law are expressions of considerations to be taken into account by a decision maker." Vining continues:

> They focus not on themselves as a self-contained system but upon decision-making activity pointing forward. Talk of rights and rules of a static kind, projecting an image of law standing off by itself, obscures the focus that legal rules have in fact, always a decision that must be made, at the edge of lives that have not been lived before, in a world that has not been seen before.[61]

Again, what the simplifications of the positivists and codifiers miss, in their efforts to get law nailed down, is that there is no law unless decisions are being made to guide conduct in the name of law. The question of what conduct is proper or permissible is a question of concrete fact, and unless we are talking about guides to conduct, we aren't quite talking about law, though we may be talking about its sources or about what evidences to it. And when it comes to what should shape and structure our guides to conduct in the inevitable thick of life's particulars, nothing is ruled out a priori, at least not absolutely.

Lawyers do not have nice specifications of what evidence can be looked to when inquiring what the law is on a matter. There is a technique, which is to focus on a canon of texts and, if they are available, upon central texts generated by an institutional arrangement that is usually hierarchical in form. But in reading those texts, reading them seriously to understand them, lawyers do not "exclude evidence" (as a litigating lawyer would say), close their eyes to evidence of meaning (or lack of meaning). Some of that evidence is of the kind we call sociological. All of the evidence is about the life of the aspirations and ways of thinking with which lawyers work. There is, as a consequence, no notion of the "purely legal." Legal discourse is not a closed system. The meaning of texts is a real meaning.[62]

Why must this be so? Because it is intelligent human life and aspirations that are at issue. We do not confront law as largely inert automatons. We come to law, and deciders create law, because of our constitutive eros to know and instantiate the valuable (and avoid the valueless). We can do less, but what essays in "law" that start some place other than with the importunate human subject miss, is that law is about us, about us as we are and might yet become. "Law" that does not respond to our genuine needs reaches us as that "unintelligible restraint." Law is a tool to assist in satisfying the human longing to discover and live by the truth and to instantiate the valuable; what fails to fulfill this function fails to be law. Like other artifacts of our human creation, law cannot be used—except perversely—to frustrate the purposes of those who create it and need it.

With respect to texts specifically, it is inevitable that those who create them today in aid of human living risk that those who come the next day will live in the past and dodge the day. But the practicing lawyer, tightly situated within the practical matrix of the work of making statements of law to be lived by, will—and, we can say, should—use the inherited texts not to dodge, but to meet, today's exigencies. That he sometimes does what he knows to be less is not an argument for settling for less, in what we do in the name of law.

This subordination of texts in law to the (life) project to which they are a part risks appearing to undervalue texts, so it will be worthwhile to emphasize why this appearance would be false. It is easy to identify the shortcomings of *Denzingertheologie* without appearing to slight the relevant texts, for no one engaged in Christian theology flirts with jettisoning sacred text. When, however, we observe that practicing lawyers regard—and argue that practicing lawyers should regard—texts as potential contributors to statements of law, not as the law itself and by itself, then we can seem to some insufficiently appreciative of text. But what good lawyers do with text is very much like what students of sacred texts do with their texts, and the reasons for this similarity, as Vining observes, overlap:

> Close reading, reading in every detail and in every way, is at the very center of what lawyers qua lawyers do, and other parts of lawyers' method and the institutional structure of law are designed to make close reading possible. Anything closely read and reread must be there some time, always aging, if only to permit rereading. The rereading of some texts, the Confucian, the Vedaic, the Torah, for example, may go on forever.
>
> But the large fact remains that in law focal texts, no matter how old, are not fixed. No legal text is immune from challenge and substitution, not even statute or constitutional provision. If one does not understand a text despite all efforts of one's own and others, if in the end it does not fit, has no resonance, it then cannot hold its place. . . .
>
> No one, again, simply mouths the words of legal texts. They are read for their meaning, translated, restated by one who, responsible for the effects of what he says and does, will give orders or contribute to orders as he believes himself to be ordered by what he hears. The search for authority is a search for a voice beyond the brute facts of the past unfolding into the present.[63]

Lawyers, like priests, turn to texts; and they pay them most careful heed. But just as the priest does not elide the text at hand with the Word of God, the lawyer does not substitute text for law. What we confront here—in this use of texts to reach what is beyond the text—is what at the outset I referred to as "the inner experience of law." Lawyers turn to texts, which they have selected and arranged; these they read assiduously, not to echo them but in aid of making a statement of law to be acted upon. But that statement, though not determined by text, is not ungoverned; it must satisfy the speaker's need to speak only what is worthy of being acted on. What gives the statement its worthiness to be acted upon? The answer, which I have been suggesting, is encapsulated in this passing observation by Lonergan: "One has only to peruse such a collection of conciliar and pontifical pronouncements as Denzinger's *Enchiridion Symbolorum* to observe that each is a product of its place and time and that each meets the questions of the day for the people of the day."[64] One can turn to texts to engage in archaeology, or to find palindromes, or to . . . One can generate texts to entertain, to edify, or to . . . Alternatively, one can turn to texts, and one can generate texts, in aid of meeting "the questions of the day for the people of the day" as concerns their living in community where, in the name of the community, justified coercion can be used to back certain kinds of conduct and eliminate others.

In this seemingly innocuous formulation—"meet[ing] the questions of the day for the people of the day"—is contained the very heart of the matter, the core of a whole philosophy of law for worthy human living. Those who would say what the law is, and thus expect obedience and not mere strategic compliance, must be meeting the questions of the day. Those not meeting the questions of the day are not worthy of being listened to by the people of the day, certainly not worthy of being obeyed by the people of the day. It would be a violation of their (our) own obligation to honor inner law to subordinate themselves (ourselves) to authorities ignoring their (our) questions. Those not meeting the questions of the day for the people of the day are, as lawyers say, irrelevant and immaterial—and perhaps even prejudicial. Those worth listening to and obeying, because they do meet the questions of the day for the persons of the day, speak with authority. Vining says of the mind that possesses authority that it possesses it in virtue of its caring. "For law, mind is caring mind. Mind that does not care is no mind to seek, no mind to take into oneself, no mind to obey: it has no authority."[65]

In the idiom I introduced at the outset, the mind possessed of authority is the human subject who is obedient to inner law. To be meeting the questions of the day for the people of the day—through all the quotidian researching, selecting, interpreting, evaluating, drafting, revising, submitting, arguing, rearguing, collaterally attacking, and so forth—is to be answering that constitutive human eros that orders us out of ourselves to discover and affirm what is and what is valuable and, then, to live accordingly. It is the very process of answering the questions that issue from our rational nature itself that generates authority. The process is not ungoverned, but neither does the constitutive criterion to which it is subject enter arbitrarily or violently. The eros for the real and the valuable enters from the lawyer's own rational subjectivity; and though we are passive with respect to its entering, it enters. It does not coerce our compliance, however, but awaits obedience. This constitutive eros for the real and the valuable, "the pure question," cannot by mistaken for the degenerate phenomenon that is idle curiosity or episodic questioning; it is, rather, the unrestricted desire to know the real and the valuable, which manifests itself in ever fresh questions that we can either meet or evade.

"Name it what you please," this eros drives and structures our worthy human living, and it does not make an exception for law, not even for "dogmatic democracy." Refusing to be dogmatic, it asks to govern the practicing lawyer's use of texts in aid of coming to decision of law to be acted upon. This is not to make the silly claim that the work-a-day practicing lawyer is thematically aware of "inner law"; the suggestion is, rather, that when he or she is struggling to speak with the requisites of authority, the practicing lawyer is obedient to inner law; and that when he or she is nagged by the injustice of unanswered questions and loose ends not tied up, it is the violation of inner law that is registering in conscience.

In sum, those living in conformity with inner law avoid the temptation to transmute our quest for law into the imposition of unintelligible restraint. Awaiting our dedication to meeting its demands, inner law does not coerce us. The "pure question" reaches us from within, not *ab extra*, and it constitutes our very rationality and intelligence; choosing to honor it is to live on the level of the dignity of our rational natures. To do less remains possible, but settling for less leaves our normative and unrestricted demand for answers to the questions unmet, our human potential denied. "Every closing off, blocking, denial of the empirically, intelligently, rationally, freely, responsibly conscious subject is also a closing off, a blocking, of the dominance of the higher aspirations of the human spirit and the human heart."[66] What we cannot do, without violating inner law, is to meet some questions arbitrarily or ignore others: "Negatively . . . the unrestricted desire excludes the unintelligent and uncritical rejection of any question, and positively the unrestricted desire demands the intelligent and critical handling of every question."[67] The human subject who dodges questions lacks authority, even in "law."

LOCATING AUTHORITY IN LAW: THE PROBLEM OF AUTHORITIES

We have traced law to authority, and authority to mind obedient to inner law; not text, but the mind that meets the questions of the day for the persons of the day speaks with authority. But not everyone who can speak with authority can bind with the coercive power of the law backed by the might of "the state." We confront, therefore, the relationship between authority and authorities.

A brute fact that frequently comes down to us from the past, and frequently obscures the line between authority and authoritarianism, concerns authorities, a fact reflected in the ambivalent connotation and denotation of this English word: "authorities." Sometimes the "authorities" are law enforcement folk conspicuous for their bluntness; other times the "authorities" are those who will get the work of justice done. When we "call in the authorities," or the authorities just arrive on the scene, we hope for the latter, but fear the former. We face the fact of men and women who ask to be regarded as authorities over us; the critical issue is to distinguish between those authorities who possess authority and those who cloak the authoritarian in legal garb. "The barbarian may wear a Brooks Brothers suit."[68]

The problem—we can call it the problem of the authoritarianism of false authorities—grows out of the conditions of cooperation. Acting alone, we can get very little done; reinventing the wheel assures either boredom or, in the alternative, an early demise. Cooperation, both across the ages and in the here and now, gets things done, and makes sustenance, and then progress, possible. Cooperation can occur quite spontaneously, but the limits of spontaneous cooperation prove to be severe. Cooperation, if it is to continue, must be regularized. The more cooperation is reticulated, ramified, and reinforced, the more powerful it becomes, and the more that can be accomplished. Spontaneity gives way to custom, and custom gives way to more formalized institutions. Offices are created, defined, and populated. Those who populate the offices we know as authorities—that is, "the officials to whom certain offices have been entrusted and certain powers delegated."[69]

As long as the authorities remain faithful to their offices and to the purposes for which those offices were created, and as long as conditions remain unchanged, things go as they did from the beginning. But conditions do not remain unchanged among the living. At the very least, new questions emerge. To take another example from administrative law, the question arises whether it would not be better for those charged with administering government benefits to proceed according to a grid rather than on a case-by-case basis? Would this not tend to assure more thoroughly informed and, therefore, intelligent results?[70] We might be able to go on doing things the old way, but these new questions invite new answers. Correlatively, the fact of new learning clarifies the possibility of, and invites satisfaction of the conditions of, progressive and cumulative learning. Cooperation is not just horizontal; as I observed above, it can be vertical and span the ages. In order to meet the questions of the day, changes will have to be made to accommodate and assure new learning (without becoming amnesiac about what we already know, condemning ourselves to reinventing the wheel).

Meeting the questions of the day for the people of the day means keeping up with new questions. To the extent, however, that offices have been designed and parceled out in a brittle way, the officeholders will lay claim to terra firma on which to resist new questions and the new directions in which they might lead. And even offices designed and parceled out with an openness to adaptation may by now be populated by authorities who have grown officious; instead of continuing the pattern of growing and ramifying cooperation that produced and populated the offices in the first place, the authorities dig in their heels and rule some challenges out of court. Today's questions are stifled; the possibility of progressive and cumulative learning, and with it more developed living, is denied. Stasis sets in and then is enforced; people begin to talk about the offices as though informed by Platonic Forms. "[M]y only authority as a judge to prevent the state from doing what may be bad things is the authority that the majority has given to the courts."

To press the mutability of offices is not to call for (what Judge Noonan once referred to as) "a roving constitutional convention"; indeed, quite the reverse. It won't do to live, as Michael Oakeshott said of Descartes, every day as though it were one's first. For the reasons I have been developing, offices need to be structured in such a way as to facilitate drawing on and further developing (and, as necessary) correcting the inherited knowledge and wisdom. Nothing short of "the stages of human historical process" depend on people's success in developing methods for becoming "more reasonable and responsible in the various arrangements of their cooperative and personal living."[71] The creation of offices that allow us to live more reasonably and responsibly, by meeting the questions of the day, is the low door in the wall that leads to a decent or perhaps even better future. As Joseph Flanagan observes portentously, "We can mark off the major periods in the history of culture by the way different historical communities control [the] functions of knowing and choosing, or by the different methods that cultures have developed to govern their personal and collective making of history."[72] The key is to keep the offices in service of living, in service—that is, not of the *status quo ante*, but of progressive and cumulative learning that meets the questions of each new day.

The original parceling out of offices, by custom and usage, were justified in fact by its contributing to meeting the questions of the day for the people of the day. As custom and usage gives way to law, the legalistic solution is always just around the regulatory corner. Legalism enjoys some of law's aura and prestige, but is much more efficient. Its peculiar genius is not to get hung up on the questions of the day; its flaw is that, at least in the long run, it would prove fatal for the persons whose questions go unmet. Of course, if we succeed in ignoring or denying, first, that persons have questions about how to live and live well, or, second, that in that failing to meet them in our collective living is to violate the inner law that we humans have in common, then we inure ourselves to some of the consequences of their going unanswered. We get used to that phenomenon identified by the philosopher-historian Eric Voegelin as the interdict on the question,[73] and so it happens that "[a] society in decline digs its collective grave with arresting efficiency."[74]

A complete anesthesia of the desire for the real and the valuable—an effective repression of the pure question—is a rare occurrence, however. Whatever the case with the neighbors (or the aliens or the poor or the disenfranchised) and what we hear said to be "good enough" for them, we have our own—and those we love and care about have their own—questions. We want to know this world, to know what is valuable. Inner law keeps inviting us to transcend the isolation of pure interiority, inviting us to answer and not interdict its questions. Our wanting to be knowers, our wanting to be people who discover the valuable—this is half, but only half, of the core of authority in law.

Not only do we desire to know the valuable, we also and concomitantly desire to instantiate it in our living. But just as knowing has its conditions (which are either satisfied or not), so, too, does instantiating the valuable. Desiring and knowing the valuable are not sufficient to the realization of its instances. There is nothing abstract or armchair about this. Concretely, succeeding—realizing the valuable in our living—requires cooperation, and cooperation works itself out in social structures. Social structures—such as economies, school districts, clubs, and corporations—succeed by helping us meet the questions of the day; they fail, and they cause us to fail, by leaving our questions unanswered, by stifling further questions.[75]

The social structure that is the legal system, our current concern, is good at getting us authorities, but the question ever remains whether the authorities are assisting us in meeting the questions of the day, questions about how to instantiate the valuable here and now, and tomorrow. Authorities who do so assist us possess authority; they lack authority who block or fail to assist our common engagement in this process of creating and developing structures that lead to instances of valuable living. In the context of law, the other half of authority's core consists of the concrete conditions in which we succeed in instantiating the valuable in our living.

The locus of authority in what we do in the name of law, then, is the community engaged in the ongoing work of asking and answering questions about the real and the valuable and creating the conditions for the progressive and cumulative entrance of knowledge about and the realization of what is truly valuable. Authority appears in the concrete judgments the community's decisionmakers—the community's "authorities"—reach in the name of the law. But though those appearances of authority are the personal achievements of individual human subjects, they would lack the authority necessary to be law for the community to the extent that they did not reflect and bear the community's inherited but cutting-edge insights into valuable living. Not for any reason having to do with the priority of "democracy," but because of the community's nonfungible accumulation of wisdom into the conditions of valuable living and ongoing engagement with the questions of the day, the community possesses authority. Descartes, by assaying to live every day as though it were his first, cut himself off from the community and thus from the possibility of meeting the questions of the day for the people, other than himself, of the day. Those who are meeting the questions of the day for the people of the day enjoy authority; those who are doing this on behalf of the community and with authorization to give it effect, even coercive effect if necessary, are the locus of authority in law.

Bernard Lonergan identifies authority with "the community that has a common field of experience, common and complementary ways of understanding, common judgments and common aims."[76] If there is a terminological trouble with this identification, it concerns Lonergan's locating authority in the community without regard to the nature and quality of that community's field of common judgments and aims.[77] On Lonergan's usage, a community of persons would enjoy authority no matter how dogmatically closed it was to further learning. Lonergan does go on at once to distinguish between "authentic" and "unauthentic" fields of common judgments and aims, and, thus, between authentic authority and unauthentic authority. Fundamentalist communities would therefore possess authority, but lack "authentic authority." Lonergan's usage is workable, but it would seem more to the point, and truer to common usage, to identify as authority—and authoritative—the community that is engaged in and committed to furthering judgments and aims that ask and answer the questions of the day, and as authoritarian the community that is collectively engaged in blocking the asking and answering of questions.

We began by inquiring "the locus of authority in what we do in the name of law." We have answered by tracing such authority to the community; more specifically, a community "living by the question"—that is, engaged in a common enterprise of asking and answering questions and then cumulatively and progressively creating the conditions that allow living by the results. Decisions guiding conduct and taken in the name of law rise to the level of law for the community by their being bearers of the community's present body of insight into valuable living and the means of its achievement. The creation and preservation of texts can aid the progressive and cumulative development of insight into such human living and the creation of conditions therefor; approached another way and with lesser purposes, the same texts can stunt or block valuable human living. If, as the possibility of progressive and cumulative results will demand, the community "transmits" its authority to agents with specific offices, thereby creating authorities, satisfaction of the conditions of authority ever remains necessary if the authorities are not to sink to the level of authoritarian bureaucrats.[78]

As to exactly how those conditions can be satisfied once such a transmission has been effected, something remains to be said in the final section. What I would emphasize first, however, is that to the extent that the authorities have given up being part of a communal project of asking and answering questions—that is, if, in Lonergan's idiom, they have given up being authentic—to that extent they have divested themselves of authority. Nor would it matter that the office "requires" this of them. Authorities may continue to wear the externalia, the badges of office that allow them to be recognized and distinguished from the vigilante; but unless they are in fact bearers of the community's learning about and quest for valuable living, they are mere authorities who lack authority. Whether someone merely wears the badges of office or actually, in addition, possesses authority—this remains always a question of concrete fact.

> Besides authority, authorities are also needed. If there are to be authorities, then over and above their authenticity there is needed some external criterion by which their position can be publicly recognized. But while this external condition is a necessary condition, it is not a sufficient condition. The sufficient condition must include authenticity. The external criterion need not be accompanied by authenticity. For in human beings authenticity always is precarious. Commonly, indeed, it is no more than a withdrawal from unauthenticity.
>
> Such, then, is the dialectic of authority.[79]

Authorities do not necessarily act with authority. There is the *ultra vires* act; more fundamentally, there is the act by the authority that, forsaking what authority it might have enjoyed, becomes officious and ceases to engage in meeting the questions of the day for the people of the day. By not allowing the questions of the day to occur, the authority decamps from authority to the authoritarian. It can be subtle, but its effect is blunt. Correlatively, authority, and with it law, is forever a fragile achievement.

THE DIALECTIC OF AUTHORITY: A SURE END TO "SOVEREIGNTY"

This dialectic, "the dialectic of authority," will come as a disappointment to some. Among the disappointed will be those who had hoped to get on in law with as little appearance of genuine authority as possible; for these, such as Scalia, the admission of authority in law, as other than a democratically sanctioned license, amounts to a necessity to be minimized. Also among the disappointed will be those who, frankly admitting the need for nonmarginal authority in the legal enterprise, would lodge and cabin it in firmly delineated offices and their officious personnel; for these, linking authority—and, with it, law—to a "dialectic" undermines the very solidity that law and its rule of rules were supposed to be about. But this dialectic, though not what many had wanted, may be just what we need; it is, in any event, the best we can do, though we often do much less.

Or, rather, seen from another angle, we often purport to do very much more. Law that is nothing short of sovereign is what Field boasted. The alternative position developed here has been that law, in the sense in which we ordinarily speak of it, is necessarily subordinate to (the dialectic of) authority and to inner law, and, therefore, never possessed of sovereignty. Of course, "sovereignty" is a slippery enough term that, with a little effort, one might be able to make it fit law that is subordinate to authority and inner law. But, as Stanley Benn concluded in his study of sovereignty, "there would seem to be a strong case for giving up so Protean a word,"[80] and that case, as made out by Jacques Maritain (1882–1973), is that "the term needed [in constructive political discourse] is not Sovereignty."[81]

The word conjures a legal regime or state that is comprehensive—a closed system from which there is no appeal. It was Maritain's judgment that "[t]he two concepts of Sovereignty and Absolutism have been forged together on the same anvil. They must be scrapped together."[82] The United States of today is no totalitarianism of the sort Maritain was reacting against, of course. However, a state in which (we are told) God takes care of the natural law, and the judge simply dispatches the democratic majority's business (except in the limit case in which he recuses himself), is a state that has smuggled sovereignty in through the back door of the courthouse. If, as Vining says, lawyers (like priests) sometimes speak for the sovereign,[83] this would be because they live in the dialectic of authority, not pretending to sovereignty but seeking authority in the only place it can be found.

> What is created in decision making by participants in the process [of law] can never be celebrated as individuals' self-governance—their own, however contingent or arbitrary, legitimate whatever it is—for it is not their own lot but others' that is being fashioned.

Knowledge of this is part of knowledge of law and continuously reconfirmed by practice in the actual operations of the organized human world. This is the strength of law, this knowledge. All are trustees, participants, and decisionmakers alike, arguing, deciding, approving, and reacting. All is discussion of value, all is drawn forward by value, all identification through time with those who are affected in the future and those who have made decisions in the past is through value. And the central concern of law, atheoretical, pretheoretical, is then connection of value and responsible mind, for value not connected by mind to responsible belief is mirage, nothing, vanishing when questioned or sought.

Thus law is at work before any political theory, and after political theory is finished speaking: nothing is secured by any tracing of power or jurisdiction to a formal source or process, kingly, judicial, legislative, or popular. Against the constant fading of the conditions of authority is what comes from law that pushes toward the personal and a context of decisionmaking in which the personal can be recognized, recognition of the personal being the only entrance to the experience of authority.[84]

In law, there is always a decisionmaker; which is why Vining is right to focus on the action of the individual's mind bringing value to bear on a decision of consequence. That individual subject acting through office in the name of the law, though he alone is responsible for satisfying the conditions that give him authority, does so by drawing on the common fund and dynamic of the community. Although the community needs its authorities, and thus to create offices, it is the community itself that is jurisgenerative—not by merely being a democratic majority, but, as I have argued, by living by the question. The common strain of thought that looks for law in the dictates of the state to the individual overlooks the true springs of authority in the community's common engagement in asking questions, answering them, and then, with the help of authorities, living by those answers.

Which brings me to the issue I reserved above, viz., how the conditions of "living by the question" are satisfied once the community has transmitted its authority to authorities. This is a complex problem, which space constraints allow me to address here only in outline. The preceding analysis has clarified that there is no authority where its conditions are not satisfied; the problem that attends the simple failure of those conditions to be satisfied is the different problem of counterfeit authorities—that is, of authoritarianism. This seems simple enough, except that the satisfaction of the conditions of authority is not, however, a scalar quantity. Most if not all concrete situations—and decisions guiding conduct are never taken apart from concrete situations—embody a messy amalgam of questions answered and questions evaded or suppressed. Lonergan suggests that sometimes what can be done in the face of such situations will amount to little more than the withdrawal from the unauthenticity and authoritarianism into which we have slipped. Most of the time we find ourselves in a world in which what inner law requires of us is not an all-or-nothing choice, but rather the choice to work as we can to be authentic ourselves and to encourage its conditions in the communities and social structures of which we are contributing members. In law, conscientious disobedience and recusal are examples of the more aggressive response that may be required. Revolution is the limit case.

In those times before revolution, and even before recusal and conscientious disobedience, one problem having to do with authority concerns how to keep the authorities—that is, the government officials who constitute "the state"—meeting the questions of the day for the people of the day. This is the problem on which most of contemporary constitutional theory of the "communitarian" or "civic republican" sorts has focused, and its focus on "dialogue" as the legitimating condition of governing has obvious parallels with my conditioning authorities' authority on their meeting the questions of the day for the people of the day.[85] The difficulties of solving this problem have largely prevented constitutional theorists of the sorts mentioned from facing that other, related problem of how such government is to create and sustain conditions in which nonstate actors can live by the question, and, doing so, shape the actions taken by their authorities.

The problem concerns not only the overt mechanisms of "self-government"; it also reaches its antecedent—that is, culture. By "culture" I mean the set of reasons and values we have for individual and collective action. Cultures are not given by nature; they have to be created and recreated (or decreated), and they are to be judged valuable, like social structures, inasmuch as they encourage us to ask questions and proceed to live by the answers.[86] A state bureaucracy fueled by intelligent asking and answering of questions will be of little value or relevance to a populace inculturated into passivity, drifting, lethargy, and rote rule-following. It has to be question-and-answer from the bottom to top; anesthetized subjects are ripe subjects for authoritarian depredations, not for authority and the law it can generate.

Because living by inner law means living in community—no one meets questions except within a common horizon of experience, understanding, knowledge, values, and aims—the state will have as part of its essential work the encouragement of communities committed to collective learning. The vitality of such communities will depend more on friendship and love than on the aid of the state, but the state, too, at least much of the time, will have a positive responsibility to nurture such communities; indeed, the nurturing of such communities will be one of the reasons that justify the very creation of that particular community of authorities that constitutes "the state." The authority of such communities does not derive from the state. On the line of analysis pursued here, the authority of any community comes from its collective obedience to inner law. The state, then, as a community of persons united by a set of questions having to do with the good of the whole body politic and empowered to give legal effect to answers to those questions, is one authority among others.

A principal problem of statecraft, when the state does not succumb to the temptation to crush competing communities and their respective authorities, and thereby deny people the opportunity to meet the questions that those communities uniquely mediate, is the one of fostering, for the common good of all, the respective authorities of the plural communities in which people live and grow (or not).[87] Arguing against a notion of the state as either the embodiment of the entire body politic or the *sui generis* controller of all subordinate communities that stand between itself and individuals, one commentator observes that "the true picture is not a pole, with the State on one end and the other associations [or communities] in the middle, but a dense web, where all the associations, State and non-State, interact with and influence each other, and in which variant meanings and value systems flourish like plants in a tropical garden."[88] To this observation I would add that "value systems" that disvalue the question and honest answers to the same should not be expected, let alone encouraged by the state, to continue. That being said, such discriminations are not in fact always easy to make.

With respect to authorities acting in the name of "the state" and its law, we should anticipate a dialectic of authority. When, then, we see Justice Scalia tilting too far in the direction of rigidity, closure, and "dogmatic democracy," we can recall Professor Glendon's reference to "our legal culture."[89] Scalia's bid for radical reform operates against a background of intelligentsia who deny—through a form of judicial imperialism that falls at the other end of the spectrum from Scalia's—that values worth living by emerge through the community's (or, rather, communities') collective inquiry (or inquiries). As we assess Scalia's attempt to redress an imbalance caused by judicial legislation in derogation from the central moral tradition of the West, we observe a case in this point of Vining's: "Disputes in constitutional or administrative law," Vining observes, "are almost always in part about the design of institutions that will make law possible," by making authority possible.[90] If we sympathize with Scalia's attempt to create a closed universe of legal texts in response to a (legal) culture that would entrust judicial actors with power that many have grown accustomed to abuse, still we must observe that the unreasonable responses that unreasonable situations call forth remain, for all that, unreasonable. "The claim of illegality, persuasively made, is always the claim that what is, even if it has always been done, has no authority."[91] Except for the appearance of prophet or saint who shocks people into new ways of aspiring and living, the transitions to be made must be one at a time, meeting the questions of the day for the people of the day.

I have emphasized the dialectic of authority, but the final word must go to what at the outset I described as the "rock" on which we can perform the necessary dialectic. That rock on which we can build is the human subject's dynamic orientation toward, by way of his primal and unrestricted desire for, the real and the good. That rock is not a theory or a text, but it provides the concrete conditions under which the subject begins to move from pure interiority and come to know the real and the valuable and, then, to instantiate the valuable in his living. A full account of our interiority lies, of course, beyond the scope of this inquiry into authority in law; the goal here has been to suggest, in a preliminary way, why nothing else than meeting the human subject's eros for the real and the valuable will supply the authority necessary to law and worthy human living.

Michael Novak once said, in a self-conscious revision of the tradition, that the unrestricted desire for the real and the valuable is our "natural law."[92] That unrestricted desire does not compel us; God does not apply the natural law—our God-given drive for intelligence about the real and the valuable awaits our response:

> We are committed [to the realm of fact and value], not by knowing what it is and that it is worth while, but by an inability to avoid experience, by the subtle conquest in us of the Eros that would understand, by the inevitable aftermath of that sweet adventure when a rationality identical with us demands the absolute, refuses unreserved assent to less than the unconditioned and, when that is attained, imposes upon us a commitment in which we bow to an immanent Anagke. . . .
>
> The critical experience can weigh all else in the balance, only on condition that it does not criticize itself. It is a self-assertive spontaneity that demands sufficient reason for all else but no justification for its demanding. It arises, fact-like, to generate knowledge of fact, to push the cognitional process from the conditioned structures of intelligence to unreserved affirmation of the unconditioned. It occurs.[93]

The conquest is subtle. History reveals the frequency with which it occurs or fails to occur, and its further occurrence remains a choice. Such is the dilemma of living, including in law. The legal analogue of *Denzingertheologie* does remain a possibility, but only for those slouching into authoritarianism.

In conclusion, it remains to be said that it is not because our constitutive eros for the real and the valuable is (we think) coextensive with the entire world in which we live, and which we might create, that the last word goes to it; it has the final say because its scope is unrestricted. Our questions concern the beyond, and what is beyond what we know and do in this world is what promises to fulfill that unrestricted desire once and for all. The question who "we" are is, as I signaled at the outset, expansive. Denying that the form and direction of our political life have anything to do with life beyond the here and now, Justice Scalia would build a wall between this world and the beyond. What this occludes is the fact that those who follow the question in the here and now are—whether they recognize it or not—on their way to what is surpassing; they are on the way to recognizing the true and only Sovereign. "The question of God," as Lonergan says, "lies within man's horizon. . . . The contemporary humanist will refuse to allow the question to arise. But their negations presuppose the spark in our clod, our native orientation to the divine."[94]

NOTES

1. Joseph Vining, *From Newton's Sleep* (Princeton, N.J.: Princeton University Press, 1995), 344.
2. Pierre Schlag, "The Problem of the Subject," 79 *Texas Law Rev* 1627, 1743 (1991).
3. Vining, *From Newton's Sleep*, 128.
4. Mary Ann Glendon, *A Nation under Lawyers* (New York: Farrar, Strauss, & Giroux, 1994), 10.
5. Reconstruction is Pierre Schlag's term. See Schlag, "The Problem of the Subject," 1661–62.
6. Some of these are among the "grand theories" canvassed and criticized by Daniel Farber and Suzanna Sherry, *Desperately Seeking Certainty: The Misguided Quest for Constitutional Foundations* (Chicago: The University of Chicago Press, 2002).
7. Paul Kahn, *The Reign of Law* (New Haven, Conn.: Yale University Press, 1997), xi and 240.
8. See Cass R. Sunstein, *Legal Reasoning and Political Conflict* (Oxford: Oxford University Press, 1996), 35–61.
9. Kevin M. Crotty, *Law's Interior: Legal and Literary Constructions of the Self* (Ithaca, N.Y.: Cornell University Press, 2000), 90.
10. Francis George, "Law and Culture in the United States," 48 *American Journal of Jurisprudence* 131, 146 (2002).
11. David M. Granfield, *The Inner Experience of Law: A Jurisprudence of Subjectivity* (Washington, D.C.: The Catholic University of America Press, 1988).
12. Bernard Lonergan, *Insight: A Study of Human Understanding* (New York: Harper & Row, 1958), 221.
13. Lonergan, *Insight*, 9.
14. The expression "rock on which to build" is Lonergan's. See Bernard Lonergan, *Method in Theology* (Minneapolis: Seabury, 1972), 19.
15. Martin Stone, "Focusing the Law," in *Law and Interpretation: Essays in Legal Philosophy*, ed. Andrei Marmor (Oxford: Clarendon Press, 1995), 31, 57–60.

16. See Patrick McKinley Brennan, "Realizing the Rule of Law in the Human Subject," 43 *Boston College Law Review* 227, 239 (2002).

17. Thomas Paine, "Common Sense," *Common Sense and Other Political Writings*, ed. Nelson F. Adkins (New York: Liberal Arts, 1953), 3, 32.

18. David Dudley Field, quoted in Brian Z. Tamanaha, *On the Rule of Law: History, Politics, Theory* (Cambridge: Cambridge University Press, 2004), 79.

19. On the move to make law to be the sovereign, see W. J. Stankiewicz, *Aspects of Political Theory: Classical Concepts in an Age of Relativism* (London: Collier Macmillan, 1976), 62.

20. Pontifical Council for Justice and Peace, *Compendium of the Social Doctrine of the Church* (Vatican City: Vatican City Press, 2004), 230, par. 408. The quotation, which itself is wholly a quotation from the encyclical *Centesimus Annus* (1991), is from the English typical edition, prepared and published in Rome. The official Latin text of *Centesimus Annus*, though it does indulge in a personification of law, hardly seems to bear the English translation given it by the drafters of the *Compendium*: "dominator potassium leges."

21. Antonin Scalia, "Common-Law Courts in a Civil Law System," in *A Matter of Interpretation*, ed. Amy Gutmann (Princeton, N.J.: Princeton University Press, 1997), 17.

22. See Farber and Sherry, *Desperately Seeking Certainty*, 29.

23. Scalia, "Common-Law Courts," 25.

24. Ibid., 17, 25.

25. Antonin Scalia, "The Rule of Law as a Law of Rules," 56 *University of Chicago Law Review* 1180, 1187 (1989).

26. Antonin Scalia, "the Common Christian Good" (presented at a symposium entitled "Left, Right and The Common Good" held at Gregorian University on 2 May 1996). Transcription available at www.learnedhand.com/scalia.htm.

27. George Kannar, "The Constitutional Catechism of Antonin Scalia," 99 *Yale Law Journal* 1297, 1345 (1990).

28. H. Jefferson Powell, *A Community Built on Words: The Constitution in History and Politics* (Chicago: The University of Chicago Press, 2002), 209. Ralph Rossum, in his sympathetic *Antonin Scalia's Jurisprudence: Text and Tradition* (Lawrence: University Press of Kansas, 2006), acknowledges that Scalia is attempting something of a revolution in order to provide "constraints" on would-be activist judges. Id., at 203–7. What Rossum overlooks is how textualism itself depends on another species of activism. See this chapter, 167–68. See also Brennan, "Rule of Law," 306–18.

29. Powell, *A Community Built on Words*, 209.

30. The irony of the creative work of the textualist is explored in Brennan, *Rule of Law*, 305–18, through the example of Justice Scalia's opinion in the case *M.C.I. v. A.T. & T.*, 512 U.S. 218 (1994).

31. See Brennan, "Rule of Law," 316–17.

32. Vining, *From Newton's Sleep*, 239–41.

33. Steven Smith, *Law's Quandary* (Cambridge, Mass.: Harvard University Press, 2004), 170.

34. Gordon Wood, "Comment," in *Matter of Interpretation*, 49, 63.

35. As this provocative admission confirms: "That is why, by the way, I never thought Oliver Wendell Holmes and the legal realists did us a favor by pointing out that all these legal fictions were fictions: Those judges wise enough to be trusted with the secret already knew it." Farber and Sherry, *Desperately Seeking Certainty*, 38.

36. The gaping exception is his disagreement with the position taken on capital punishment in the encyclical letter by Pope John Paul II *Evangelium Vitae* (1995) and then in the *Catechism of the Catholic Church*, revised edition, with amendments following the publication of the *Edito Typica* (Vatican City: Libreria Editrice Vaticana; Washington, D.C.: United States Catholic Conference, 1997).

37. See John Finnis, "The Truth in Legal Positivism," in *The Autonomy of Law: Essays on Legal Positivism*, ed. Robert P. George (Oxford: Oxford University Press, 1996), 195.

38. Kannar, "The Constitutional Catechism of Antonin Scalia," 1313. The Baltimore Catechism was prepared for religious instruction in the United States at the request of the bishops of the Third Plenary Council of Baltimore (1884). It emerged first in 1891, and in its various editions and "numbers" (the higher the number, the more elaborated the presentation) structured most Catholic catechesis in the United States until it fell out of favor following the Second Vatican Council.

39. Lonergan, *Method in Theology*, 330–31.

40. In the thirty-sixth edition of the book, published in 1965 (Rome: Herder), the quotations numbered 3999. By the time of the thirty-eighth edition in 1995 (Bologna: Edizioni Dehoniae Bologna; edizione bilingue), the number had risen to 5041, thanks to the inclusion of texts from the Second Vatican Council.

41. Kannar, "Constitutional Catechism of Antonin Scalia," 1315–17.

42. Bernard J. F. Lonergan, "Pope John's Intention," in *A Third Collection: Papers of Bernard J. F. Lonergan, S.J.*, ed. Frederick Crowe (New York: Paulist Press, 1985), 224, 233.

43. Lonergan, *Method in Theology*, 331.

44. J. M. O'Hara, *Curiosity at the Center of One's Life* (Montreal: Thomas More Institute, 1987), 426.

45. Lonergan, *Method in Theology*.

46. See Bernard Lonergan, "The Transition from a Classicist World-View to Historical-Mindedness," in *Bernard J. F. Lonergan, S.J., A Second Collection*, eds. W. Ryan and B. Tyrrell (Philadelphia: Westminster, 1974), 1–9.

47. Austin Flannery, O.P., ed., *Second Vatican Ecumenical Council: The Conciliar and Post Conciliar Documents, Dei verbum* (1965) par. 8 ("crescit enim tam rerum quam verborum traditorum perceptio") (Boston: Costello, 1980), 754.

48. See e.g., John T. Noonan Jr., *A Church that Can and Cannot Change* (Notre Dame, Ind.: University of Notre Dame Press, 2005), 193–96.

49. Flannery, *Second Vatican*, 754.

50. For a helpful survey of these issues, with a particular emphasis on Scalia's normative argument for originalism/textualism, see Richard H. Fallon Jr., *Implementing the Constitution* (Cambridge: Cambridge University Press, 2001), 13–25.

51. David Tracy, *Plurality and Ambiguity: Hermeneutics, Religion, Hope* (Chicago: University of Chicago Press, 1987), 11.

52. Mary Ann Glendon, "Comment," in *Matter of Interpretation*, 113.

53. Vining, *From Newton's Sleep*, 239.

54. Mary Ann Hinsdale, for example, describes Denzinger's Enchiridion as "a comprehensive catalogue of official pronouncements of popes and councils." Mary Ann Hinsdale, "Infinite Openness to the Infinite: Karl Rahner's Contribution to Modern Catholic Thought on the Child," in *The Child in Christian Thought*, ed. Marcia Bunge (Grand Rapids, Mich.: Eerdmans, 2001), 406, 414n29.

55. See Gary Lawson, "On Reading Recipes . . . and Constitutions," 85 *Georgetown Law Review* 1823 (1997).

56. Vining, *From Newton's Sleep*, 227.

57. Ibid., 26.

58. See *Sugar Cane Growers Cooperative of Florida v. Ann M. Veneman*, 289 F.3d 89 (D.C. Cir. 2002); *Allied-Signal Inc. v. United States Nuclear Regulatory Commission*, 988 F2d 146 (D.C. Cir. 1993); *Checkosky v. SEC*, 23 F3d 452 (D.C. Cir. 1994).

59. Vining, *From Newton's Sleep*, 128.

60. Ibid., 110.

61. Joseph Vining, *The Authoritative and the Authoritarian* (Chicago: University of Chicago Press, 1986), 217–18.

62. Vining, *From Newton's Sleep*, 75, 76.

63. Ibid., 115.

64. Lonergan, *Method in Theology*, 296.

65. Vining, *From Newton's Sleep*, 32.

66. Bernard Lonergan, "The Human Good as Object: Differential and Integration," in *The Collected Works of Bernard Lonergan*, eds. Robert M. Doran and Frederick Crowe (Toronto: University of Toronto Press, 1993), 10: 63.

67. Lonergan, *Insight*, 638.

68. John Courtney Murray, *We Hold These Truths* (New York: Sheed & Ward, 1960), 12.

69. Bernard J. F. Lonergan, "Dialectic of Authority," in *A Third Collection*, 7.

70. See, e.g., *Heckler v. Campbell*, 461 U.S. 458 (1983).

71. Joseph Flanagan, *Quest for Self-Knowledge: An Essay in Lonergan's Philosophy* (Toronto: University of Toronto Press, 1997), 256.

72. Ibid., 222.

73. Eric Voegelin, *Order and History*, vol. 4, *The Ecumenic Age* (Baton Rouge: Louisiana State University Press, 1980), 330.

74. Bernard J. F. Lonergan, "Dialectic of Authority," in *A Third Collection*, 7.

75. For this phenomenon understood as sin as a component in social structures, see *The Collected Works of Bernard Lonergan*, 10: 60–61.

76. Bernard J. F. Lonergan, "Dialectic of Authority," in *A Third Collection*, 18.

77. Max Weber identified "authority" with "domination," and then distinguished "authority" from "legitimate authority," thereby beginning a tradition that tends to assimilate authority to domination. For Weber's usage, see Max Weber, *Economy and Society* (Berkeley: University of California Press, 1968), 1:31, 53. Cf. Vining, *From Newton's Sleep*.

78. On the history and philosophy of the "transmission" theory of authority, see, e.g., Yves Simon, *Philosophy of Democratic Government* (Notre Dame, Ind.: University of Notre Dame Press, 1951), 158–75.

79. Bernard J. F. Lonergan, "Dialectic of Authority," in *A Third Collection*, 11.

80. Stanley Benn, "The Uses of 'Sovereignty,'" *Political Studies*, 109, 122 (1955).

81. Jacques Maritain, *Man and the State* (Chicago: University of Chicago Press, 1951), 49.

82. Ibid., 53.

83. Vining, *From Newton's Sleep*, 263.

84. Ibid., 281.

85. See e.g., Paul Kahn, "Community in Constitutional Theory," 99 *Yale Law Journal* 1 (1989).

86. See Flanagan, *Quest for Self-Knowledge*, 200; Thomas Kohler, "The Integrity of Unrestricted Desire," in *Autonomy and Order*, ed. Edward W. Lehman (Lanham, Md.: Rowman & Littlefield, 2000), 61–65.

87. See Hittinger in this volume. See also Franklin Snyder, "Sharing Sovereignty: Non-state Associations and the Limits of State Power," 54 *American Law Review* 365 (2004).

88. Snyder, "Sharing Sovereignty," 377–78.

89. Glendon, *A Nation under Lawyers*, 113.

90. Vining, *From Newton's Sleep*, 312.

91. Ibid., 112.

92. Michael Novak, "Bernard Lonergan: A New Approach to Natural Law," XLI, Proceedings of the American Catholic Philosophical Association 246 (1967).

93. Lonergan, *Insight*, 331–32.

94. Lonergan, *Method in Theology*, 296. It may well be, as Smith suggests (in this volume) that we have become as a people almost incapable of recognizing the spiritual element in our constitution, but our ignorance does not alter that essential constitution.

10

"Hollow Men"? Law and the Declension of Belief

Steven D. Smith

"All men by nature desire to know," Aristotle maintained[1]; but he might more aptly have said that all men—or all women and men—desire, and need, to *believe*. Of the two—"believing" and "knowing"—believing seems to be the more imperative, and the more distinctively human.

THE HUMANNESS OF BELIEVING[2]

In fact, among the many qualities that supposedly distinguish us from other animals—or from androids, or angels, or gods—our capacity and propensity to *believe* is arguably the most central and cogent. Consider some other leading candidates. Man is supposedly the "rational animal." But computers engage in operations that can be described as *reasoning*; so do some animals—probably—and angels. Or take emotions. Except in science fiction stories like "I, Robot," computers cannot *feel*—cannot experience emotions such as love or hatred—but animals and angels surely can. Or sociability. Man is a *social* being, it is often and truly said; but then so are bees and ants—not to mention the celestial company of the seraphim and cherubim.

All of these qualities we share with other beings and species. But only humans can truly and genuinely *believe*. Even if computers *think*, as some philosophers argue, they surely do not believe; if someone remarks, "This laptop *says* the figures add up to 46.59, but I wonder whether it really *believes* that," we will think he must be joking. Nor do dogs or cats or cows believe, except perhaps in the most rudimentary sense.

Not even God believes, properly speaking. God knows too much. So "What does God believe about this?" is not a sensible question to ask.

Believing, it seems, is at the very core of what it means to be a human being, and it reflects our distinctive relation to *truth*—to truth not just in the sense of mundane facts ("It's raining outside"; "Tomorrow is Friday"), but to Truth in the upper case. Richard Rorty explains that "[u]ncapitalized, 'truth' and 'goodness' name properties of sentences, or of actions and situations. Capitalized, they are the proper names of objects—goals or standards which can be loved with all one's heart and soul, and mind."[3] Rorty offers this remark with a derisive tone, but Thomas Aquinas might have said much the same thing but without the sarcasm. Thus, Thomas declared that "[t]he ultimate end of the universe must . . . be the good of an intellect. This good is truth. Truth must consequently be the ultimate end of the whole universe, and the consideration of the wise man aims principally at truth."[4] One of the most important encyclicals of the spiritual leader for whom the Pope John Paul II Cultural Center is named begins: "The splendour of truth shines forth in all the works of the Creator and, in a special way, in man, created in the image and likeness of God. . . . Truth enlightens man's intelligence and shapes his freedom, leading him to know and love the Lord."[5]

These are exhilarating declarations—and, I believe, true ones. And yet, lest they mislead us, I think they need to be tempered with the gloomier observation from Psalm 39 that "verily every man at his best state is altogether vanity."[6] We are creatures oriented to truth, and yet in our mortal, finite, fallen condition, our grasp of truth is tenuous. For the most part, we walk by faith, seeing "through a glass, darkly,"[7] believing as well and as truly as we can: that seems to be our distinctive fate and our special glory. And what we most essentially are—as individuals, as societies—is to a significant extent determined by what we centrally believe. Thus Chesterton's comment that "the most practical and important thing about a man is still his view of the universe. . . . The question is not whether the theory of the cosmos affects matters, but whether, in the long run, anything else affects them."[8]

If believing makes us what we are and anchors our humanity, then the loss of belief (or an inability to believe) detracts from that humanity. In the life without belief there is a sort of hollowness. Imagine a generation that on the central questions cannot muster up or maintain any real conviction: it would be a "lost generation," a whimpering generation of "hollow men."[9] In a similar vein, in Orwell's *1984* an essential part of the Party's program is to make people incapable of genuine belief, so that they will simply parrot whatever propositions the Party fills them with. Winston Smith, the protagonist, is at the outset a more real or full person than most of his fellows are, mainly because he still has the capacity to believe—he believes that two plus two is four, whatever the Party says, and that Oceania was not always at war with Eurasia, despite the Party's contrary propaganda. So the Party sets out to correct this humanizing capacity. And O'Brien, who applies the Party's methods to Winston, explains what the outcome of this process will be:

> Everything will be dead inside you. Never again will you be capable of love, or friendship, or joy of living, or laughter, or curiosity, or courage, or integrity. You will be hollow.[10]

By the end of the book, we can see that O'Brien is right. Winston has been violently conditioned to say and think whatever the Party says, and he no longer is capable of genuine belief—or of any genuinely human quality. Winston is, as O'Brien predicted, hollow.

THE CORROSION OF BELIEF

For many people, in many times and places, believing seems as natural as breathing. But other people in other settings seem to suffer from a kind of epistemic asthma, or creedal paralysis. For many people, our own place and period seem to be one such setting. So we are told that ours is an Age of Disbelief.[11] "Doubt," Felipe Fernandez-Armesto asserts, "is the truth of our times."[12] These dark descriptions seem to me slightly off base, though. Outside the university, belief still seems to flourish. And looking around the universities that I have studied or worked in for most of my adult life, I would say that although particular beliefs obviously vary greatly from person to person, if there is a prevailing mind-set here it is not so much one of outright disbelief or doubt as of belief (sometimes almost childlike trust, it seems to me) in a *naturalistic worldview* and in *science* as the preferred method of reliable understanding. But for many purposes this naturalistic belief system seems very much akin to doubt—and hence generates the sort of descriptions I've just noted—because it does effectively amount to rejection of many of the classical or traditional commitments that informed people's core, orienting beliefs that life has meaning, that we have dignity, that we are subject to moral obligations, and so forth. These implications of the naturalistic worldview are usually either resisted or ignored—more on that in a moment—but we also see occasional confessions bemoaning that most of what we regard as virtuous, lovely, or praiseworthy is simply not credible, or not even intelligible, on modern naturalistic assumptions.[13]

One such cry of anguish from my own discipline occurs at the end of a lecture given by one of my law school professors, Arthur Leff. After arguing basically that morality depends upon a God in whom we can no longer believe, Leff closed with this plaintive and oft-quoted plea:

> All I can say is this: it looks as if we are all we have. Given what we know about ourselves and each other, this is an extraordinarily unappetizing prospect; looking around the world, it appears that if all men are brothers, the ruling model is Cain and Abel. Neither reason, nor love, nor even terror, seems to have worked to make us "good," and worse than that, there is no reason why anything should. Only if ethics were something unspeakable by us, could law be unnatural, and therefore unchallengeable. As things now stand, everything is up for grabs.
>
> Nevertheless:
>
> Napalming babies is bad.
>
> Starving the poor is wicked.
>
> Buying and selling each other is depraved.
>
> Those who stood up to and died resisting Hitler, Stalin, Amin, and Pol Pot—and General Custer too—have earned salvation.
>
> Those who acquiesced deserve to be damned.
>
> There is in the world such a thing as evil.
>
> [All together now:] Sez who?
>
> God help us.[14]

SALVAGING (HALF-) BELIEF

So, if believing is central to what makes us human but our central, almost constitutive beliefs come under challenge, how do we respond?

Perhaps the most obvious response is to engage in apologetics—to collect evidence or muster arguments that serve to rebut the assaults. I do not mean the term "apologetics" to have any pejorative connotation here, but rather to describe what can be a straightforward, honest effort to meet the criticisms, examine them, and show that they are unfounded. This is perhaps our most natural and responsible way of meeting challenges to belief; if it succeeds, the challenges are deflected and our beliefs remain intact.[15]

Suppose our apologetic efforts fail, though; the contrary evidence or arguments seem (at least to some of us) more compelling than our attempts at rebuttal. In this case, it seems, the purest response would be to modify our beliefs so that they are more in accord with what evidence and argument plausibly support. We might simply abandon discredited beliefs, or we might amend them so that they conform to reality as we now perceive it.

If belief were a matter of practical indifference—if, that is, people were merely detached and dispassionate agents seeking to find and profess the most supportable beliefs—then these two responses (apologetics and the modification or abandonment of discredited beliefs) might exhaust the possibilities. Obviously, though, life is hardly that simple. As I have noticed already, we do not merely believe; we *need to believe*. Relinquishing old beliefs may be painful or, for practical purposes, simply unacceptable. Not many people will be able to live with the sort of desperate skepticism expressed by Arthur Leff; it is not certain whether or how well Leff himself (who, tragically, died at a young age) could have lived with it. So when apologetics fail but the modification or abandonment of belief is unacceptable, we may adopt a variety of less pure responses to an assault on belief.

For present purposes, we can group these less pure strategies into two general categories. Probably the most familiar of these strategies could be called "distorting the record," or "fudging the facts." We may simply misrepresent the evidence; or we may carefully neglect to consider some damaging pieces of evidence while placing undue weight on other, more favorable items. We "bend the truth," as they say, and thereby preserve a precarious ability to believe what we want or need to believe.

This sort of "truth bending" is perfectly common; we all perceive *other people* doing it all the time—even (though you may be shocked to hear it) presidential candidates and (more shocking still) lawyers. I suspect that this practice has its costs, though—not just to the pursuit of truth (in a trial, for example, or a public debate), but also to our very *capacity to believe*. Probably we are at least vaguely aware that we are screening out some evidence—how else could we manage to perform the screening?—or that we are dispensing with the usual procedures for ascertaining factual truth; this nagging awareness will likely mean that even as we persist in *affirming*, we are no longer really *believing* in the same wholehearted way that we did before the assault on our beliefs occurred. And like a person who has been proven dishonest in some particular affair or transaction, our very judgment—or our faculty for believing—may become suspect; we are no longer sure that it is being entirely straight with us. As Dostoyevsky's character Father Zossima explains, "Above all, don't lie to yourself. The man who lies to himself and listens to his own lie comes to such a point that he cannot distinguish the truth within him, or around him, and so loses all respect for himself and for others."[16]

So, is there any way to avoid this kind of "truth bending" or "fact fudging," with the attendant injury to our capacity to believe? It seems that there is, though the alternative strategy requires a bit more implicit philosophical sophistication than more mundane forms of fudging. The alternative is suggested in the biblical account of Jesus's examination before Pilate.[17] In response to a question, Jesus had said that everyone who is "of the truth" would hear his voice, and Pilate dismissed this assertion by asking, "What is truth?" and then quickly leaving the room.[18] Voltaire, in commenting on this incident, remarked that "Pilate had very little curiosity."[19] But there is a more plausible reading of the story: Pilate, it seems, was becoming increasingly distraught about Jesus and his claims, and especially about what he, Pilate, was being successfully pressured to do—namely, execute a man he knew to be innocent—and Pilate tried to dispel these concerns, not by bending the truth to make Jesus appear guilty, but rather by adopting a cynical attitude toward the very notion of truth.

The story illustrates a tempting possibility: When our beliefs are challenged, we might try to retain them not by fudging *facts* or distorting evidence (so that our beliefs appear to be in accord with truth) but rather, more radically, by adopting what I am calling a declension strategy—that is, by revising downward the very concepts of "truth" and of "belief" themselves. What is it for something to be "true"? What does it mean to "believe"? There is room to maneuver here.

THE PRAGMATIC TURN

It seems to me that modern thought is filled with such declensions—with revisions calculated to permit us to continue to profess cherished beliefs even though these beliefs will no longer have the same wholehearted, full-blooded character they had before. This is not the place (and I am not the person) to offer any comprehensive survey of these revisionist strategies. If we were to limit ourselves to the area Arthur Leff was troubled by, for example—that is, morality—we would need to discuss the various forms of expressivism, quasi-realism, and fictionalism that modern philosophers have proposed to justify us in continuing to issue moral judgments that at least *look like* statements of belief even though, as the proponents of these theories contend, these judgments are not and could not really be assertions about what is *true*. For present purposes, it will be enough to mention one more generic version of the truth-adjusting strategy that probably informs most of the others as well.[20] We can call this version of the strategy the pragmatic turn.

More specifically, we might understand ourselves not so much as creatures with a special relation to truth, but rather as products of random evolutionary development with "interests"—especially including an interest in survival—that we need or want to satisfy. *Believing* (along with thinking, running, fighting, mating, and so forth) is one of the functions that evolution has equipped us to perform, and its justification lies in its ability to satisfy our interests.[21] We should therefore believe what it is in our interests to believe, and should understand "truth" in these same pragmatic terms.

Thus, in a renowned series of lectures William James explained that "truth is *one species of good. . . . The true is the name of whatever proves itself to be good in the way of belief.*"[22] From this conception it followed that "[t]ruth in science is what gives us the maximum sum of satisfactions, taste included"—though James hastened to add (perhaps inconsistently with his own announced conceptions) that "consistency both with previous truth and with novel fact is always the most imperious claimant."[23] The pragmatist would be open to the possibility of religious truth as well, though in a sense that might leave the traditional believer a bit queasy: "*If theological ideas prove to have a value for concrete life, they will be true, for pragmatism, in the sense of being good for so much.*"[24]

With this conception of "truth" in mind, one can readily imagine a defense of traditional religious beliefs along the following lines: "It is good for people to believe that the Bible is the literal and infallible revelation of God. The belief is good because it gives people meaning and comfort and makes them happier and better behaved. But you keep asking if the belief is 'true.' Don't you get it? If it is good for people to believe this, then the belief *is* 'true.' *That's what it means* for a belief to be true."

Of course a similar account might be offered for virtually any other cherished belief that is under challenge from what seems contrary evidence. Is the theory of creationism, or the theory of evolution, "true"? Are there differences in natural aptitudes among races? Are "all men created equal"? Do we have a moral obligation to do unto others as we would have them do unto us? Perhaps these questions are debatable, but the important point is that the debate should be over what it's good for people to believe; there is no *independent* question of "truth."

If he could hear what I've just said, William James would probably protest that I have misunderstood and mischaracterized his position[25]; and as an admirer of James, I would like to think that I have (though I think it more likely, as Arthur Lovejoy powerfully argued, that pragmatists like James tend to equivocate in their use of terms like "truth"—and pragmatism).[26] For our purposes, in any case, the important thing is not to figure out exactly what James meant or whether "pragmatism" (which surely has been a source of a variety of valuable insights) is plausible or not. The important point is that the sorts of pragmatic adjustments I have mentioned are perfectly familiar, and they reflect a significant revision—I think it is fair to say declension—in our understanding of truth and belief.

"Truth," in this modern view, is something we construct to serve our ends. In this spirit, Richard Rorty criticizes objectivist or correspondence theories of truth: "true sentences," he explains, "are not true because they correspond to reality, and so there is no need to worry what sort of reality, if any, a given sentence corresponds to."[27] A proposition is true, rather, if it is one that is good to assert, and "[t]he question of what propositions to assert, which pictures to look at, what narratives to listen to and comment on and retell, are all questions about what will help us get what we want (or about what we *should* want)."[28]

So why do I describe these pragmatic conceptions of truth and belief as a kind of "declension"? As I've noted, these conceptions are sometimes offered as a way of preserving religious or moral beliefs that we hold dear but have trouble defending on old-fashioned, objectivist grounds. So it is sometimes suggested that by contrast to an older, more hard-boiled "Enlightenment" rationality, what is sometimes called the "postmodern" mind-set is more hospitable to religious beliefs.[29] If all beliefs are "true" not because they correspond to an objective reality "out there" but only in the sense that they engage our interest and support for a variety of reasons, then what excuse is there for discriminating against religious beliefs that so engage us?

But the crucial question, I think, is whether affirmations made within this sort of antiobjectivist framework can meaningfully be called "belief." Can the statement "I believe in God the Father, the creator of heaven and earth" be reformulated without loss into "I find it useful and satisfying to affirm the idea of God the Father, the creator of heaven and earth"? Does someone who understands the creed in this more modern (or "postmodern") sense *really believe* it? I doubt it; moreover, I think the reformulated declaration is not only different in meaning but also self-undermining, because someone who can say only that it is useful and comforting to affirm an idea will eventually find that he does not and cannot actually affirm it.

With reference to one particular version of this pragmatic turn—namely, a "neo-Wittgensteinian" but antiobjectivist conception of truth that understands "truth" to be the product of "language games"—John Hick notes both the promise and the terrible cost of the revisionist response to challenge: "[W]hen a Humanist or Marxist tells a believer that it is foolish to pray to God, because there is no God to pray to, the neo-Wittgensteinian philosopher of religion will tell both atheist and believer that they are playing different language games and that there can therefore be no controversy between them. The believer is thus left secure in his belief, protected from outside attack." However, the believer can make this defense, Hick explains, "only on the understanding that his beliefs do not depend for their validity upon the universe being structured in one way (a theistic way) rather than another (an atheistic way)." But this concession is in fact catastrophic; it "cuts the heart out of both belief and practice." That is because "the importance of religious beliefs to the believer lies ultimately in the assumption that they are substantially true references to the nature of reality."[30]

H. Richard Niebuhr expressed the basic point succinctly: "the instrumental value of faith for society is dependent upon faith's conviction that it has more than instrumental value."[31] Consequently, "[t]he godliness which is profitable to all things becomes unprofitable when profit rather than God comes to be its interest. This ancient dilemma is not solved by any doctrine of necessary fictions but only by the recognition that objectivism rather than pragmatism is the first law of knowledge."[32]

I admit that in the real world, it might be that many people who profess belief—to others, and even to themselves—manage to do so by adopting some such declension strategy. Still, it seems to me that this course necessarily involves the believer—or the half-believer—in self-deception, or at least in a sort of Orwellian double-think. That is because if a pragmatic belief is "true" only in the sense that it is useful, it is useful only because and to the extent that the person who holds it believes it to be *true*—true in some objective sense. The person must hold the belief to be true *much of the time*, at least, or *when acting on it*; otherwise, what would be the point? So this sort of attitude is at best a kind of half-belief. And the people who live on such a basis would be, if not exactly "hollow men," at least half-hollow.

Can human beings actually live on this basis? It seems so; what *is* done *can be* done. But it seems to me that this is a shadowy, unsatisfactory, hollow kind of existence. I doubt that many generations could persist, or that *any* generation or person could flourish, on this understanding of things. We may sometimes find ourselves in this condition, but we ought not to become complacent about it. Rather, we should strive to place our lives on some firmer foundation. That at least is my belief.

BELIEVING IN LAW[33]

My comments thus far have been a long preparation for a more specific assessment of what is supposed to be my own field of expertise—that is, law. And the trajectory of the discussion would suggest that at this point I should proceed to argue that modern law has resorted to declensionist strategies in order to maintain a belief in law. But that argument is at once surprisingly easy, almost superfluous, but also exceedingly difficult or even futile; this is because modern lawyers and legal thinkers have managed to adopt what Harvard law professor Duncan Kennedy describes as "[t]he simultaneously critical and 'believing' character of American legal consciousness, its paradoxical combination of skepticism and faith."[34] In some contexts, modern lawyers self-consciously announce and even celebrate their embrace of declensionist notions; I am not sure whether there is another discipline so generally candid, or so brazen, about this development. But lawyers also pervasively deny that they have done this, or at least that there is anything at all problematic about their doing so. And if they (or I suppose I should say *we*) practice self-deception (as I believe we do), our admissions mean that it is a sort of open, candid self-deception, which of course seems paradoxical. Addressing the matter is complicated, and anything one says on the subject is likely to provoke, at the same time, impatient, peremptory denials, but also yawns: "So what? Tell us something we don't already know."

So let me try to approach the subject in this way. For centuries, it was a common view among Western legal thinkers that law was a manifestation of something that transcended mundane human enactments and judicial decisions. Judicial decisions in particular were not "law," exactly, but rather "evidence" of law. In this vein, Blackstone explained that "the decisions of courts . . . are the *evidence* of what is common law."[35] A famous American case expressed what sounds like a similar view. "[I]t will hardly be contended," Justice Joseph Story wrote for the Supreme Court in *Swift v. Tyson*,[36] "that the decisions of courts constitute laws. They are, at most, only *evidence* of what the laws are; and are not of themselves laws."

So then what was that deeper or larger reality of which judicial decisions were merely "evidence"? The immediate answer of a jurist like Blackstone might have invoked "custom," but ultimately the question led back to that part God's providential plan for the cosmos sometimes described as the "law of nature." "This law of nature," Blackstone explained, "being co-eval with mankind and dictated by God himself, is of course superior in obligation to any other . . . no human laws are of any validity, if contrary to this: and such of them as are valid derive all their force, and all their authority, mediately or immediately, from this original."[37]

In saying this, Blackstone was not asserting anything especially radical or even novel, but rather was simply reciting a long-established and widely accepted view. Thus, over a century before Blackstone, Edward Coke, that learned and feisty champion of the common law, had explained that a common law decision "agrees with the judicial law of God, on which our law is in every point founded."[38] Still earlier, Sir John Fortescue, the great fifteenth-century theorist and Chief Justice of the King's Bench, declared that "all laws that are promulgated by man are decreed by God"; hence, "to learn the laws, even though human ones, is to learn laws that are sacred and decreed of God."[39] In his treatise on the subject Fortescue repeatedly cited Aquinas,[40] who of course had provided the classic account of this understanding of law in the thirteenth century.[41]

Today, by contrast, it is hard to imagine leading scholars or judges explaining law in anything like these terms. Just when the change occurred is impossible to pinpoint, but Oliver Wendell Holmes gave typically vivid and influential expression to the change in conceptions. Holmes mocked the classical view for holding that law is some sort of "brooding omnipresence in the sky,"[42] a view he emphatically rejected as "fallacy and illusion."[43] Instead, Holmes proclaimed that law is a purely human affair. "When we study law," he declared in the first sentence of a notable lecture that became the most cited law review article in history, "we are not studying a mystery but a well known profession."[44] The imperative, as Felix Cohen later put it, was to "redefine supernatural concepts in natural terms."[45]

Nearly all lawyers and legal scholars today would account for law in just those natural terms. So positivist accounts in a variety of shapes and sizes have dominated modern thinking about law. The problem is that although law clearly *does* have its positivist dimensions, and although positivist accounts *can* plausibly account for a good deal of what we do and say under the heading of "law," there is also a good deal that fits awkwardly at best, or not at all, with those accounts, and that in fact resonates better with the more classical understandings of law as a reflection of something that preexists or transcends it. I have argued for this position at some length elsewhere[46]; here I will briefly mention only two such features.

First, I think that a careful, candid examination of the way judges and lawyers use precedent—a practice central to law-talk that distinguishes it from other less exotic forms of "practical reason"—reveals that despite our denials, we still treat judicial decisions not so much as "law" in themselves as "evidence" of something that lies beyond them. Lon Fuller, though no proponent of the classical view, acknowledged this fact.

> [I]t is not too much to say that the judges are always ready to look behind the words of a precedent to what the previous court was trying to say, or to what it would have said if it could have foreseen the nature of the cases that were later to arise, or if its perception of the relevant factors in the case had been more acute. There is, then, a real sense in which the written words of the reported decisions are merely the gateway to *something lying behind them* that may be called, without any excess of poetic license, "unwritten law."[47]

"Judges," Fuller observed, "are apt to talk as if they were all working together in bringing to adequate expression a *preexisting thing called 'The Law.'*"[48]

In a similar vein but with more of the "poetic license" that Fuller eschewed, the historian and law professor Norman Cantor observes that the common law is sometimes treated as if it were "a kind of fixed heavenly firmament, its procedures and principles shining down like beautiful and remote stars, infinitely set apart from the anxieties, confusions, and passions of particular human lives."[49]

A second feature of legal practice that suggests a continuing presupposition of an independently existing "law" lies in the common judicial practice of treating decisions as retroactively applicable even to events occurring before the decisions were rendered.[50] The longstanding assumption has been that despite our standard condemnation of *ex post facto* laws, it is nonetheless appropriate to subject past actions to a newly announced judicial ruling, so that you or I can be sued for all we're worth for violating a legal rule that was unknown and unarticulated at the time we violated it: this is because the ruling merely announces or declares what "the law" *is* (in a portentously expansive sense in which "is" describes a sort of perpetual present reaching back into the indefinite past). This practice is usually followed even in so-called cases of first impression and—most strikingly—even when a decision explicitly overrules a prior decision.[51] The new decision is said merely to declare "the law" that obligated parties all along—even though a previous judicial opinion mistakenly declared otherwise.[52]

These are particular features of law that resonate with the classical conception. But more generally, lawyers and judges routinely talk about "the law" as something that exists independent of their talk and their decisions. Brian Simpson, the eminent legal historian, summarizes our current situation.

> For lawyers, to quote E. P. Thompson, writing in 1975 of what he calls "the greatest of all legal fictions," "the law itself evolves, from case to case, by its own impartial logic, true only to its own integrity." There is, of course, a sense in which *nobody really believes this any more*, but it remains the case that much legal behaviour proceeds on the assumption that the law is like that. For example, all legal argument in court makes this assumption.[53]

Simpson describes law as we talk about and practice it as a "fiction," much in the way the philosopher Richard Joyce describes morality as a valuable fiction. We talk and think "as if" morality were real, Joyce argues, even though it isn't.[54] In his famous lecture Holmes said much the same thing about law. Lawyers and judges talk *as if* legal conclusions follow from legal premises—as if the precedents or rules or doctrines *require* particular results—but the apparent logic of judicial opinions is misleading. In most cases, Holmes said, an equally plausible legal argument can be constructed to justify just the opposite conclusion. "You can give any conclusion a logical form. You can always imply a condition in a contract. But why do you imply it?" The apparently deductive quality of legal reasoning is largely illusory,[55] in short, and to accept that reasoning as the real basis of a decision is to fall victim to "the fallacy of logical form."[56] What really determines the outcomes in cases, Holmes thought, is not the parsing of precedents and rules and doctrines, but rather an underlying "judgment as to the relative worth and importance of competing legislative grounds," or "some opinion as to policy."[57] Though often "inarticulate and unconscious," this sort of policy judgment is in reality "the very root and nerve of the whole proceeding."[58] This view of law has by now become familiar to the point of being platitudinous.[59]

But of course lawyers still do not write briefs and judges do not render decisions explained mainly in terms of "social policy"; as Simpson points out, they still *talk* as if their arguments and decisions were statements of *the law*. So in order to take this view of law, we have to do just what Holmes did: we need to suppose that what lawyers and judges say in their briefs and opinions is a kind of elaborate cover for the real or "policy" bases of decisions. We need to suppose, in other words, that lawyers and judges are engaged in a sort of epic charade.

In this vein, Judge Posner asserts that "the true grounds of legal decision are concealed rather than illuminated by the characteristic rhetoric of opinions."[60] Posner's arch-antagonist, Ronald Dworkin, agrees; though insisting that the "true grounds" of decisions are or should be moral philosophy rather than economics or social policy, Dworkin likewise contends that judges who present their decisions as the product of conventional legal reasoning (which is to say, virtually *all* judges) are "guilty of a costly mendacity."[61] Grant Gilmore was describing this understanding of law when he remarked, with his usual flair, that "[f]or two or three generations past it has been the merest truism, in much American legal writing, that the doctrine which may be found enshrined in case report and treatise is neither important nor relevant."[62]

As I have said, this view which sees the legal reasoning that lawyers and judges engage in mainly as a cover for some significantly different mode of decisionmaking has become yawningly familiar. And yet it ought to strike us as astounding. First of all, if we pause to contemplate it, the depiction of a vast enterprise of hundreds of thousands of lawyers and judges of diverse views, temperaments, and backgrounds writing millions of pages of briefs and opinions in one set of terms while in fact acting on an almost wholly different set of considerations seems quite fantastic. And then there is the question of motivation: *Why* on earth would we carry on such a charade for generation after generation?

Of course, Holmes and many of his descendants have not exactly favored maintaining the charade. Usually they have called for a more honest discourse that would replace or at least supplement conventional law-talk with a more open acknowledgment of economics or moral philosophy or whatever. And they have expected such a transformation of discourse to occur promptly. But more than a century after Holmes, the revolution still has not happened; legal discourse is not so different than it was a century ago—or maybe even five centuries ago. Thus, Norman Cantor asserts that "[a] London barrister of 1540, quick-frozen and revived in New York today, would need only a year's brush-up course at NYU School of Law to begin civil practice as a partner in a midtown or Wall Street corporate-law firm."[63]

So it seems that the need for law and law-talk runs deep. And once again we face the question of *why*?

That question, though rarely addressed directly, has festered underneath (and given rise to) a great deal of modern jurisprudence, and it has provoked legal analogues to the sorts of positions that have arisen in moral philosophy, such as expressivism, fictionalism, and more generally pragmatism. But I think the question inevitably points us to a perceived or at least dimly intuited need for deception. Maybe we in the legal profession need the general public to believe that we are acting on grounds others than the ones that (in the modern view, at least) we actually *are* acting on. Or maybe *we ourselves* need to believe that we are acting on grounds other than the ones we are ostensibly acting on. We need to believe in law in something like the classical sense even though we understand (or think we understand) that law in the classical sense does not actually exist.

In this vein, Duncan Kennedy diagnoses modern law as the product of a conflict between our commitment to "rule of law" and our knowledge that in fact law does not and cannot actually be what we need it to be. Judges resolve this conflict by presenting decisions as deductive, and by half-believing that law in fact has this character, even though at another level they know this is not so. They do not engage in "conscious, deliberate, strategic misrepresentation," and probably *could not* do so, because law "would then have the instability of any conspiracy that involves many thousands of people and has to constantly renew itself by recruiting new Grand Inquisitors."[64] Instead, they practice a deception that is "half-conscious, or conscious and unconscious at the same time."[65] Nor is the practice limited to judges; it engulfs us all—perhaps for our benefit:

> Judges keep the secret, even from themselves, in part because participants in legal culture and in the general political culture want them to. Everyone wants it to be true that it is not only possible but common for judges to judge nonideologically. But everyone is aware of the critique, and everyone knows that the naive theory of the rule of law is a fairy tale.[66]

In short, we manage to maintain faith (albeit "bad faith") in the law because we think "the rule of law is . . . a beneficent illusion."[67]

Some may dismiss Kennedy as a left-leaning Crit. But Kennedy may have a surprising ally—Justice Scalia. In a recent book Daniel Farber and Suzanna Sherry suggest that although Scalia usually advocates a rigorously formalist view of law, "there is some evidence that he views [this account of law] . . . as a sort of noble myth to which judges ought to give their allegiance even if it is not wholly true." Farber and Sherry quote a provocative statement in which Scalia observes: "That is why, by the way, I never thought Oliver Wendell Holmes and the legal realists did us a favor by pointing out that all these legal fictions were fictions: Those judges wise enough to be trusted with the secret already knew it."[68]

A CHRISTIAN JURISPRUDENCE?

So, how should we appraise this situation from a Christian perspective? Let me say immediately that I don't think there is any single or orthodox Christian response to the state of affairs I have been discussing.[69] But I can briefly mention three directions that I think a Christian jurisprudence might take.

First, it sometimes used to be noticed with amusement that the common acronym for the radical, leftist Critical Legal Studies movement—CLS, as it was usually called—was the same as that for the Christian Legal Society, so that a law student looking for "the CLS meeting" (of either sort) might accidentally find herself in very unexpected company. But in fact I think the divergence is not as radical as it may seem. More specifically, I think a Christian position might well sponsor a "Critical" jurisprudence—and one that would be more searching and true than the criticism that emanated from the typical Crits of the 1980s and 1990s. From this Christian perspective, the situation I have been describing—with its deception and self-deception and double-think—might be viewed as a predictable consequence of human fallenness, or perhaps as a sort of object lesson in what happens when fundamental truths are denied. To be sure, at bottom the Christian Crit would maintain a good deal more cosmic optimism—faith, hope, and charity—than the traditional Crit did. But they might travel together for a very long way.

Other Christian legal thinkers would be inclined to take a more redemptive approach to law, and Christian teaching might also provide the materials to do that. More specifically, the decisive break between the classical view of law and the modern view (as expressed by figures like Holmes) is the modern rejection of, as Blackstone put it, the "law of nature" deriving from God's providential plan. To the secularist the notion of any such transcendent law seems untenable, of course—but not to the Christian. So a different, perhaps more constructive, Christian approach might seek to reestablish law, more or less as we know and practice it, but on more secure metaphysical foundations.

A third and even more visionary possibility might be to use law as a base for attempting to resist or roll back the darkness of doubt in modern thought more generally. Suppose we think we have rejected the premises necessary for particular conclusions but find that we cannot relinquish the conclusions themselves: one possibility is that at some level we still believe the premises after all. Go back to Arthur Leff. Leff contended that morality makes sense only if there is a God, and his problem was that although he thought he (or we) no longer believe in that God, he also thought that he (and we) cannot give up on—cannot *disbelieve* in—morality. It would at least be worth encouraging Leff to introspect and ask himself how sure he is that he does not believe in God.[70] In a similar vein, if the ways we talk about and practice law make sense on the assumption of a transcendent law derived from a providential plan, and if we find that despite a century of sustained effort we cannot let go of that kind of law, then perhaps we believe in that transcendent law and author even though we say and *consciously think* we don't.

This suggestion may sound paradoxical, but it has been developed with great subtlety by Joseph Vining, one of the more difficult but also more probing Christian legal thinkers of our time. I hesitate to try to summarize Vining's views in a few words, but perhaps it is permissible to say that Vining sees in the activities of lawyers a search for authority—a search that presupposes the reality of authority. But authority is necessarily personal. Moreover, no merely human authority would have the capacity to claim our respect across generations and jurisdictions. So lawyers search for—and presuppose the reality of—an author that Vining describes as "spirit," or the "transcendent."[71] "Lawyers are caught by legislation and their reading of it," Vining argues. "Either they must believe what they do with legislation is often foolish and deceptive; or they do believe and confess a belief in *an informing spirit* in the legislated words that is *beyond individual legislators*." Vining adds that "[a]s in all large matters, there is mixture, the usual combination, of doubt and belief, made easier to live with, as usual, by strong doses of self-deception."[72]

Approached in this way, Vining concedes, law becomes "an object of amazement to the modern and postmodern mentality."[73] And he points out that, reflectively studied, law and its presuppositions will be "subversive" of twentieth-century thought—of the materialism evident in so much work in the sciences and social sciences, but also of "what goes by the name postmodernism in literary and philosophic studies."[74] In essence, Vining sees in law a possible source of a revival of faith and of a response to the modern ways of thought that have undermined faith.

So there are various directions in which a Christian jurisprudence might develop in response to the kind of declension I have been describing. Despite my admiration for Vining's work, I have to admit that my own thinking runs less in the redemptive and more in the "Christian Crit" channels. What most impresses itself on me is the hollowness in so much modern legal thought—a hollowness that manifests itself in various ways and places: in a legal professoriate that resembles, in Roberto Unger's famous description, "a priesthood that had lost their faith and kept their jobs,"[75] and in Supreme Court opinions that seem ever more arrogant and ever less worthy of respect as the generations pass. I've sometimes thought, for example, that it would be a harsh penance (worthy, if not of hell, then at least of purgatory) to be sentenced to sit in a comfortable, air-conditioned office perpetually reading opinions by Justice O'Connor or Justice Kennedy.

But let's not dwell on that prospect, which is horrible to contemplate and hardly a happy scene on which to end here. Instead, let me finish by alluding to a well-known Hopkins poem.[76] Holmes's famous essay was called "The Path of the Law," and Holmes's Path is one that for generations now we "have trod, have trod, have trod." The path leads to a dead end, I think, and so at the moment the picture can be a dispiriting one. The whole enterprise "wears man's smudge and shares man's smell." Yet even here, if with Vining we pay close attention to the underlying commitments and presuppositions that pervade law and that we seem constitutionally unable to relinquish, we may glimpse "the dearest freshness deep down things." "[T]hough the last lights off the black West went," even so, transcendence "will flame out, like shining from shook foil." And so we can say that the world—and even the law—is "charged with the grandeur of God." That vision is at least part of what a Christian jurisprudence should help us see.

NOTES

1. Aristotle, "Metaphysics," in *Introduction to Aristotle*, ed. R. McKeon (New York: The Modern Library, 1947), 980a1, 243.

2. Much of the first section of this chapter is distilled from Steven D. Smith, "Believing Persons, Personal Believings: the Neglected Center of the First Amendment," 2002 *University Illinois Law Review* 1233 (2002). For a helpful argument to similar effect from a sociological perspective, see Christian Smith, *Moral, Believing Animals: Human Personhood and Culture* (Oxford: Oxford University Press, 2003), 45–61.

3. Richard Rorty, *Consequences of Pragmatism* (Minneapolis: University of Minnesota Press, 1982), xiv.

4. St. Thomas Aquinas, *Summa Contra Gentiles*, Book. I, trans. Anton C. Pegis (Notre Dame, Ind.: University of Notre Dame Press, 1975), 60.

5. Pope John Paul II, Encyclical *Veritatis Splendor*, Introduction (1993).

6. Psalm 39:5.

7. I Cor. 13:12.

8. Quoted in Joseph Vining, "The Cosmological Question," 94 *Michigan Law Review* 2024, 2025 (1996). See also David F. Swenson, "The Dignity of Life," in *The Meaning of Life* rev. ed., ed. E. D. Klemke (New York: Oxford University Press, 2000), 22 ("A view of life is . . . a personal expression of what a man essentially is in his own inmost self"). Richard Weaver quotes Thomas Carlyle to similar effect: "But the thing a man does practically believe (and this is often enough *without* asserting it even to himself, much less to others); the thing a man does practically lay to heart, and know for certain, concerning his vital relations to this mysterious Universe, and his duty and destiny there, that is in all cases the primary thing for him, and creatively determines all the rest." Richard M. Weaver, *Ideas Have Consequences* (Chicago: University of Chicago Press, 1948), 18. See also ibid., 3 (asserting that "world view is the most important thing about a man").

9. Cf. T. S. Eliot, "The Hollow Men," in David Lehman, ed., *The Oxford Book of American Poetry* (New York: Oxford University Press, 2006), 365.

10. George Orwell, *1984* (New York: Signet Books 1950), 211.

11. See, e.g., Huston Smith, *Why Religion Matters: The Fate of the Human Spirit in an Age of Disbelief* (San Francisco: HarperCollins, 2001); Gregg Easterbrook, *Beside Still Waters: Searching for Meaning in an Age of Doubt* (New York: William Morrow, 1998).

12. Felipe Fernandez-Armesto, *Truth: A History and a Guide for the Perplexed* (New York: St. Martin's Press, 1997), 206. Fernandez-Armesto's book aims to give a brief history of "how our society has come to lose faith in the reality of [truth] and lose interest in the search for it"—a condition he believes to be "the unique predicament of our times." Ibid., 2, 3.

13. Half a century ago, Princeton philosopher Walter Stace observed that "[n]o one any longer effectively believes in moral principles except as the private prejudices either of individual men or of nations or cultures. This is the inevitable consequence of the doctrine of ethical relativity, which in turn is the inevitable consequence of believing in a purposeless world." W. T. Stace, *Man Against Darkness and Other Essays* (Pittsburgh: University of Pittsburgh Press, 1967), 10. Stace acknowledged that many people suppose "the world can go on just the same as before, as if nothing had happened," but this supposition was "shallow." Ibid., 4. The loss of belief in a cosmic order entailed "the ruin of moral principles and indeed of all values." Ibid., 9. "If the scheme of things is purposeless and meaningless," Stace argued, "then the life of man is purposeless and meaningless too. Everything is futile, all effort is in the end worthless." Ibid., 7.

14. Arthur Allen Leff, "Unspeakable Ethics, Unnatural Law," 1979 *Duke Law Journal* 1229, 1249 (1979).

15. See Avery Cardinal Dulles, S.J., "The Rebirth of Apologetics," 2004 *First Things* 18 (May 2004). Found at http://www.firstthings.com/ftissues/ft0405/articles/dulles.html.

16. Fyodor Dostoyevsky, *The Brothers Karamazov*, trans. Constance Garnett (New York: Signet Books 1959), 53. Father Zossima goes on: "And having no respect he ceases to love. And in order to distract himself without love he gives way to passions and coarse pleasures and sinks to bestiality in his vices—all this from continual lying to other men and to himself."

17. John 18:28–19:16.

18. Ibid., 18:37–38.

19. Ben Ray Redman, ed., *The Portable Voltaire* (New York: The Viking Press 1968), 215.

20. See Richard Joyce, *The Myth of Morality* (New York: Cambridge University Press 2001), 135–231 (justifying "fictionalism" in morality on pragmatic grounds).

21. See also Edward O. Wilson, who states, "Traditional religious beliefs have been eroded, not so much by humiliating disproofs of their mythologies as by the growing awareness that beliefs are really enabling mechanisms for survival." Edward O. Wilson, *On Human Nature* (Cambridge, Mass.: Harvard University Press 1978), 3.

22. William James, "Pragmatism," in *Pragmatism and Other Essays* (New York: Washington Square, 1963), 36.

23. Ibid., 96.

24. Ibid., 35.

25. James protested against people who described pragmatism as authorizing "saying whatever you find it pleasant to say and calling it truth"; this depiction, he insisted, was "an impudent slander." Ibid., 103. And indeed, he sometimes described the pragmatic conception of truth in what seem more traditional, less liquid terms. He maintained, for instance, that "[o]ur ideas must agree with realities, be such realities concrete or abstract, be they facts or be they principles, under penalty of endless inconsistency and frustration." Ibid., 93. And he conceded that "copying" is after all "one genuine mode of knowing." Ibid., 104. Critics might claim, however, that James's more "objectivist"-sounding language amounted to mere backsliding, and that they have understood the implications of his positions better than he did. See infra note 26.

26. Lovejoy carefully delineated an array of different and often incompatible things that pragmatists like James occasionally seemed to mean in talking about pragmatic notions of meaning or truth. Lovejoy insisted that each of these strands "should manifestly be given a name of its own if confusion in future discussion is to be avoided." Arthur O. Lovejoy, "The Thirteen Pragmatisms," in *The Thirteen Pragmatisms and Other Essays* (Baltimore: Johns Hopkins Press 1963), 28. But he doubted that pragmatists would be willing to unpack their position: "I suspect that all the charm and impressiveness of the theory arises out of the confusion of its alternative interpretations. It gets its appearance of novelty and of practical serviceableness in the settlement of controversies from its one meaning; and it gets its plausibility entirely from the other." Ibid., 10.

27. Rorty, *Consequences of Pragmatism*, xvi.

28. Ibid., xliii.

29. See, e.g., Frederick Mark Gedicks, "Spirituality, Fundamentalism, Liberty: Religion at the End of Modernity," 54 *DePaul Law Review* 1197, 1206 (2005) (asserting that "[t]he displacement of modernity by postmodernity has been an ambiguous blessing for religion. To be sure, it has re-opened space for religious belief that had previously been almost entirely and aggressively filled by reason and science. Religion need no longer confine itself to the gaps in our knowledge that reason and science cannot fill, because many of their purportedly universal explanations turn out to be local").

30. John Hick, "Seeing-as and Religious Experience," in *Faith*, ed. Terence Penelhum (New York: Macmillan Publishing Co., 1989), 183, 184.

31. Martin E. Marty, introduction to *The Kingdom of God in America*, by H. Richard Niebuhr (1937; reprint, Middletown, Conn.: Wesleyan University Press, 1988), 12.

32. Ibid.

33. Much of this section is distilled from Steven D. Smith, *Law's Quandary* (Cambridge, Mass.: Harvard University Press 2004), especially chap. 3 and 4.

34. Duncan Kennedy, *A Critique of Adjudication (fin de siecle)* (Cambridge, Mass.: Harvard University Press 1997), 79.

35. William Blackstone, *Commentaries on the Laws of England*, vol. 1 (1765; reprint, Chicago: The University of Chicago Press, 1979), 70 (emphasis added). See

also Matthew Hale, *The History of the Common Law of England* (London: John Walthoe, 1716), 67 (asserting that judicial decisions "are less than a Law, yet they are greater Evidence thereof, than the Opinion of any private Persons").

36. *Swift v. Tyson* 41 U.S. 1, 18 (1842) (emphasis added).

37. Blackstone, *Commentaries*, 41. See generally ibid., 38–41.

38. Quoted in Jonathan Rose, "Doctrinal Development: Legal History, Law, and Legal Theory," 22 *Oxford Journal of Legal Studies* 323, 334 (2002).

39. Sir John Fortescue, *On the Laws and Governance of England*, ed. Shelley Lockwood (1471; reprint, New York: Cambridge University Press, 1997), 7. Fortescue went on to observe that "because this law cannot work in you [the Prince] without grace, it is necessary to pray for that above all things." Ibid., 13.

40. Ibid., 17–18, 53, 83.

41. See Thomas Aquinas, *Summa Theologica*, I–II, Questions 90–105.

42. *Southern Pacific Co. v. Jensen*, 244 U.S. 205, 222 (1917) (J. Holmes dissenting).

43. *Black & White Taxicab Co. v. Brown & Yellow Taxicab Co.*, 276 U.S. 518, 532–33 (1928) (J. Holmes dissenting).

44. Oliver Wendell Holmes, "The Path of the Law," 10 *Harvard Law Review* 457 (1897).

45. Felix Cohen, "Transcendental Nonsense and the Functional Approach," 35 *Columbia Law Review* 809, 830 (1935).

46. See Smith, *Law's Quandary*.

47. Lon L. Fuller, *Anatomy of the Law* (New York: F. A. Praeger, 1968), 92 (emphasis added).

48. Ibid., 98 (emphasis added).

49. Norman F. Cantor, *Imagining the Law: Common Law and the Foundations of the American Legal System* (New York: HarperCollins 1997), 377.

50. In statutory cases, new interpretations are applied to events occurring before the interpretation was announced but usually not to events that occurred before the statute was enacted.

51. For discussion and collected materials on this practice, see William N. Eskridge Jr. and Philip P. Frickey, *Cases and Materials on Legislation: Statutes and the Creation of Public Policy*, second ed. (St. Paul, Minn.: West Publishing Co., 1995), 441–57.

52. For a time it appeared that a selective practice of prospective rulings might develop. See, e.g., *Chevron Oil Co. v. Huson*, 404 U.S. 97, 106–7 (1971); *Linkletter v. Walker*, 381 U.S. 618 (1965). More recently, though, not only the traditional practice but also the classical rationale for that practice have firmly reasserted themselves. Thus, Justice Souter observes that retroactive application of decisions is "overwhelmingly the norm." *Jim Beam Distilling Co. v. Georgia*, 501 U.S. 529, 535 (1991). Souter goes on to explain that this practice is grounded in the view that "the function of the courts [is] to decide cases before them based upon their best current understanding of the law"—a view that in turn reflects "the declaratory theory of the law, according to which the courts are understood only to *find the law, not to make it*." Ibid., 535–36 (emphasis added). In the same case, Justice Scalia, writing for an unusual coalition including himself and Justices Marshall and Blackmun, goes even further; he maintains that retrospective

application of decisions is constitutionally required because the courts' function is simply "to say *what the law is*." Ibid., 549 (quoting *Marbury v. Madison*, 5 U.S. 137, 177 (1803)) (emphasis added). Two years later, in *Harper v. Virginia Department of Taxation*, 509 U.S. 86, 97 (1993), a majority of the judges reconfirmed this rule of retroactivity.

53. A. W. Brian Simpson, *Leading Cases in the Common Law* (New York: Oxford University Press, 1995), 10 (emphasis added).

54. See generally Joyce, *Myth of Morality*.

55. See Holmes, "The Path of the Law," 466. ("[T]he logical method and form flatter that longing for certainty and for repose which is in every human mind. But certainty generally is illusion, and repose is not the destiny of man.")

56. Ibid., 468.

57. Ibid., 466.

58. Ibid.

59. "Since the legal realist movement," Edward Rubin observes, "most scholars have been convinced that law is a social instrumentality. . . . [I]t is a system whose components are derived from social policy, not from either a universal moral order or the collective wisdom of the ages." See Edward Rubin, "Legal Scholarship," in *A Companion to Philosophy of Law and Legal Theory*, ed. Dennis Patterson (Cambridge: Blackwell Publishers, 1996), 565.

60. Richard A. Posner, *Economic Analysis of Law*, third ed. (Boston: Little, Brown, 1986), 21.

61. Ronald Dworkin, *Freedom's Law: The Moral Reading of the American Constitution* (Cambridge, Mass.: Harvard University Press, 1996), 37.

62. Grant Gilmore, *The Ages of American Law* (New Haven, Conn.: Yale University Press, 1977), 13.

63. Cantor, *Imagining the Law*, 192.

64. Kennedy, *A Critique of Adjudication*, 193, 192. However, a few judges may be guilty of conscious lying. Ibid., 202.

65. Ibid., 200.

66. Ibid., 192.

67. Ibid., 206. Kennedy acknowledges that the illusion confers a dangerous authority on judges. But who knows?—if the illusion were shattered, then perhaps "judges would tyrannize us worse than they do already." Ibid.

68. Daniel A. Farber and Suzanna Sherry, *Desperately Seeking Certainty: The Misguided Quest for Constitutional Foundations* (Chicago: University of Chicago Press, 2002), 38.

69. For a rich diversity of perspectives, see the essays collected in Michael W. McConnell, Robert F. Cochran Jr., and Angela C. Carmella, eds., *Christian Perspectives on Legal Thought* (New Haven, Conn.: Yale University Press, 2001).

70. For an interesting exploration of the question, see Samuel Wolfe Calhoun, "Grounding Normative Assertions: Arthur Leff's Still Irrefutable, But Incomplete, 'Sez Who?' Critique," XX *Journal of Law and Religion* 31 (2005).

71. Joseph Vining, *From Newton's Sleep* (Princeton, N.J.: Princeton University Press, 1995), 157, 222.

72. Ibid., 200 (emphasis added).

73. Ibid., 110.

74. Ibid., 208.

75. Roberto M. Unger, "The Critical Legal Studies Movement," 96 *Harvard Law Review* 561, 675 (1983).

76. Gerard Manley Hopkins, "God's Grandeur," in John Pick, ed., *A Hopkins Reader* (New York: Image Books, 1966), 47.

Index

About the Contributors

Patrick McKinley Brennan was awarded a B.A. in philosophy by Yale College and earned an M.A. in philosophy at the University of Toronto. Professor Brennan earned his J.D. from Boalt Hall School of Law, University of California, Berkeley. He currently holds the John F. Scarpa Chair in Catholic Studies at Villanova University School of Law, where he is also professor of law. After law school, he clerked for the Honorable John T. Noonan Jr. of the United States Court of Appeals for the Ninth Circuit. Professor Brennan teaches and writes in the areas of jurisprudence, Catholic social thought, federal jurisdiction, administrative law, and criminal law. He is the author of more than thirty articles, essays, and book chapters, as well as the coauthor of *By Nature Equal* (Princeton University Press, 1999) and the editor of *The Vocation of the Child* (W.B. Eerdmans, 2008).

J. Budziszewski graduated from University of South Florida with a B.A and M.A. He then earned his doctorate from Yale University in 1981, and has specialized in the relations among ethical theory, political theory, and Christian theology. He currently is a professor in the departments of government and philosophy at the University of Texas at Austin. The focus of his current research is natural law and moral self-deception. His books include *The Resurrection of Nature: Political Theory and the Human Character* (Cornell, 1986), *The Nearest Coast of Darkness: A Vindication of the Politics of Virtues* (Cornell, 1988), *True Tolerance: Liberalism and the Necessity of Judgment* (Transaction, 1992), *Written on the Heart: The Case for Natural Law* (InterVarsity, 1997), *The Revenge of Conscience: Politics and the Fall of Man* (Spence, 1999), and *What We Can't Not Know: A Guide* (Spence, 2003).

John E. Coons received his B.A. from the University of Minnesota. He received his J.D. from Northwestern University, where he taught until moving to the University of California, Berkeley, Boalt Hall, in 1967, where he is currently the Robert Bridges Professor of Law Emeritus. He has taught courses in jurisprudence, the sociology of law, and contracts. Professor Coons has written dozens of articles and chapters, and has coauthored *By Nature Equal: The Anatomy of a Western Insight* (Princeton University Press, 1999), *Education by Choice: The Case for Family Control* (Educator's International Press, 1999), *Scholarships for Children* (Institute of Governmental Studies Press, 1992), and *Private Wealth and Public Education* (Harvard University Press, 1970).

Avery Cardinal Dulles, S.J., graduated from Harvard College in 1940 and shortly thereafter served in the U.S. Navy. Upon his discharge from the Navy in 1946, Avery Dulles entered the Jesuit Order, and was ordained to the priesthood in 1956. After a year in Germany, he studied at the Gregorian University in Rome, and was awarded the doctorate in sacred theology in 1960. He was created a Cardinal of the Catholic Church in Rome on February 21, 2001, by Pope John Paul II. Cardinal Dulles is currently the Laurence J. McGinley Professor of Religion and Society at Fordham University. The author of over seven hundred articles on theological topics, Cardinal Dulles has published twenty-two books, including *Models of the Church* (Doubleday, 1974), *Models of Revelation* (Doubleday, 1983), *The Catholicity of the Church* (Clarendon Press, 1985), *The Craft of Theology: From Symbol to System* (Crossroad, 1992), *The Assurance of Things Hoped For: A Theology of Christian Faith* (Oxford University Press, 1994), *The Splendor of Faith: The Theological Vision of Pope John Paul II* (Crossroad, 1999), *The New World of Faith* (Our Sunday Visitor, 2000), and *Newman* (Continuum, 2002). The fiftieth anniversary edition of his book, *A Testimonial to Grace*, was republished in 1996 by the original publisher, Sheed & Ward, with an afterword containing his reflections on the past fifty years.

Russell Hittinger received his B.A. from the University of Notre Dame and both his M.A and Ph.D. in philosophy at St. Louis University. He is currently the Warren Professor of Catholic Studies in the Department of Philosophy and Religion at the University of Tulsa, where he also serves as a research professor in the School of Law. He presently serves on the editorial board of *First Things: A Monthly Journal of Religion and Public Life*. His publications include *The First Grace: Rediscovering Natural Law in a Post-Christian Age* (ISI, 2003) and *A Critique of the New Natural Law Theory* (University of Notre Dame Press, 1987). He edited *Linking the Human Life Issues* (Regnery-Gateway, 1986).

Thomas C. Kohler was awarded his B.A. from Michigan State University and his J.D. from Wayne State University. His LL.M is from Yale University. He is currently a professor of law at Boston College, where he was named concurrent professor in law and philosophy in 2004. He teaches a variety of labor and employment law courses as well as "Foundations of Western Law." The author of many articles and essays in jurisprudence and labor law, among his most recent publications is the coauthored "Bonding and Flexibility: Employment Ordering in a Relationless Age," in the *American Journal of Comparative Law.*

H. Jefferson Powell graduated from St. David's University College, University of Wales, with a B.A., and then went on to receive an A.M. and a Ph.D. from Duke University, an M.Div. from Yale Divinity School, and a J.D. from Yale Law School. Since 1989, he has been professor of law and divinity at Duke Law School. In addition to dozens of articles, book chapters, and essays, Professor Powell is the author of such books as *The Moral Tradition of American Constitutionalism* (Duke University Press, 1993), *The Constitution and the Attorneys General* (Carolina Academic Press, 2002), and *A Community Built on Words: The Constitution in History and Politics* (University of Chicago Press, 2002; rev. ed. 2005). Professor Powell has twice served in the Office of Legal Counsel, United States Department of Justice. He also served as principal deputy solicitor general during the Clinton administration.

Steven D. Smith earned his B.A. at Brigham Young University and his J.D. at Yale University Law School. He is currently the Warren Distinguished Professor of Law at the University of San Diego School of Law. Previously, he has served on the faculties of the University of Notre Dame Law School and the University of Colorado, Boulder, School of Law. In addition to many articles in the nation's leading law reviews, he is the author of *The Constitution and the Pride of Reason* (Oxford University Press, 1998), *Foreordained Failure* (Oxford University Press, 1995), and *Law's Quandary* (Harvard University Press, 2004).

Glenn Tinder is Professor of Political Science Emeritus at the University of Massachusetts at Boston. In addition to many articles and essays, Professor Tinder has published *The Political Meaning of Christianity* (Louisiana State University Press, 1989), *Community: Reflections on a Tragic Ideal* (Louisiana State University Press, 1980), *The Fabric of Hope* (Scholars Press, 1999), *Against Fate: An Essay on Personal Dignity* (Notre University Press, 1981), *Crisis of Political Imagination* (Scribner, 1964), and *Tolerance and Community* (University of Missouri, 1995).

Joseph Vining earned his B.A. at Yale University and his J.D. at Harvard Law School. He holds an M.A. in history from Cambridge University. He is currently the Harry Burns Hutchins Professor of Law at the University of Michigan Law School. He has served in private practice and as an attorney at the Department of Justice and on the President's Commission on Law Enforcement and the Administration of Justice. He teaches and writes in the fields of legal philosophy, administrative law, corporate law, comparative law, and criminal law. In addition to many articles, essays, and book chapters, he is the author of *Legal Identity* (Yale University Press, 1978), *The Authoritative and the Authoritarian* (University of Chicago Press, 1986), *From Newton's Sleep* (Princeton University Press, 1995), and *The Song Sparrow and the Child* (University of Notre Dame Press, 2004).

Michael J. White was awarded a B.A. in anthropology by Arizona State University. He earned an M.A., C.Phil, and Ph.D. in philosophy at the University of California, San Diego. He is currently a professor of philosophy and professor of law at Arizona State University. Professor White has served as a fellow at the National Humanities Center and was the recipient of a National Science Foundation Grant. In addition to authoring numerous articles, his other works include *Agency and Integrality: Philosophical Themes in the Ancient Discussions of Determinism and Responsibility* (D. Reidel Publishing Company, 1985), *The Continuous and the Discrete: Ancient Physical Theories from a Contemporary Perspective* (Clarendon Press, 1992), *Certainty and Surface in Epistemology and Philosophical Method: Essays in Honor of Avrum Stroll* (Edwin Mellen Press, 1991), *Partisan or Neutral? The Futility of Public Political Philosophy* (Rowman & Littlefield Publishers, 1997), and *Political Philosophy: An Historical Introduction* (Oneworld Publications, 2003).